HOW TO
MAKE
MONEY
SELLING
STOCKS
SHORT

Founded in 1807, John Wiley & Sons is the oldest independent publishing company in the United States. With offices in North America, Europe, Australia and Asia, Wiley is globally committed to developing and marketing print and electronic products and services for our customers' professional and personal knowledge and understanding.

The Wiley Trading series features books by traders who have survived the market's ever changing temperament and have prospered—some by reinventing systems, others by getting back to basics. Whether a novice trader, professional or somewhere in between, these books will provide the advice and strategies needed to prosper today and well into the future.

For a list of available titles, please visit our Web site at www.WileyFinance.com.

How to Make Money Selling Stocks Short

William J. O'Neil

with
Gil Morales

WILEY
John Wiley & Sons, Inc.

Credits

My heartfelt thanks goes out to the team that put in many hours of hard work to produce this book: Gil Morales, Sarah Schneider, Angela Han, Gail Crozier, Michelle Oviedo and Karen Siegler. In particular, I am grateful to Gil Morales, Chief Market Strategist and internal Portfolio Manager for William O'Neil + Co., Inc. who undertook the tremendous task of rewriting, revising and updating this work, which was originally published in 1976 in pamphlet form, and who, in the process, contributed much of his own research on the topic of short-selling.

Table of Contents

Foreword

Over 40 years ago, when I was a 29-year-old stock broker for a major New York Stock Exchange member firm, I got my start by being 100% out of the stock market by April 1, 1962 and then selling short. By the end of 1962, I showed a net profit when almost everyone around me was down substantially in one of the worst stock market breaks of the 1950s and 60s. It was a year later that I bought a seat on the New York Stock Exchange and started my own firm, William O'Neil + Co., Inc., and two decades later when I founded *Investor's Business Daily*. Throughout all of this, doing well at times, making my share of mistakes, working with individual investors, hiring portfolio managers, and observing hundreds of professional portfolio managers working for other institutional clients, I have concluded that there is a material lack of knowledge and some very human, but very major psychological blocks when it comes time to sell stocks, much less to sell stocks short.

After the 1973–74 bear market, we conducted a study for one institutional investment client that showed institutional research firms were heavily biased toward buy and hold advice. During that difficult and drawn-out bear market, we found that buy and hold recommendations outnumbered sell recommendations four to one. During the recent 2000–2002 bear market, the worst since 1929, investors found that Wall Street analysts had fifty different ways to say "buy" while they remained mute with respect to sell recommendations. Long after the great bull market of the 1990s had topped in March of 2000, most Wall Street analysts continued to recommend purchase of former high-flying leaders all the way down. This occurred even as these former leaders came down as much as 90% or more off of their bull market highs, or, in some cases, were in the process of going bankrupt. The evidence strongly suggests that there are few investors, even professionals, who know how to sell and will actually take decisive action to sell when they should. This implies that, for most investors, selling short is even more difficult.

It takes real knowledge and market know-how as well as lots of courage to sell, and particularly to sell short, because you will make many mistakes. However, I don't see how anyone can really do well in the market and protect assets if they don't learn how, when, and why stocks should be sold. If an investor doesn't know how to recognize when a stock has topped and should be sold, how can she be sure that the very stocks she is buying aren't actually giving off indications that they should be sold? Buying without the ability to sell is like a football team that is all offense with no defense. To win, you must understand and execute both.

I have never subscribed to market letters and never made any money listening to analysts or economists. You can learn more about the market by reading a couple of good books like Gerald Loeb's *Battle for Investment Survival* or Edwin Le Fevre's *Reminiscences of a Stock Operator* (or even my own best-seller, *How to Make Money in Stocks*), studying the few successful investors or groups you know in the market, and plotting and analyzing on charts all of your own past decisions.

Good luck.

William J. O'Neil

PART 1

HOW AND WHEN TO SELL STOCKS SHORT

I f you are like most investors, everyone is always telling you about good stocks to buy, and most of your investment study and research time is spent looking for that one big, winning, buy idea. That's fine if the overall market is consistently positive and strong. But the market has had periods where it has spent as much time in a bear market as in a bull market. There are two sides to everything—except the stock market! In the stock market there is only one side, and it isn't the bull side OR the bear side, but the RIGHT side.

Few investors really understand how to buy stocks successfully. Even fewer investors understand when to sell stocks. Virtually no one, including most professionals, knows how to sell short correctly.

Selling Short

A short sale is one in which you sell shares of a company's stock that you don't own. You "borrow" the stock certificates through your stockbroker in order to make delivery to the buyer of the shares you sold short. It is simply the opposite of buying first and selling later. You sell first and buy back later, hopefully at a lower price, in which case you will have made a profit, less commissions. Of course, if you are wrong, you will have to buy those shares back at a higher price and take a loss.

Before you sell short, have your broker check to be certain that he or she will be able to borrow the stock you are selling short. Since you are selling a stock you don't own, your broker will have to borrow the stock to deliver to the person that buys the stock from you when you sell it short. You will also have to pay to the purchaser of the stock you short any dividend that is declared while you are short the stock. Your broker will handle this for you. It isn't a major risk since the stock normally drops in price by the amount of the dividend when the stock goes ex-dividend. In addition, since you are required to use a margin account to sell short, you don't pay interest on the amount of borrowed margin money. This is due to the fact that the broker doesn't have to loan you money because he obtains the proceeds from the stock you sell.

The mechanics of short selling are relatively simple. If you believe the price of ABC Company's common stock is headed lower, all you do is give your stockbroker an order to sell short 100 shares of ABC. Because short sales can only be executed on a price increase, your order will be executed on the first plus-tick or zero-plus-tick that occurs in the price of the stock. A plus-tick is a trade that occurs at a higher price from the immediate, prior trade[1]. A zero-plus-tick is a trade that occurs at the same price as the previous trade when the previous trade itself was a plus-tick (price increase) from the prior trade. The Time & Sales Table 1.1 for a hypothetical stock illustrates both of these concepts.

---

[1] At the time of this writing, the SEC was considering whether to eliminate the "uptick" rule for some stocks considered highly liquid, large-capitalization issues that are not easily subject to price manipulation by short sellers.

Table 1.1. Determining the "Tick" for a Stock

```
TIME          SIZE    PRICE
12:18:53P     2000    54.45
12:19:05P     1500    54.44   < MINUS-TICK
12:19:10P     400     54.46   < PLUS-TICK
12:19:16P     700     54.46   < ZERO-PLUS-TICK
12:19:22P     1000    54.40   < MINUS-TICK
12:19:29P     200     54.42   < PLUS-TICK
12:19:32P     500     54.48   < PLUS-TICK
12:19:38P     200     54.48   < ZERO-PLUS-TICK
```

In the above example for a hypothetical stock, we can see the time and sales report for trades that occurred around 12:19 P.M. on the New York Stock Exchange on that particular day. The first column shows the exact time the trade was made in hours, minutes and seconds. The second column shows the size of the trades in terms of number of shares, and the last column shows the actual price at which each trade took place. We can see that at 12:18:53 2,000 shares traded at $54.45, followed by a 1500-share trade twelve seconds later at $54.44. Since this price, $54.44, is lower than the prior trade at $54.45, this is a "down-tick" and therefore a short sale could not be made on this trade. However, the very next trade of 400 shares is made at a price of $54.46, which is two cents higher than the prior trade and therefore constitutes an "up-tick" or "plus-tick" on which a short sale may be made. The next trade of 700 shares at the same price of $54.46 constitutes a "zero-plus-tick" since the stock, after trading up on the previous trade, trades at the same price as the prior "plus-tick." A short sale could also have been made on this "zero-plus-tick" trade. The next trade is then made at $54.40, lower than the prior trade at $54.46 and therefore a "minus-tick" at which NO short sales may be made. The next three trades, however, are all plus-ticks or zero-plus-ticks and all constitute trades at which a short sale could have been made.

Sell Short in the Correct Market Environment

The tricky part is determining the right time to sell short. Cardinal Rule #1 is to sell short only during what you believe is a developing bear market, not a bull market. The reason is quite simple. In a bull market, most stocks go up. In a bear market, almost everything will go down, sooner or later. The key is to learn to recognize the type of market you are in, according to the trend and condition of the general market averages (Dow Jones Industrial, S&P 500, NASDAQ Composite, etc.). If you spot a bear market developing, selling short can be a profitable endeavor. However, selling short during a bull market is swimming against the tide, which is rarely profitable.

Bear markets occur about once every three years, and, when they do, the decline occurs at a much faster pace than the previous rise. More profit potential can be had in a three-month period, if your timing is correct, than may have occurred in the prior year of an up market. In my view, there are only two things you can do in a bear market: either sell most or all of your stocks and get out, keeping your money in cash or cash equivalents like U.S. Treasury Bills or money market funds, or sell stocks short.

When you liquidate your stocks after riding them up in a bull market, they will probably be 10 to 15 percent off their peak values before you recognize the deteriorating general market and onset of a developing bear market. Short selling could gain back some of this amount and even some additional profits. The result of both moves in a bear market, if done correctly, should be that your portfolio is in a less damaged position, armed with cash, uncluttered with former disastrous mistakes, and ready to capitalize on the next bull market and its fresh crop of exciting new leaders.

What Goes Up Must Come Down

Stocks that hold up in price and seem to defy a bear market will sooner or later break down. In a major bear market, they virtually all come down; therefore, it is a fallacy to try to shift your portfolio and buy higher quality blue chips or seemingly defensive issues because they are resisting the downtrend. These stocks are just postponing the inevitable and will normally break in price later. With this strategy you may end up losing less than the market averages, but you still end up losing money.

Once caught in a bear market, many investors, both individual and institutional alike, employ the face-saving crutch that they are actually long-term investors and therefore correct in their judgement because they are still getting dividends on their stock holdings. This is not only naïve, but also foolish and risky, since the money received in dividends can be wiped out in one day's correction. The person who sells nothing at all when a bear market begins will find the pressure building steadily as the months of decline continue. It is just this person who may be finally overcome by fear and panic, only to sell out at the bottom with tremendous losses.

How to Use the General Market Averages

The General Market Averages (Dow Jones Industrial, S&P 500, NASDAQ Composite, etc.) are important because they represent for the most part some of the largest and most well-established companies in the American economy.

Watching several major indexes at the same time is important because not only will it help you recognize important market tops, but it will also enable you to spot a divergence where one index will noticeably lag another or fail to confirm new highs shown in the other index.

It is best to time your short selling with the action and movement of the general market averages. After they show definite signs of weakness, only then does it become a question of the selection and timing of the individual stocks to sell short. There are several charts of the daily market averages in *Investor's Business Daily* every day. Four charts are shown each day, and these are rotated among the following major market indexes: Dow Jones Industrial, S&P 500, S&P 600, NASDAQ Composite and IBD New America Index. These charts are stacked one on top of the other on one page, making it easy to spot divergences between various market indexes and indicators.

Top formations in the general market indexes will occur in one of two ways. The first way is for the market averages to move up and make a short-term, new high in price on mediocre or low volume. This tells you that demand for stocks is poor at that point and that the rally will soon be overcome by selling. The second way also involves topping while the averages are still in an up trend. What happens is that there will suddenly be one, two or three days where the daily volume on the New York Stock Exchange or NASDAQ increases from the prior day, but the market averages actually make very little to no price progress (this is known as "churning") or even close down in price versus the prior day's close. We call these "distribution days," and when three, four or five of these begin to show up in a two- to four-week period, it's time to start raising cash and re-evaluating your current stock holdings.

The 1984 Market Top was a double-top type of formation that was actually under distribution while it continued moving higher. Studying Chart 1.1 closely reveals that numerous distribution days, with the Dow down for the day on increased volume from the prior day, were occurring as the market was moving higher, leading up to Point A on the chart. At Point A the market traded increased heavy volume for two days but failed to make significant upside progress, indicating that the market was churning at that point. Four days later at Point B, the Dow index moved into new high ground intraday, only to close lower on extremely heavy volume—a major distribution day. The market then began to roll over, logging five more distribution days before it found its footing and began to rally back to the highs at Point C, where the market again traded heavy volume but was unable to make upside progress. Another day of churning action occurred at Point D, after which the market began to sell off again, logging five more distribution days that took the index down through its 200-day moving average. This marked the start of the 1984 bear market.

Chart 1.1. Dow Jones 1984 Top Daily Chart

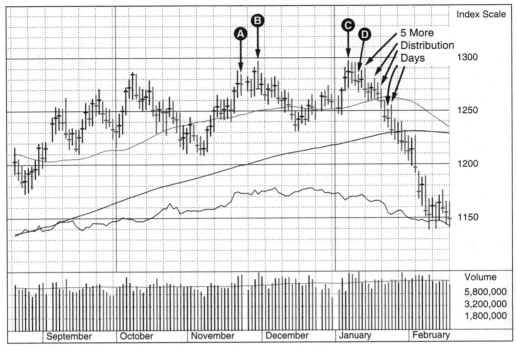

Chart 1.2. Dow Jones 1990 Top Daily Chart

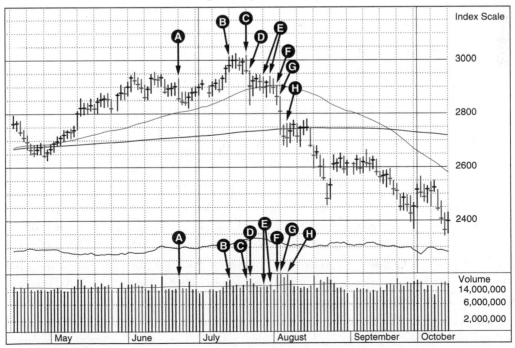

The Dow's top in 1990 was similar to 1984. Distribution showed up while the market continued to move into new high ground. Point A on Chart 1.2 identifies one day where the market traded very heavy volume as it attempted to move higher, but rolled over and closed lower for the day, marking a day of distribution. From that point the market then stabilized and again moved into new high ground. At Point B the market traded increased heavy volume but closed in the lower part of its range for that day to end up making very little upside progress for the day—a day of churning action. At Points C and D volume picked up sharply as the index began to roll over. The market held up for another week and a half, logging two more distribution days at the points marked E, but giving alert investors time to bail out of their long positions, after which volume again picked up in earnest at Points F, G, and H as the market broke wide open.

Chart 1.3. NASDAQ Composite Index 2000 Top Daily Chart

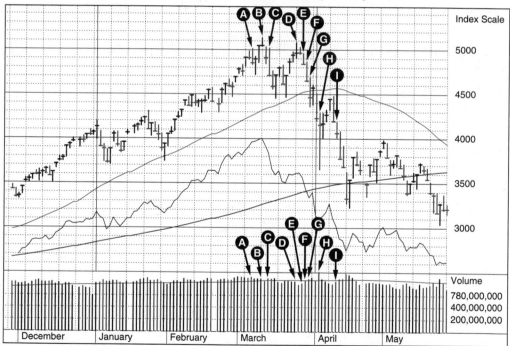

The market top in 2000, as shown in the NASDAQ index chart above, was another classic double-top type of formation that looked very powerful as it was rallying into new high ground. By the time it reached its ultimate top, the NASDAQ had doubled from its October 1998 bottom, breaking through the 5,000 level and eliciting wild fanfare and predictions of higher levels for the NASDAQ. The Internet stocks were all ripping to the upside, rising 10, 20, or even 40 points in a single day during what turned out to be final, climactic, topping moves. Notice that as the market was advancing up to Point A on the chart, volume was picking up. Volume increased for several days right around Point A, but the index faltered as it hit the 5,000 level for the first time with volume picking up as the index reversed and closed lower for the day. The next three days saw the NASDAQ climb into new high ground, trading above-average volume for three days, but stalling on the third day at Point B. At Point C volume again picked up as the index sold off and logged a third day of distribution. The NASDAQ then found its feet again at around the 4,500 level, whereupon it again rallied above the 5,000 level, but not as high as the levels reached two weeks earlier. However, notice that at this juncture, labeled Point D on the chart, the index thrust itself above the 5,000 level, but volume remained relatively light in comparison to its first move above 5,000 around Point A—a subtle clue that demand was waning at this level. The first down day after Point D occurred on light volume, but for the next three days, Points E, F & G on the chart, volume picked up as the index sold off sharply. At this point, the NASDAQ had logged seven distribution days right around the top. Investors got a one-day reprieve as the NASDAQ temporarily halted its slide at the 50-day moving average, only to roll over the next day on lighter volume. At Point H the NASDAQ traded tremendous volume and broke sharply but closed high in its daily range, causing many technical analysts to call a "capitulation bottom" for the NASDAQ. However, this day was in fact another distribution day as the "capitulation bottom" lasted all of three days before the index failed in its attempt to rally back above its 50-day moving average. Notice that the three days on which the NASDAQ rallied after Point H occurred on successively light volume—a sign that demand was waning as the index tried to recover. Beginning with the day labeled Point I, the NAS-DAQ then logged four straight days of distribution as it began to plummet on expanding volume. Thus began one of the most brutal bear markets in history.

It is important to note that after the market averages have topped, you do not have to see a large increase in volume as the market starts to move to the downside for the first few days. This is important to recognize since most technicians are trapped into thinking that a correction is normal when there is initially no real pick-up in downside volume. For more examples of market tops, see my book, *How to Make Money in Stocks*.

What to Do with a Rally

Following one or sometimes two or three volume distribution days at the top, the general market will frequently sell off for four or more consecutive days. Within a few days, a rally will be attempted. This is your next opportunity to evaluate the condition and strength of the market averages at a new, lower level. You should watch to see if the market can rally on higher volume. The first three days of any rally off a short-term bottom in the daily market averages should be disregarded unless all three days make tremendous price progress on heavy volume. Genuine upturns in the market averages will, in 85% of the cases, have a strong price and volume "follow-through" day. This usually occurs anytime from the fourth to the tenth day of the attempted rally when at least one of the major indexes is up 1.7% or more on increasing volume from the prior day. In a few instances, you may have a strong follow-through day and the market will still fail. When this occurs, it usually happens rather fast and can be figured out in a few days. The key reason for you to wait and watch for a follow-through before turning bullish is to avoid being fooled by the one- and two-day rallies that never follow through. If the market is making very little price progress on decreased volume, or if it abruptly begins to fail badly after a sharp, one-day rally, you are probably at another short selling point, as far as the general market averages are concerned. Chart 1.3 offers a good example of why the first three days of a rally attempt can be misleading. Note that after Point H in that example, the market rallied off its lows for three days but was unable to put in a follow-through day and soon failed.

Chart 2.1. NASDAQ Failed Follow-Through in 2002 Daily Chart

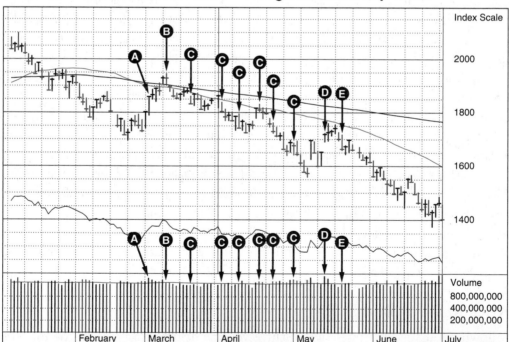

Once the market puts in a follow-through to the upside, it is important to monitor the indexes to see if the follow-through fails. Failed follow-through attempts generally offer secondary shorting opportunities. In Chart 2.1 above, the NAS-DAQ signals a turn to the upside with a follow-through on the seventh day of the rally attempt at Point A. It is likely that this rally attempt with the index popping some 12% off its low would force you to cover your short positions as your stop-loss points are hit. However, the rally begins to wane at Point B as volume declines and the market cannot make further upside progress. Distribution days begin to show up at the points labeled "C" as the index approaches and then breaches its near-term low. A few days later the market bottoms and puts in what appears to be a very strong follow-through day at Point D. However, the index begins to stall the very next day and then begins to roll over as volume increases at Point E. Over the next two weeks, four distribution days follow, and the NASDAQ plummets to new lows. It is important to note that you only need to see one or two distribution days soon after the follow-through day to know that the rally attempt has failed.

Chart 2.2. S&P 500 Index Failed Follow-Through in 1982 Daily Chart

In the above example, Chart 2.2, the S&P 500 puts in a very strong, fourth-day follow-through at Point A, but four days later volume picks up from the prior day and the index closes down, marking the first of four distribution days that occur over the next week and a half at Point B, stopping the attempted rally in its tracks. This example actually has a couple of failed follow-through days in it, and I will leave it to the reader to study this chart and identify them as a simple exercise.

The point of understanding failed follow-through days is that they often coincide with laggard, shortable stocks rallying up into areas of overhead resistance which can offer optimal secondary shorting points. You should be alert to follow-through days that occur without fundamentally sound stocks staging fresh breakouts from sound base formations. Often, a questionable follow-through can be identified by a dearth of such breakouts which results in a noticeable lack of new leadership. A sound follow-through day is generally accompanied by strong breakouts among a number of fundamentally sound stocks, so when this doesn't happen, be alert to the possibility that the follow-through may likely fail.

How Cycles Occur

Bear markets and panics are normally brought on by deteriorating basic conditions or unusual, specific events. The 1962 break in the market, for example, began after the SEC announced it was going to conduct a special study of the stock market. The economic and monetary statistics at that time were not negative, but many professional investors, uncertain about the outcome of the SEC investigations, withdrew from the market and sold stock. President Kennedy then made a strong move against the steel companies after the absolute top, which added more fuel to the fire that had been ignited. More recently, in 1998, the collapse of Long-Term Capital Management, a highly leveraged hedge fund managed by several Nobel Laureates, created fears of a market meltdown, which sent the market into a three-month tailspin.

In normal market cycles, money becomes tight after the third or fourth increase in the Federal Reserve Board Discount Rate. Further expansion of business, particularly in the housing sector, is choked off.

Topping markets are also characterized by a number of stocks that will break out of chart base formations, only to fail a few weeks later. Most of these chart patterns, upon closer investigation, are actually faulty, improper formations. However, few investors, professionals included, are able to distinguish between proper and improper base formations. Most of these faulty formations fall within one of the following types: 1) third or fourth "late-stage" bases—the third or fourth time a major price base is formed during an overall up trend, which makes the base obvious to everyone; 2) cup-type formations that form a narrow "V" in the bottom of the cup where the stock breaks straight down and then rallies straight back up without rounding out and putting in time in the bottom of the formation; 3) wide and loose price formations with wide weekly price spreads, particularly when compared to the prior two or three bases in the same stock; 4) upward wedging handles that do not drift down but instead "wedge" slightly upward with each successive weekly low closing slightly higher than the preceding week; and 5) handles within cup with handle patterns that form in the lower half of the overall cup base structure. Examples of failure-prone chart patterns are explored on the following pages.

Examples of Failure-Prone Bases

Calpine's chart (Chart 3.1) in June of 2001 offers a classic example of an obvious, late-stage base failure. Calpine's big move from $2.60 to nearly $60 a share occurred with several, well-formed bases from which the stock continued to break out during its upward trek. Notice how the first five bases that the stock formed on the way up were relatively well-contained, and the fifth base was a reasonably well-formed cup with handle with a rounded bottom and handle that drifted downward. The sixth turned out to be a late-stage base that took on a notable change in character in that it was wider and looser than any of the previous bases formed by the stock on the way up. Rather than rounding out a nice cup-like bottom, the stock jerks back and forth along the bottom of the cup, moves up, and then attempts to break out again, only to fail. This type of base is fairly obvious to most investors at this point, and as we know, what is obvious to all in the market is rarely what it appears to be. It is interesting to note that very near to Calpine's ultimate top, the infamous California Energy Crisis of 2001 which resulted in "rolling blackouts" was in full swing and getting widespread publicity, fueling bullish sentiment for energy stocks like Calpine. But all of this, combined with a faulty, late-stage base made Calpine all too obvious. As we have already seen, what is obvious in the market rarely works.

Numerical Technologies (Chart 3.2) is a good example of a wide, loose, faulty base structure. Notice how the stock forms several V-shaped cup formations with improper handles, finally failing after a breakout attempt from the last V-shaped cup with handle at Point A.

Applied Micro Circuits (Chart 3.3) trended higher in a well-contained uptrend channel throughout its big move in the 1998–1999 bull market. Once it reached the price area denoted by Point A, the stock began to give signals of potential trouble by swinging widely back and forth and then attempting to break out straight up from the bottom of the base formation. Note the wide weekly price ranges in comparison to the relatively tight weekly ranges the stock exhibited during its uptrend. Ultimately the stock's breakout attempt from this formation failed and the stock formed a second base. This base was also improper, with the stock forming a cup with handle formation that was over 50% deep and which had a handle that formed in the lower half of the pattern. The stock then attempted to break out from this improper base and failed for good, plummeting over 85% over the next eleven weeks.

After putting in a climax top at Point A, Charles Schwab (Chart 3.4) then formed two bases as it tried to stabilize and reset. However, both of these bases were faulty. The first, big cup with handle, forms its handle in the lower half of the chart pattern at Point B. The stock then breaks out and moves higher for four weeks

Chart 3.1. Calpine Corp. 2001 Weekly Chart

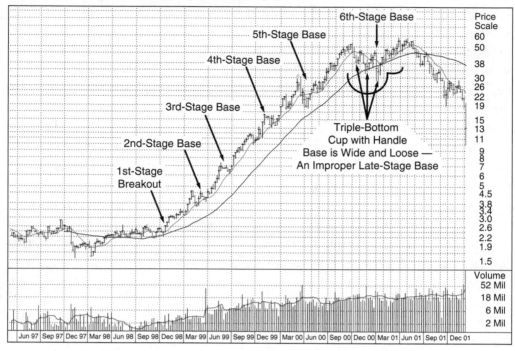

Chart 3.2. Numerical Technologies, Inc. 2002 Weekly Chart

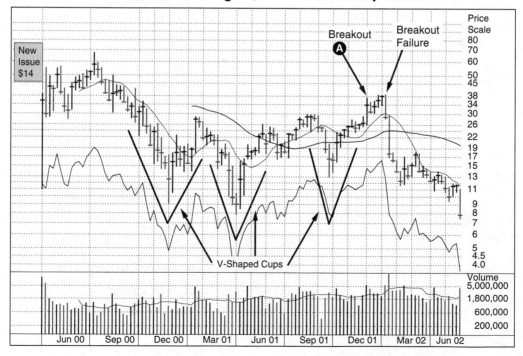

Chart 3.3. Applied Micro Circuits Corp. 2001 Weekly Chart

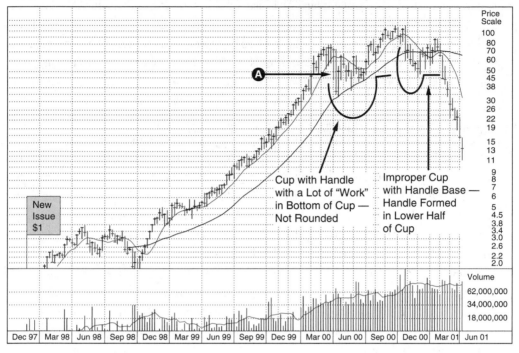

Chart 3.4. Charles Schwab Corp. 2001 Weekly Chart

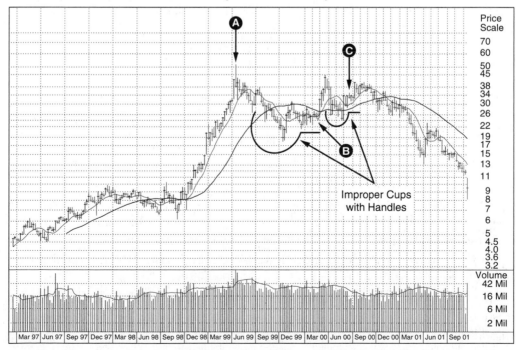

before failing and forming another cup with handle with the handle again forming in the lower half of the cup pattern at Point C. The stock breaks out from this formation, but there is little upside volume in the pattern as the stock comes up the right side of the cup, indicating a lack of real power and demand for the stock at this point. A few weeks later, the stock fails and begins a downtrend that took it all the way back to its October 1998 breakout point.

Watch the Stocks as Well as the Market

Bull markets don't top out in just one week or one month. A top is a process that requires months to complete. You can easily be premature in short selling. If so, you will be forced to cover and cut your losses. But don't give up or lose your nerve because the market could develop severe weakness within two or three months and you should once again move to establish short positions. As with anything else, successful short selling requires discipline and persistence.

Sometimes companies will increase their dividend, report good news, declare a stock split, or show good earnings during a bear market environment. Don't be misled by seemingly positive news. Intelligent professionals will probably use the positive news as an opportunity to sell more stock. Corporations frequently increase dividends in a weak market, feeling that this will help their stock's price performance. Normally, it is exactly the wrong thing to do, as professionals will use this as an opportunity to sell stocks. The key is to follow the stock's price and volume action. Frequently, a rally in a stock that is caused by positive news or announcements will take the stock right back into a proper shorting position, enabling you to use this "news rally" to your advantage!

What to Sell Short

The stocks you select to sell short should primarily be the big leaders from the immediately preceding bull market. That is, stocks that have had very large percentage increases. They should have acquired a large, increased number of institutional sponsors like mutual funds, banks, and pension funds. Our studies have shown that more institutions own more shares of former leaders as much as one to two years AFTER they top than they do during the stock's big run and period of outstanding price performance. This creates huge amounts of potential selling supply as these stocks continue to move lower—everybody owns them, and all that is left are potential sellers who are loaded up with stock.

It is also helpful if a stock has recently split, and the larger the split, the better. It is even better if it is the stock's second split during the last couple of years. The second time a stock splits is usually at a much later stage in the stock's overall move.

This is normally too obvious to the crowd to be a rewarding situation. The reason stock splits are helpful to the short seller is that if an institution owns 500,000 shares and the stock then splits 3 for 1, now this institution owns 1,500,000 shares, creating more supply should it decide to sell. This effect is multiplied when large numbers of institutions own the stock. Like everything else in the stock market, it is a simple issue of supply and demand with a large potential supply of stock that could be offered for sale in the marketplace. Oftentimes a stock will top in price after the second or third stock split in a year.

Huge institutional sponsorship of a stock can also be a liability for a stock once a bear market sets in. Normally you would want to see strong institutional sponsorship in a stock during a bull market. However, in a bear market, stocks that are heavily owned, and in some cases "over owned," by institutions can suffer if these sources of potential supply decide to unload their positions. This over-ownership usually occurs in leaders that have long since topped. For example, AOL-Time Warner (AOL) at its absolute top in December 1999 had 815 mutual funds owning approximately 362 million shares. Over two years later, after the stock had plummeted from over $90 to under $10, over 1,000 mutual funds reported ownership of a total of 886 million shares! This proves that most mutual fund managers are late to the party, and foolishly buy hundreds of thousands of shares of a former leader well after it has topped, creating excessive over-ownership of the stock as it is going down. This late, after-the-fact buying of a former leader creates an excess of supply that will eventually lead to a situation where the stock under-performs for many years or even completely collapses.

One technique to help in the selection and timing of specific stocks to sell short is to look at stocks within the context of belonging to various industry groups. Even if the general market has topped, all groups do not top at the same time. Therefore, for one group it might be proper, timing wise, to sell short, while another group might be premature by two or three months. Be patient. This group's time will come and the market will give you the clue when it is time for you to act. If one or two stocks that have institutional sponsorship break badly and do not rally, or show highly abnormal weakness, then you should look at the other leaders in the same group, since they may likely follow suit. *Investor's Business Daily* provides a table (see Table 2.1) that breaks the market into 197 industry groups and tracks their performance on a daily basis, enabling you to identify groups that might contain short selling candidates. For added perspective, IBD also shows industry group rankings from the prior week and six months, helping to identify groups that are strengthening or weakening in group rank.

Table 2.1. Sample Industry Group Rankings

IBD's 197 Industry Group Rankings

Industry Groups are ranked 1 through 197 on price performance of all stocks in the industry in the latest 6 months (1=best performance). Top 10 industries in performance yesterday are boldfaced. Worst 10 are underlined. Studies show most top-performing stocks are found in the top quartile of groups and that group action determines at least half of a stock's performance.

Rank 3 This Wk	Last Fri	3 Mo Ago	Industry Name	No of Stocks In Grp	% Chg Since Jan 1	Daily % Chg
1	1	1	**Steel-Specialty Alloys**	10	+34.9	+0.9
2	2	9	Food-Meat Products	13	+39.7	−0.6
3	3	5	Steel-Producers	27	+20.0	−1.0
4	5	15	Metal Proc & Fabrication	50	+11.7	−0.9
5	6	3	Oil&Gas-U S Expl&Prod	82	+23.3	−0.6
6	4	53	Textile-Mill/Household	8	+35.2	−0.7
7	7	2	Comml Svcs-Security/Sfty	52	+28.3	−0.5
8	21	152	Computer-Manufacturers	16	+15.0	−2.3
9	11	22	Oil&Gas-Field Services	53	+12.4	−1.0
10	9	43	Oil&Gas-Refining/Mktg	23	+12.3	−0.6
11	14	41	Transportation-Svcs	11	+21.7	−0.7
12	19	39	Bldg-Hand Tools	10	+24.0	−0.6
13	8	132	Retail-Major Disc Chains	12	+15.3	−1.1
14	20	56	Retail-Mail Order&Direct	15	+16.6	−1.5
15	24	84	Machinery-Tools & Rel	7	+12.9	−1.0
16	12	21	Energy-Other	31	+11.6	−0.4
17	26	40	Metal Prds-Distributor	5	+19.6	−0.3
18	16	23	Oil&Gas-Cdn Expl&Prod	54	+17.3	−0.1
19	10	4	Transportation-Ship	27	+30.9	+0.1
20	22	86	Comml Svcs-Advertising	33	+16.0	−0.4
21	13	11	Oil&Gas-Machinery/Equip	29	+26.0	−1.0
22	32	8	**Bldg-Wood Prds**	22	+7.2	+0.4
23	27	100	Elec-Military Systems	14	+14.6	−0.7
24	18	141	Oil&Gas-U S Integrated	5	+21.4	−1.1
25	25	6	Leisure-Gaming/Equip	43	+12.4	−0.4
26	15	68	Oil&Gas-Intl Expl&Prod	24	+7.7	−0.9
27	36	103	Real Estate Operations	39	+16.6	−0.3
28	41	14	**Bldg-Mobile/Mfg & Rv**	20	+16.3	+3.2
29	35	78	Machinery-Gen Industrial	48	+7.3	−0.7
30	30	75	Medical/Dental-Services	50	+12.9	−0.7
31	29	176	Transport-Air Freight	9	+13.4	−1.1
32	28	99	Transportation-Truck	32	+10.7	+0.1
33	17	62	Beverages-Soft Drinks	17	+10.4	−3.1
34	56	36	**Funeral Svcs & Rel**	8	+17.3	+0.5
35	43	24	Chemicals-Specialty	55	+3.3	−1.2
36	57	144	Beverages-Alcoholic	32	+6.4	−0.3
37	39	48	Retail-Clothing/Shoe	64	+5.5	−0.9
38	38	26	Medical-Hlth Maint Org	20	+13.8	−1.9
39	37	13	Medical-Systems/Equip	91	+7.1	−0.9
40	23	16	Internet-Content	35	+13.0	−3.0
41	40	27	Medical-Outpnt/Hm Care	31	+19.5	−1.0
42	31	12	Cosmetics/Personal Care	45	+10.1	−1.8
43	44	58	Auto/Truck-Replace Parts	10	+10.7	−1.5
44	63	94	Retail-Super/Mini Mkts	34	+9.4	−0.5
45	42	55	Financial Services-Misc	39	+9.5	−0.6
46	54	163	Oil&Gas-U S Royalty Tr	18	+8.2	−0.1
47	46	125	**Bldg-Cement/Concrt/Ag**	17	+8.1	+0.5
48	45	47	Retail-Leisure Products	26	+6.5	−1.3
49	60	101	Diversified Operations	79	−2.5	−0.6
50	51	32	Retail-Restaurants	75	+2.3	−1.2
51	53	112	**Leisure-Hotels & Mot**	23	+12.8	+0.9
52	76	118	Containers	25	+5.7	−0.6
53	62	52	**Food-Dairy Products**	9	+17.8	+0.6
54	92	185	Retail-Drug Stores	8	−1.8	−0.9
55	48	42	Leisure-Products	27	+5.9	−1.0
56	70	127	Banks-West/Southwest	93	+4.6	−0.4
57	49	138	Food-Confectionery	7	+8.1	−1.2
58	69	30	Auto/Truck-Tires & Misc	6	+12.8	+0.1
59	75	20	Pollution Control-Svcs	33	+7.4	−1.0
60	52	105	Insurance-Acc & Health	9	+12.7	0.0
61	66	54	Leisure-Services	33	+8.8	−1.0
62	33	76	Insurance-Brokers	12	+9.8	−1.3
63	72	157	Pollution Control-Equip	24	+4.6	+0.2
64	64	83	Retail/Whlsle-Bldg Prds	19	+6.1	−0.5
65	47	69	Oil&Gas-Drilling	23	+11.4	−1.4
66	55	97	Chemicals-Fertilizers	11	+18.1	−1.8
67	79	123	Aerospace/Defense Eqp	51	+5.0	+0.2
68	67	46	Medical/Dental-Supplies	28	+7.3	−0.6
69	61	111	Paper & Paper Products	44	−1.6	−1.3
70	102	116	Real Estate Development	20	+7.8	−0.2
71	80	162	Media-Cable/Satellite Tv	30	−12.3	−1.2
72	59	25	Medical-Ethical Drugs	88	+2.2	−1.2
73	74	48	Apparel-Clothing Mfg	51	+3.0	−0.9
74	73	158	Utility-Electric Power	88	+0.4	−0.5
75	86	131	Office Supplies Mfg	11	+10.0	−0.9
76	91	33	Telecom-Wireless Equip	61	−13.7	−2.3
77	108	104	Comml Svcs-Market Rsrch	19	+6.2	−1.6
78	83	150	Banks-Midwest	83	+0.8	−0.4
79	71	10	Telecom-Wireless Svcs	73	+9.9	−0.7
80	77	149	Soap & Clng Preparatns	6	+5.6	−1.8
81	90	51	Chemicals-Basic	21	+3.2	−0.7
82	68	67	Medical-Products	134	−0.2	−1.2
83	107	31	Internet-E Commerce	44	+0.6	−2.4
84	50	107	Finance-Consumer/Cml Lns	43	+5.3	−1.7
85	113	93	**Comml Svcs-Leasing**	14	+4.9	+0.3
86	88	44	Bldg-Constr Prds/Misc	40	+3.1	−0.0
87	97	71	Computer-Integrated Syst	36	−4.2	−0.9
88	65	81	Oil&Gas-Intl Integrated	22	−1.2	−0.9
89	34	28	Chemicals-Plastics	19	+2.7	−1.7
90	123	147	Leisure-Movies & Rel	19	−2.3	−0.9
91	87	70	Food-Flour & Grain	12	+6.4	−0.5
92	94	175	Aerospace/Defense	7	+8.2	−0.0
93	78	77	Comml Svcs-Misc	57	−2.2	−0.4
94	81	90	Retail-Miscellaneous	25	+4.6	−0.5
95	84	64	Computer-Peripheral Eqp	15	+0.9	−0.7
96	99	18	Apparel-Shoes & Rel Mfg	18	+8.5	−0.4
97	82	135	Retail-Department Stores	14	+1.6	−0.4
98	101	154	Banks-Southeast	142	−0.8	−0.6
99	95	180	Utility-Gas Distribution	38	+2.5	−0.7
100	116	136	Comml Svcs-Printing	16	+7.2	−0.5
101	114	137	Computer Sftwr-Educ/Entr	22	+15.1	−2.2
102	89	80	Agricultural Operations	23	+4.3	−0.8
103	85	181	Finance-Reit	205	+1.2	−0.8
104	138	115	**Trucks & Parts-Hvy Duty**	11	+4.9	−2.0
105	147	19	Machinery-Constr/Mining	9	−1.6	−0.4
106	112	153	Transportation-Rail	14	−1.5	−0.9
107	96	164	Retail/Whlsle-Jewelry	11	−5.2	−0.4
108	110	29	Consumer Products-Misc	21	+5.4	−1.3
109	58	34	Metal Ores	44	−4.9	−1.0
110	106	66	Comml Svcs-Healthcare	22	−3.4	−0.9
111	105	165	Oil&Gas-Transprt/Pipelne	33	+1.2	−0.4
112	98	108	Insurance-Prop/Cas/Titl	108	+2.9	−0.8
113	111	143	Insurance-Diversified	14	+8.2	−0.2
114	140	124	Electrical-Equipment	30	−5.0	−2.0
115	104	174	Media-Periodicals	11	+6.2	−1.2
116	122	96	Transportation-Equip Mfg	12	+10.6	−0.2
117	109	139	Food-Misc Preparation	46	−3.5	−1.2
118	100	74	Machinery-Farm	9	+0.0	−0.4
119	134	145	Oil&Gas-Cdn Integrated	5	+3.0	−0.2
120	93	38	Elec-Scientific/Msmg	50	−1.7	−2.2
121	120	122	Machinery-Mtl Hdlg/Autmn	19	+0.6	−2.2
122	103	159	Metal Prds-Fasteners	6	−0.4	−0.7
123	125	189	Banks-Super Regional	17	−2.0	−0.5
124	146	106	Telecom-Services Frgn	67	−7.0	−1.1
125	130	128	Retail/Whlsle-Autos/Prts	27	−6.5	0.0
126	127	65	Medical-Nursing Homes	19	−8.0	−1.0
127	155	188	Leisure-Toys/Games/Hobby	15	−8.1	+0.2
128	118	37	Comml Svcs-Staffing	32	+0.3	−0.3
129	119	57	Comml Svcs-Schools	18	+3.1	−2.0
130	126	102	Hsehold/Office Furniture	29	+2.1	−1.1
131	149	129	**Bldg-A/C & Heating Prds**	12	+2.8	+1.2
132	133	155	Insurance-Life	30	+3.9	−0.4
133	141	82	Media-Books	13	+5.1	+0.1
134	117	110	Tobacco	14	0.0	0.0
135	137	170	Finance-Savings & Loan	166	−2.8	−0.2
136	148	171	Telecom-Services	43	−12.7	−0.4
137	132	146	Banks-Northeast	140	−3.2	−0.3
138	128	85	Finance-Investment Mgmt	63	−4.1	−0.6
139	121	140	Medical-Hospitals	11	+2.3	−0.3
140	142	114	Household-Consumer Elec	18	0.0	−0.8
141	124	190	Medical-Drug/Diversified	2	−2.3	−1.2
142	150	172	Auto Manufacturers	9	−13.4	−1.3
143	139	87	Media-Diversified	26	+1.4	−0.6
144	172	35	Elec-Parts Distributors	10	+3.4	−2.0
145	129	89	Comml Svcs-Consulting	21	+0.8	−0.8
146	143	73	Retail/Whlsle-Office Sup	9	−3.8	+0.1
147	144	179	Retail-Home Furnishings	23	−6.8	−1.0
148	136	182	Finance-Mrtg&Rel Svc	21	+2.2	−0.9
149	151	95	Elec-Component/Connectr	33	−6.0	−1.3
150	115	17	Medical-Biomed/Biotech	242	−10.1	−1.7
151	152	167	Finance-Idx Tracking Fd	160	−1.7	−1.0
152	145	191	Metal Ores-Gold/Silver	61	−24.9	−2.8
153	153	88	Bldg-Maintenance & Svc	10	−0.6	−0.6
154	157	7	Computer Sftwr-Security	35	−10.2	−2.5
155	159	121	Finance-Publ Inv Fd-Frgn	78	−7.3	−0.7
156	160	91	Computer-Tech Services	86	−10.9	−1.4
157	164	126	Retail/Whlsle-Cmptr/Cell	28	−3.0	−1.4
158	166	45	Elec-Misc Products	48	−12.4	−2.1
159	189	16	Internet-Isp	35	−15.9	−3.1
160	165	101	Auto/Truck-Original Eqp	43	−9.7	−0.0
161	170	183	Banks-Money Center	20	−4.9	−0.9
162	158	63	Finance-Investment Bkrs	44	−3.2	−0.6
163	135	109	Office-Equip & Automatn	9	−5.1	−0.7
164	131	130	Bldg-Resident/Comml	23	−5.9	−0.8
165	154	113	Bldg-Heavy Construction	21	−4.6	−1.2
166	161	166	Bldg-Paint & Allied Prds	6	−9.1	−4.5
167	174	117	Retail/Whlsle-Food	15	−1.0	−1.1
168	169	187	Finance-Publ Inv Fd-Eqt	109	−7.7	−0.4
169	175	120	Banks-Foreign	26	−7.6	−0.6
170	182	178	Medical-Whlsle Drg/Suppl	14	−7.5	−0.5
171	176	192	Finance-Publ Inv Fd-Bond	436	−6.3	+0.1
172	185	142	Media-Radio/Tv	43	−20.9	−0.8
173	167	160	Utility-Water Supply	16	−3.9	−0.6
174	173	134	Retail-Consumer Elec	11	−4.9	−1.4
175	168	177	Household-Housewares	7	−8.0	−1.4
176	178	168	Computer Sftwr-Design	19	−11.4	−1.3
177	156	92	Computer Sftwr-Medical	33	−8.9	−2.0
178	181	173	Media-Newspapers	15	−8.3	−0.6
179	163	169	Computer Sftwr-Desktop	17	−6.5	−1.4
180	162	72	Internet-Software	60	−23.6	−4.0
181	171	49	Computer Sftwr-Enterprse	164	−20.6	−1.6
182	179	50	Household-Appliances	11	−5.6	−1.1
183	184	61	Telecom-Equipment	82	−10.5	−1.8
184	183	133	Computer Sftwr-Financial	31	−9.2	−2.2
185	186	79	Internet-Network Sltns	21	−14.4	−6.7
186	188	195	Mining-Gems	5	−21.3	−0.5
187	177	59	Medical-Genetics	44	−13.4	−2.4
188	180	98	Medical-Generic Drugs	22	−21.5	−1.3
189	190	197	Retail-Discount&Variety	6	−26.7	−1.7
190	191	194	Leisure-Photo Equip/Rel	6	−28.4	−0.5
191	193	151	Computer-Networking	53	−26.8	−0.5
192	195	119	Elec-Semiconductor Mfg	140	−24.0	−2.9
193	187	186	Transportation-Airline	34	−29.5	−1.4
194	192	148	Elec-Semiconductor Equip	66	−31.9	−2.8
195	194	196	Telecom-Fiber Optics	23	−19.8	−1.4
196	196	193	Computer-Data Storage	27	−25.0	−1.9
197	197	161	Elec-Contract Mfg	28	−31.0	−2.8
0	0	0	S&P Midcap 400 Ind		−0.8	−1.2
0	0	0	S&P 500 Index		−2.3	−1.0

Common Sense Should Prevail

Common sense and business understanding may help you in selecting certain types of companies that could be ideal short sales during a developing bear market. These include stocks in notoriously cyclical industries such as railroads, hotels, capital equipment, basic materials, etc., if they have had major price increases during the last one or two years. The stock of a now defunct retail company named Certain-Teed proved to be an excellent short sale in the 1962 market break, and MGIC and Kaufman & Broad (now known as KB Home), both housing-related stocks, proved likewise in the brutal bear market of 1973–1974.

Common sense also implies that the stocks with the best downside potential are the very ones that have been big leaders in the prior bull market. Things can get carried away and overdone in the stock market just as they do in other phases of life. In the bear market that developed after the market top in 2000, many tech stocks, which had insanely huge moves that ended in textbook "climax" tops, offered some highly profitable short selling opportunities as many of these stocks plummeted 90% or more off their bull market peaks.

Examples of Climax Tops

In Charts 4.1–4.6, three big leaders of the 1998–2000 bull market, HGSI, QCOM, and AOL, are shown. Each of these stocks ended their huge runs in classic "climax" tops. Sometimes a stock's advance gets so active that it has a rapid price run-up for two or three weeks on a weekly chart (eight to ten days on a daily chart). Often times this final run-up is accompanied by several upside "gaps" in the daily chart. The price spread from the stock's low to high for the week will be greater than in any prior week since the beginning of the original move many months earlier. In a few cases, near the top of a climax run a stock may retrace the prior week's large price spread from the prior week's low to its high point and close the week up a little, with volume remaining very high. I call this "railroad tracks" because on a weekly chart you will see two parallel vertical lines. Chart 4.1 shows this concept at the very peak of Human Genome's move. This is a sign of continued heavy volume distribution without material upside price progress for the week.

Often, a climax top in a leading stock will be accompanied by some major, positive news announcement, or a plethora of Wall Street analysts raising their price targets on the stock. In March 1999, when Charles Schwab & Company finally topped out in a classic climax run just above the $160 price area, one major brokerage firm's analyst raised his price target on the stock to $200. Once again, an analyst's opinion was utterly irrelevant to what was really happening in the stock—it was topping, never to see the $160 price level again, much less $200!

Careful study of these examples should help you identify climax tops when they occur in leading stocks. Understanding when a big leader has topped is the first step in identifying a potential short selling opportunity. Once a big leader has topped, you should monitor its price and volume action over the next several months for a proper shorting point.

What Not to Sell Short

It is extremely dangerous to sell short companies with very thin capitalizations (e.g., a small number of shares outstanding and a small floating supply of shares in the market), or with small trading volume. When the market suddenly turns up, thin stocks tend to advance rapidly on only a little buying and create quick, large losses. Pinpointing the turn is also difficult since these stocks trade less frequently. It is better to short stocks with a larger number of shares outstanding that trade, for example, one to ten million shares a day or more, and that have institutional ownership.

A stock should never be sold short just because its price or price/earnings ratio seems "too high." It is better to develop a system and set of rules to guide your stock market operations, and to stick to this system rather than to work from personal opinions or feelings. Likewise, it can be suicidal to sell a stock short when its price

Chart 4.1. Human Genome Sciences, Inc. 2000 Weekly Chart

Chart 4.2. Human Genome Sciences, Inc. 2000 Daily Chart

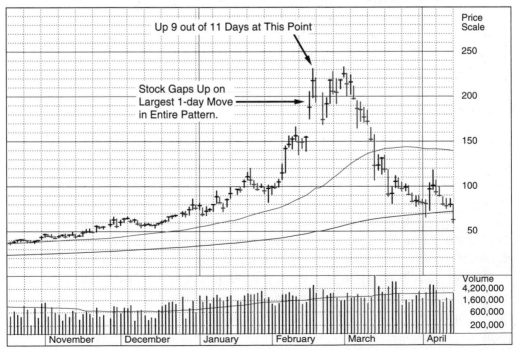

Chart 4.3. Qualcomm, Inc. 2000 Weekly Chart

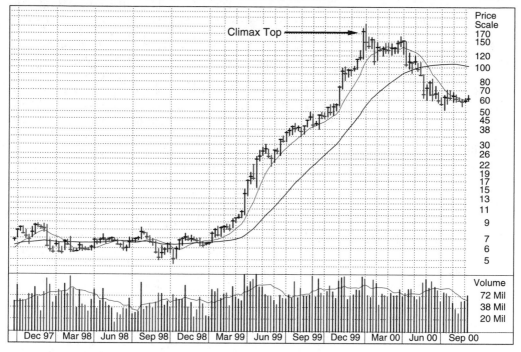

Chart 4.4. Qualcomm, Inc. 2000 Daily Chart

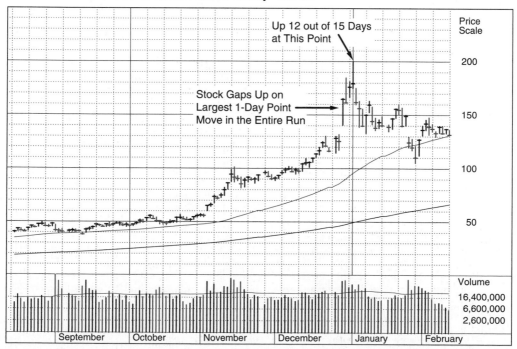

Chart 4.5. AOL Time Warner, Inc. 1999 Weekly Chart

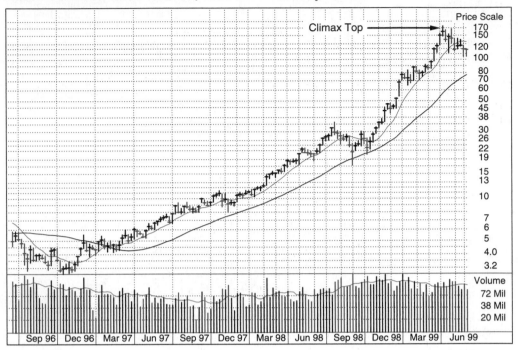

Chart 4.6. AOL Time Warner, Inc. 1999 Daily Chart

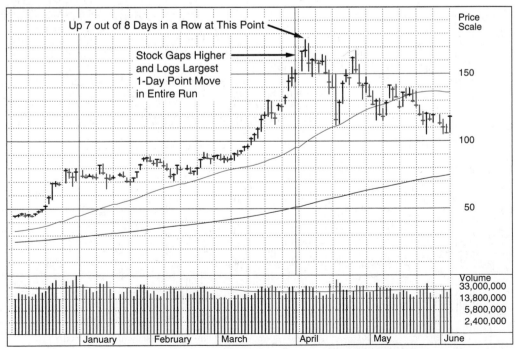

goes into new high ground. In May of 2003, one money manager I know made an appearance on a major financial news station where he triumphantly announced that he was shorting Jet Blue Airways Corp. in the mid-$30 price range because the stock was "really worth" some price "in the low 20s." Seventeen weeks later the stock was trading at over $70 a share! This offers a vivid example of how these situations have an uncanny knack of going higher! Your job is not to argue with the market, but to study it, recognize when it is weakening, and go along with it. Additionally, don't sell short because you've heard a rumor about some "bad news" on a particular company that may be announced. Chances are the stock may actually rally when and if the "bad news" is made public.

Also, do not sell a stock short on the basis that an overbought-oversold indicator on the stock says that it is "overbought." Using a single indicator like this to determine a short selling point is very dangerous. Often, a stock that is "overbought" stays "overbought" for several days or weeks as it races higher, which, if you are short the stock, can cause you to get squeezed and take a severe loss. In March of 2003, several of our institutional clients were using a newly-contrived overbought/oversold indicator which was giving sell signals on several "overbought" stocks. One of these stocks was eBay, Inc., which, according to this indicator, was "overbought" in the $80 price range. A few weeks later the stock was trading over $110.

Another common mistake is that after selling a stock they have owned outright, investors sometimes consider selling the same stock short. In general, this isn't a wise policy. The fact that a stock makes a good sale doesn't necessarily translate into making it a good short sale. Likewise, when you cover your short sale by buying it back, it is not necessarily a wise policy to reverse the position and go long the stock.

Finally, selling short too many stocks too quickly is also not wise. It is better to take time and achieve one or two gains before attempting to short a number of stocks. Be patient. Let the market tell you if you are really on the right track. This caution also avoids taking huge losses on many positions if you happen to be premature, in terms of the direction of the general market, on your timing of short sales.

Timing Your Short Sales

Once you have determined that the general market is in a downtrend and have selected several individual candidates for selling short, you can then monitor the stocks to determine the proper time to begin selling short.

To determine the exact timing of your short sale, you should analyze a good daily or weekly chart of the individual stock's price and volume movement during the last year. The point is not to sell short at the top, but at the right time. After the first abnormal or serious break in price, there will usually be two or three rallies in price. This is typically the best point to sell short and should coincide with your timing of the general market averages.

Oftentimes, a stock will, after topping, have a sharp break to the downside through its 50-day moving average. When this occurs, the stock will often attempt two to four rallies back through the 50-day moving average to the upside. It is at this point that the stock should be monitored very closely for a sharp, high-volume break back down through the 50-day moving average. When this second break occurs, confirming the downtrend that was set in motion by the first break off the top, you should begin initiating your short position as close to the break through the 50-day moving average as possible.

A very important and key concept in successfully timing short sales is that the optimal shorting point will, in the majority of cases, present itself **five to seven months or more after the absolute peak in the stock**. In the same way that we never buy a stock off of its absolute bottom, preferring instead to allow for a prior up trend and proper base to form before determining a proper buy point, we do not try and short a stock right off of its absolute peak.

The primary reason this needs to occur is that bullish sentiment will remain in a former big leader for a period of time after the absolute peak. Investors, both individual and professional alike, who watched the stock rocket higher but never got on board now see the lower price of the stock as a "bargain." This sort of "bargain hunting" can induce several waves of buying which create a series of rallies, normally back above a key moving average, usually the 50-day moving average. These rallies run in premature short sellers and bring in the last, late bargain-hunting buyers.

It is not until all of these premature short sellers and late-comers to the stock are worn down and worn out that the stock finally will begin to break significantly. A useful way to determine when this has finally occurred is to watch the 50-day moving average. When this moving average crosses the 200-day moving average and moves below it, a sharp break will often occur within a week to two months, and it is this moving average "cross" that can help narrow the timing window for a short sale. If you monitor a stock very closely after the 50-day moving average crosses below the 200-day moving average, you should be able to react to the first signs that the stock is now going to break sharply.

Examples of 50-Day Moving Average Breaks

The two examples shown here, Lucent Technologies and C-cor, Inc., illustrate 50-day moving average breaks. These types of breaks can be identified on a daily or weekly chart, and the astute short seller should monitor both types of charts to determine when a stock is finally going to break sharply to the downside.

Chart 5.1. Lucent Technologies, Inc. 2000 Daily Chart

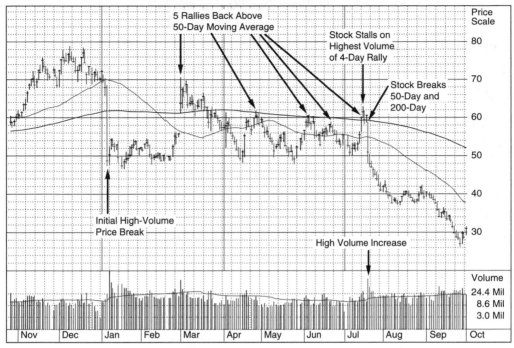

5 Rallies Back Above
50-Day Moving Average

Stock Stalls on
Highest Volume
of 4-Day Rally

Stock Breaks
50-Day and
200-Day

Initial High-Volume
Price Break

High Volume Increase

Price Scale
80
70
60
50
40
30

Volume
24.4 Mil
8.6 Mil
3.0 Mil

Nov | Dec | Jan | Feb | Mar | Apr | May | Jun | Jul | Aug | Sep | Oct

Chart 5.2. C-cor, Inc. 2000 Weekly Chart

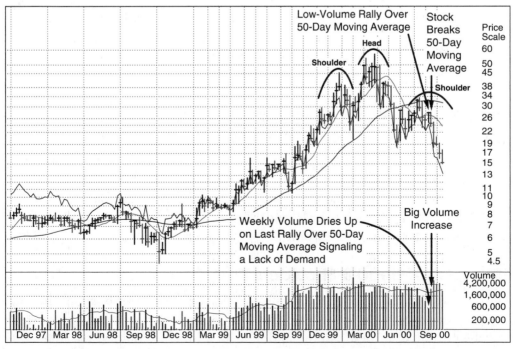

Low-Volume Rally Over
50-Day Moving Average

Stock
Breaks
50-Day
Moving
Average

Head

Shoulder

Shoulder

Weekly Volume Dries Up
on Last Rally Over 50-Day
Moving Average Signaling
a Lack of Demand

Big Volume
Increase

Price Scale
60
50
45
38
34
30
26
22
19
17
15
13
11
10
9
8
7
6
5
4.5

Volume
4,200,000
1,600,000
600,000
200,000

Dec 97 | Mar 98 | Jun 98 | Sep 98 | Dec 98 | Mar 99 | Jun 99 | Sep 99 | Dec 99 | Mar 00 | Jun 00 | Sep 00

The daily chart of Lucent Technologies (Chart 5.1) shows a very clear short selling point when the stock breaks both the 200-day and 50-day moving averages on a huge price break that occurs on significant downside volume. Note that this occurs after the fifth rally back above the 50-day moving average after the initial high-volume price break off the top. This fifth rally lasts for four days, and the fourth day shows the highest volume of the four-day rally. Notice how this last day of the four-day rally looks impressive, but the stock actually shows signs of stalling, closing in the middle of the daily range for that day.

The chart of C-cor, Inc. (Chart 5.2) shows a big head & shoulders top, and the proper shorting point presents itself as the stock rolls over on the right-side shoulder, breaking the 50-day moving averages as volume picks up sharply. Note carefully that the stock makes one final rally above the 50-day moving average on the lowest weekly volume for the stock in over a year. This indicates that this final rally is occurring on declining demand for the stock and provides a clue that the stock is on its last gasp.

Overhead Supply

The price action shown in the following examples is often due to "overhead supply." The principle of overhead supply becomes very important when you are analyzing potential short sales. By studying the charts, you should be able to determine the approximate overhead price areas where owners of the stock will likely begin to sell. Overhead supply is defined on a price chart as areas where the stock has traded for a period of time that are above where the stock is currently trading. As a stock rallies and moves up into these areas, investors who purchased the stock in these zones of overhead supply and then experienced the pain of watching it go down will be looking to sell in order to try and get out "even."

Examples of Overhead Supply

AOL Time Warner's chart (Chart 6.1) shows that the stock had trouble getting through the tremendous overhead supply at Point A and ultimately ended up rolling over to new lows.

Qlogic (Chart 6.2) attempted to rally after a bad break, but ran into a wall of overhead supply at Point A, which sent the stock back to new lows. A second rally attempt meets a similar fate at Point B.

Examples of Head & Shoulders Tops

The classic short sale price structure on a chart is called a "head & shoulders top." Many investors have probably heard of a head & shoulders pattern, which resembles the outline of a "head" in the middle with a lower "shoulder" on either side.

Chart 6.1. AOL Time Warner, Inc. 2002 Weekly Chart

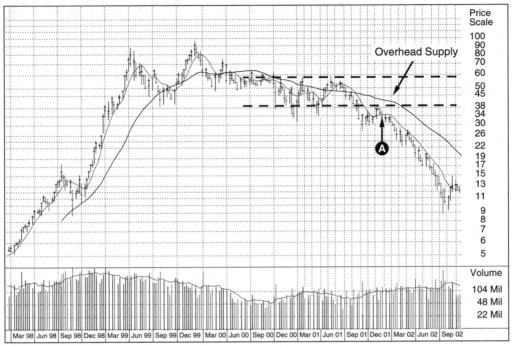

Chart 6.2. Qlogic Corp. 2002 Weekly Chart

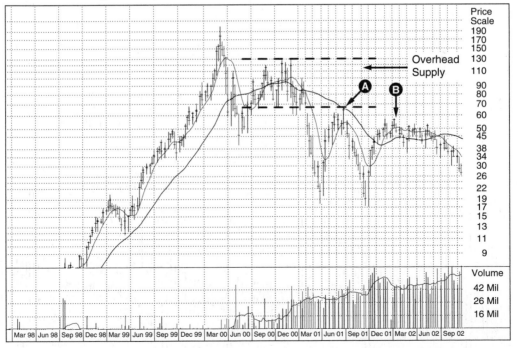

Chart 7.1. IDEC Pharmaceuticals, Inc. 2001 Weekly Chart

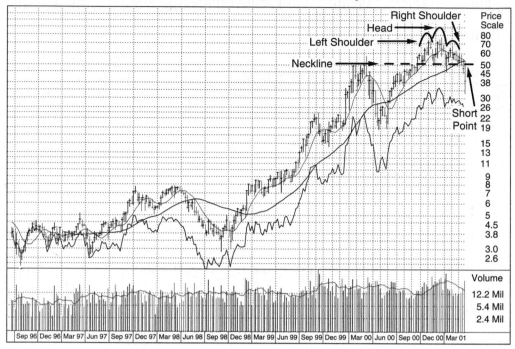

Chart 7.2. Timberland Co. 2001 Weekly Chart

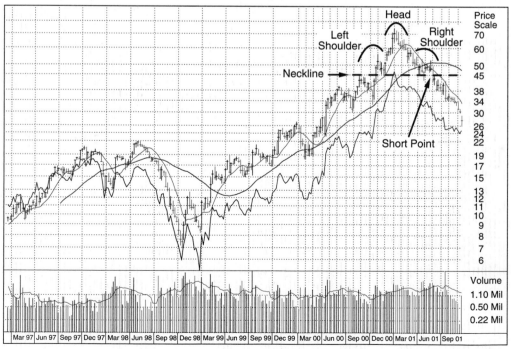

A textbook head & shoulders pattern should have the right shoulder lower than the left shoulder, and the general volume pattern in the head & shoulders should show increasing volume as the pattern moves from left to right, but this is not absolutely necessary. Referring to the examples 7.1 and 7.2, we can see that a trend line drawn along the lows of the head & shoulders pattern yields a "neckline" on the right shoulder. Normally trying to short at the neckline is too obvious, which is why we use 50-day moving average breaks to determine proper short points.

If you are a careful "tape watcher," experience teaches you that there will be times, after an initial bad break in a stock, when tremendous volume will trade while the stock is advancing in price, creating an overwhelming impression of strength. This sometimes occurs on the right shoulder of a head & shoulders price formation, near the end of the second or third rally attempt. It serves the purpose of running in other short sellers who timed their short selling incorrectly. The buying that occurs at these pullback points is what knowledgeable pros term "poor quality buying," although they can be guilty of it as well.

Study the charts of former leaders from the past that topped and then broke down severely. There are many parallel examples of stocks topping in past markets that you can use as current models. What happened in the past will happen again— stock markets have been around for hundreds of years. Correct timing is more important than any other factor in short selling, so put 80 percent of your effort into learning to start at the right time.

How to Set a Price Limit

When entering your short sale order in a weakening market, it may be best to place a price limit a half point or so below the last price for the stock. For example, if a stock last traded at $50, you might place a limit of $49.50. This type of limit order says that you are willing to sell short at any price down to $49.50, but no lower. This limit will prevent your order from being executed one or two points lower if the stock trades down substantially before an up-tick. But if the general market is rallying, it is normally better to place your short selling orders "at the market," rather than placing price limits on your orders. The object is to get your position on the short side and not quibble for an extra 10 or 20 cents which almost always leads to your totally missing the market and not getting your short selling orders off at all.

Learn by performing a post analysis of each trade. Take a red pen and plot on a set of individual stock charts exactly when and where you bought and sold each one of your stocks during the last two years. You will learn more about proper stock selection and timing from this objective analysis of your own decisions and mistakes than from anything else you will ever do in the market. Get smart. Find out what you are doing right and wrong—it is this type of post analysis that will make you a sharp buyer and seller, even short seller, of stocks.

When to Buy Back and Cover Your Short Sale

Before you sell any stock short, decide at the start the price at which you will buy back your position and cut your loss if the stock rallies against you. In many cases, the loss-cutting limit should be a little less than the normal eight percent loss limit used for long positions. This should force you to take greater care in initiating your short sale at exactly the right time. If you time the short sale wrongly, the stock may rally up 15 to 25 percent in price very rapidly, as professional buyers attempt to run in the shorts, even if the stock is ultimately going much lower. If the general market turns back to the upside with tremendous power and huge volume in several key institutional stocks, and if you have not made any real, profitable progress in your short position, you should, in most cases cover the positions quickly rather than waiting for it to reach your predetermined covering price. In particular, if you have been in a downtrend for some time, and the market signals a change in its trend by putting in an upside follow-through day, a lack of decisive action to cover short positions could cause severe losses. You must act quickly as an insurance policy against the possibility that you are wrong on the direction of the general market, which could be undergoing a major turn once an upside follow-through occurs. In the stock market, there are the quick, and there are the dead.

If the market has been steadily declining, then a day will come when either bad news hits the stock market or several stocks will experience delayed openings on the downside. A few stocks may gap down in price (e.g., open down sharply from the prior day's close), or the market may be off substantially for the day. Often times a sharp down opening will also be accompanied by some high readings in some indicators like the Put/Call Ratio or the CBOE Volatility Index (VIX). Readings in the Put/Call Ratio over 1.0 often signal excessive fear in the market which is associated with short- and long-term bottoms, while a sharp spike in the VIX over 40 and as high as 60 to 70 is also associated with such market bottoms. This is an excellent time to cover your short positions by buying your stocks back while there is a weak or panicking market. When you cover your short position, you should cover at the market. If you have a large position short, then it becomes even more crucial to buy back during market weakness because you have to cover when you have the opportunity, due to the size of your position.

Some investors suggest that if you sell short, you should follow the axiom, "Cut your losses quickly and let your winners run." However, when shorting, I have found it better to cut your losses even more quickly and take your profits when they have reached the specified percentage objective. The reason for this is that bear markets tend to break very fast and then stage short, sharp rallies which can run you in and cause any profits you have in a short position to evaporate. The percentage objective for covering your short and taking profits should be at least double the percentage limitation you use for cutting and taking losses. This allows you to be wrong twice for each time you are right and still not get into financial trouble.

Others also suggest that if a profit begins to build after selling a stock short, you should use stop-loss orders (orders entered with the specialists or market makers to automatically buy at the market if a certain price is reached) and progressively move the buy stop-loss order down along with the stock as it declines. This is what is known as a "trailing stop." I don't believe that this is the most intelligent approach because it frequently stops you out (buys back the stock you are short and covers your short position) during normal fluctuations and rallies with only smaller gains and losses. A better practice is to cut all of the losses short when you are wrong or have reached the maximum percentage loss that you set before taking your short position, and on the profit side cover and take your profits when the stock declines and hits your predetermined profit percentage objective. If you have a profit of 20 to 30 percent in a particular short position, it is probably best to take the entire profit or at least a good portion of it, rather than run the risk of having to give back a worthwhile gain.

Don't Run with the Crowd

When it becomes obvious to sell short to everyone around you and they are all doing it, you should stop and cover your short positions because it is then too late and they will probably be wrong in their timing. You are better off to trade alone, trusting your own analysis and study of timing and selection of proper short sale price patterns. Following the crowd in the stock market rarely works.

Puts and Calls

If you believe a stock is going down in price and don't want to sell common stock in the marketplace, or find it difficult to get stock short in the market, it is possible to use put options to achieve the same purpose. Don't buy any put or call without at least studying the earnings and price-chart history of the underlying stock, just as you would with the stock itself. If put options are used, you should definitely limit the proportion of your overall investment account you will commit to option trading. A prudent investor or trader should never expose all or even the majority of his or her capital to options.

Short Interest Reporting

Short interest in individual stocks on the NYSE and NASDAQ is reported once a month and published in a number of publications, including *Investor's Business Daily* and Daily Graphs®. If the short interest in a stock is very large and has been increasing recently, then that stock may not be your best candidate for selling short. Some large traders watch short interest building up in stocks and may attempt to run in the shorts by buying heavily the instant a general market turn to the upside occurs. Short interest is usually reported as the "Number of Days Volume Short" in a stock. For example, if the stock of ABC Company trades an average of 100,000 shares a day, and the current total number of ABC shares that are held short is 500,000, then it would, theoretically, take short sellers five days of average daily volume to cover their short positions in ABC. Therefore, the short interest in ABC Company in this example would be described as "5.0 days."

Short interest in stocks at the peak in 1929 and in early 2000 was extremely small. Edward Meeker, the Economist for the New York Stock Exchange during the depression of the 1930s, studied short interest at the market peak in 1929 and found that stocks with negligible short interest fell much harder during the Crash of 1929 than stocks that had a larger short interest. Large short interest does provide some cushion during declines, although it doesn't necessarily prevent declines per se.

Risk is Always Present

Finally, always remember that all common stocks are speculative and involve substantial risk. You must be willing to take many small losses in order to avoid the risk and possibility of substantially larger losses. Consider it as your fire insurance premium against catastrophic reverses. Bernard Baruch said, "If a speculator is correct half of the time, he is hitting a good average. Even being right three or four times out of ten should yield a person a fortune if he has the sense to cut his losses quickly on the ventures where he has been wrong."

Short Selling Checklist

Let's review our short selling principles as a checklist that the aspiring short seller should run through before making that first short sale:

1. The general market should be in a bear trend, and preferably in a position that is relatively early in the bear trend. Shorting stocks in a bull market does not offer a high probability of success, and shorting stocks very late in a bear period can be dangerous if the market suddenly turns to the upside and begins a new bull phase.

2. Stocks that the would-be short seller has identified as candidates for short sales should be relatively liquid. They should have sufficient daily trading volume so as not to be subject to rapid upward price movement if the stock experiences a sudden rush of buyers that can result in a significant short squeeze. A general rule of one million shares or more traded per day on average is a reasonable liquidity requirement.

3. Look to short former leaders from the prior bull cycle. Stocks that offer the best short sale opportunities in a bear market tend to be the very same stocks that led the prior bull phase and had huge price run-ups during the bull market.

4. Watch for head & shoulders top formations and late-stage, wide, loose, improper bases that then fail. These are your optimal short sale chart patterns.

5. Look to short former leaders five to seven months or more after the stock's absolute price peak. Often, the optimal shorting point will occur after the 50-day moving average has crossed below the 200-day moving average, a so-called "black cross," and this may take several months to develop. Once a former leading stock has topped, monitor it closely and be prepared to take action when it signals an optimal shorting point.

6. Set 20–30% profit objectives, and take profits often!

A LOUD WARNING TO THE WISE!

If stocks have been in a bear market for one-and-a-half to two years or more, and many former leaders from the prior bull cycle have corrected 70–90% or more off their bull market peaks, you may be late to the party if you start trying to short the market at such a late stage. Selling stocks short in the late phases of a bear market can be dangerous, if not outright disastrous. Always exercise extreme caution whenever you decide to sell stocks short, particularly if you have been late in identifying the start of a new bear market and are merely following the crowd when it becomes obvious. In other words, if the stock market has been acting terribly and in a downtrend for some time, and you've just bought this book because you have decided you are now going to sell short and cash in on the action—watch out!

PART 2

THE ANATOMY OF A SHORT SALE

Now that we've covered the nuts and bolts of selling short, it's time to put it all together by analyzing real-world examples and developing a practical understanding of exactly what to look for when deciding to sell stocks short.

We can begin with Diagram 1, on page 39, which serves as a type of "template" for the head & shoulders short sale set-up.

All good short ideas start out as outstanding buy ideas. To the extent that the stock market mirrors the U.S. economy, we can expect that the virtuous cycle of creation and destruction that is observed in the U.S. economy exists in the stock market as well.

This is demonstrated by the fact that a very high percentage of stocks that were big winners in a particular bull cycle turn out to be the best short selling situations in the ensuing bear cycle. We can think of most big, winning stocks as having a "life cycle" which plays out during the course of, first, a bull cycle and, second, the bear cycle that follows.

During the bull cycle, the winning stock is likely a new or existing company with new products, new management, or new industry conditions that begin to drive a new cycle of growth. Institutional investors such as mutual funds and pensions funds become aware of the company, and they begin to establish positions in its stock, driving it higher and higher in price as they continue to buy the stock during its prime growth phase. During this phase, the stock will form several price consolidations or bases on the way up, and each new breakout from each new base attracts the attention of more and more investors.

Eventually, after the stock has formed three to four bases or more in its uptrend, it will begin to become obvious to everyone. At this late stage in the stock's move, several Wall Street analysts are likely to be raising their price targets on the stock, or it may be featured several times in the broadcast and print media, or you may start to hear other people talking up the stock. Now that the stock is obvious to everyone, and everyone is running around talking about how wonderful it is, it tops.

It should be noted that while an outright bear market offers the best opportunities to sell stocks short, occasionally one can make money selling stocks short during an intermediate correction. Most bull markets consist of one sharp, initial leg up, followed by an intermediate correction and then a second, less sharp, leg up to a final market top. Depending on the severity of the intermediate correction, some leaders in the first leg of a bull market can be short sale candidates during an intermediate correction. For example, the 1995–1997 bull market's first leg up in 1995 to early 1996 was led, in part, by semiconductor stocks like C-Cube Microsystems, for example, which topped in late 1995 to early 1996 and in several instances offered excellent short sale opportunities. Likewise, the Chinese Internet and industrial stocks, U.S. educational stocks, and some technology stocks like Omnivision Technologies were excellent short sale opportunities in 2004.

Let's take a look at your basic short sale scenario. As Diagram 1 shows at Point 1, the initial top occurs as the stock is hammered on heavy volume from a point at or near its all-time highs. Major price breaks that occur on volume that is either the highest or nearly highest in the stock's entire move are clues that a stock is under significant distribution. Generally this occurs as the stock breaks out of a faulty, late-stage base and fails, reversing back through its pivot point, or the stock will simply drop out of the bottom of a late-stage base it may still be in the process of forming. Either way, the stock will come down fairly quickly on big volume over the course of one to five weeks or more, undercutting a prior basing or consolidation area where it will draw in short sellers who see the stock breaking a major "support" level at Point 2. However, what is obvious to most in the stock market seldom works, and the stock abruptly turns to the upside and stages a sharp rally, making a run at and usually clearing its 50-day moving average.

At this point, you should place the stock on your watch list and begin monitoring the stock as a short sale candidate. After five to seven months or more from the stock's absolute price peak, and after the stock rallies two to four times back above its 50-day moving average, the proper time and price point to execute the short sale will present itself at Point 3. After the first few rallies back above the 50-day moving average, there will come one final rally, which usually occurs on lighter volume than the prior rallies, and the volume appears to diminish as the stock moves higher. This can also be accompanied by stalling action. This is indicating that demand for the stock is finally waning, and the first high-volume turn to the downside is your signal to sell short. If you are alert, and the market is moving to the downside at the same time, possibly failing on a follow-through attempt, occasionally you can sell short as the stock is rallying on light volume, just before it dives. This is tricky and a little riskier than waiting for the downside volume to come in, but it can give you a slight head start.

Some exceptions will occur, however, and in rare instances a stock will have only one rally back up over the 50-day moving average or it may have several rallies that trade up to the 50-day moving average without actually getting above it. You may ask how you can tell which rally is the stock's last rally, and the honest answer is that you never know for sure. The key point is that each rally back above the 50-day should be analyzed within the context of the general market environment as well as the technical "quality" of the specific rally. For example, is the rally showing severe stalling or is it "wedging" higher on lighter and lighter volume, and does this technical action distinguish it from the prior rallies back above the 50-day? Has the market been rallying for the past few days into overhead resistance and is simultaneously rolling over as the stock's final rally gives way? These can be clues that a failed rally could be the correct time to short.

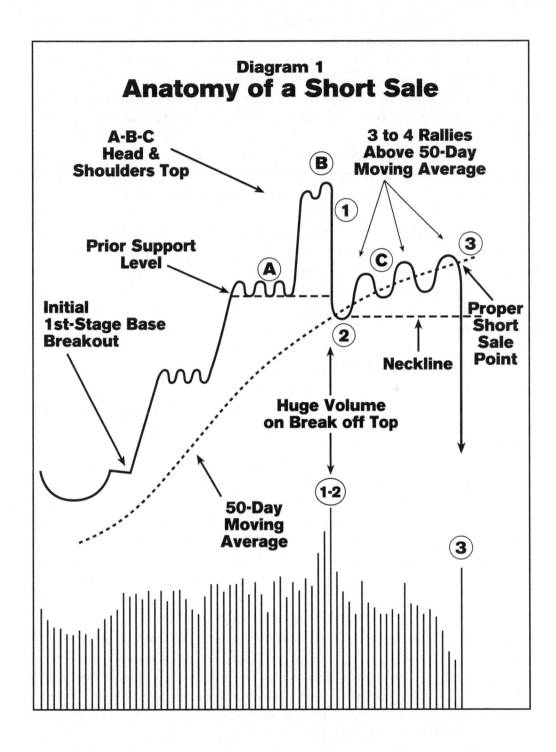

Diagram 1
Anatomy of a Short Sale

Patterns with only one rally are much harder to decipher than those with three to four, and it is possible that you may be stopped out of premature short sales when you attempt to sell short on a stock's first breach of the 50-day moving average following an initial rally back above the moving average. The odds of success increase with each successive rally back above the 50-day moving average, so naturally your odds are higher with stocks that have had three to four rallies or more above the 50-day moving average than those with only one or two. If you can afford to be very selective, then by all means do so and stick to those short sale candidates that have put in three to four rallies or more.

This entire pattern traces out an A–B–C "head & shoulders top" with A and C indicating the left and right shoulders, respectively, and B, the head. In general, the right shoulder should form lower than the left shoulder, and several bouts of heavy downside volume should be evident in the right shoulder so that the overall pattern has increasing average volume as it forms from left to right.

Head & shoulders top patterns can form over the course of five to seven months or more. The "size" or duration of the pattern is not as important as the price and volume action of the pattern itself. If a stock forms a head & shoulders top over the course of only three months and is giving all the technical signals that indicate it should be sold short, then the short sale should be made.

It is not always necessary that a stock form an exact head & shoulders topping pattern in order to qualify as a short selling candidate. A slight variant to our short selling template in Diagram 1 is the following as shown in Diagram 2, the late-stage base failure short sale set-up.

In this case, a left shoulder does not form, but the price and volume action from the peak price high onward, which normally forms the "head" in a head & shoulders top, is very similar to Diagram 1.

In this type of set-up, the stock's final top is marked by a late-stage base failure that is similar to the head & shoulders top in that it is a fast, furious, and deep sell-off that occurs in huge volume. After this sell-off, which usually undercuts a narrow support area in the stock's prior uptrend, the stock will usually stage several rallies back up through the 50-day moving average. On occasion, you may see only one or two rallies to or above the 50-day moving average

This type of pattern can offer the would-be short seller two potential, correct short points. The first occurs right as the stock is failing off of its peak, either experiencing a high-volume breakout failure that sends it back into its base, or simply falling through the lows of its late-stage, improper base on huge volume. The second can occur after several rallies form a right "shoulder" and the stock begins to roll over as volume begins to pick up.

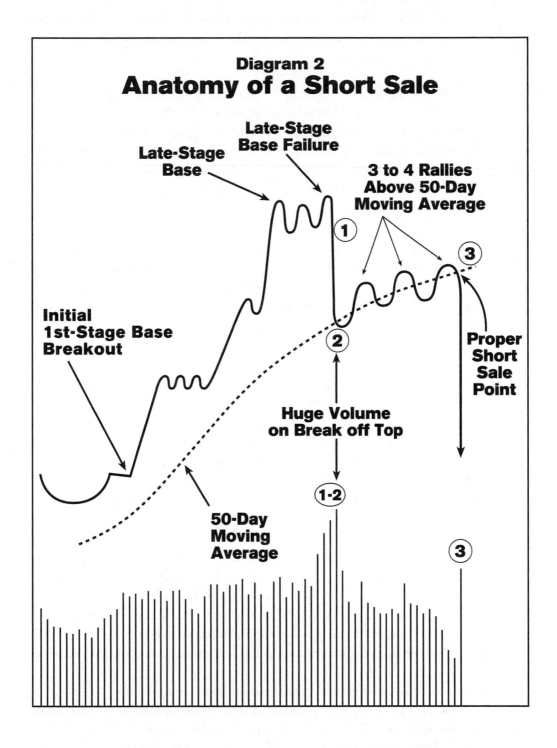

Be aware of subtle clues within a stock's chart pattern that can be telling you the stock is about to roll over. To summarize, the types of technical action to watch for are:

1. Stalling, or price action that occurs when a stock is rallying but closes below the mid-point of its weekly price range for one to three weeks on the way up, can be a clue that a rally is being met by systematic selling which will soon overcome the rally and send the stock downward again. In particular, stalling on a third or fourth rally above the 50-day moving average on the right shoulder of a head & shoulders top can be a strong sign that a downside break is imminent.

2. Wedging, or a rally that trades on successively lighter and lighter volume as the stock moves higher, is a sign that there is a lack of buying demand for the stock. Like stalling, wedging action that occurs on a third or fourth rally above the 50-day moving average on the right shoulder of a head & shoulders top formation can be a major clue that the stock is ready to break to the downside.

3. "Railroad tracks" occur when a stock trades up sharply one week and then the next week completely retraces the price range of the previous up-week, closing near the peak for the week on high volume. This gives the appearance of two lines running parallel to each other like, of course, railroad tracks. Such a high-volume retracement can indicate that a stock is under distribution, even though the action seems to indicate that the stock was supported on heavy volume since it closes at or near the highs for both weeks.

4. "Island" tops, which are characterized by a stock that has a final gap up after a rally of two to three weeks or more, and then trades in a tight range for the gap week. This has the appearance on a weekly chart of a little, square cross that is isolated and "floating" out all by itself, hence the term, "island top." It can indicate that a rally has exhausted itself as the gap runs into sellers so that the stock churns in a tight range despite closing up for the week.

5. Watch for breakouts from late-stage bases that occur on low volume. If a stock, after a long price run, forms a wide, loose, and improper late-stage base, be alert for a low-volume breakout attempt from this base. A low-volume breakout attempt that reverses on sharply increasing volume can offer an early short sale point. Sometimes this type of low-volume breakout

from a late-stage, improper base occurs after a stock has had a climax top. Following a climax top, a stock may turn up and build a big, wide and loose base and attempt to break out again. If this breakout occurs on very little volume, it very likely will fail and signal that the stock has topped for good.

Be alert to price areas that may represent prior support, as many chartists will short a stock once it breaks a support level, only to see the stock undercut the support level and then turn and rally sharply higher, running in the premature short sellers. Part of the reason this occurs is because technical analysis and the use of charts to interpret stock price action has such a wide following that many individuals act upon the same information at the same time. Since a breach of a support area is considered a bearish signal in the mainstream of technical analysis, everyone on the planet who is reading charts gets short, creating all at once a mass of short sellers at that point. Once they are all short, they effectively create a near-term floor for the stock in that they are now would-be buyers in the event they have to cover their short position. When everyone is leaning one way on a stock on the short side, they will invariably get run in. Often the best place to cover a short position is right as the stock is undercutting a prior low or area of support, because the stock will often turn and rally from that point, enabling you to wait and watch for another opportunity to short the stock.

It is important to understand that successful short selling requires relentless determination and persistence. There will be many times when you will be stopped out of your short position, and when you are you must cut your losses quickly and decisively. But, undaunted, you must continue to monitor those same stocks that you were stopped out of and which continue to fit our short selling templates, because eventually the proper short selling point will present itself, and you must be alert to catch it as it unfolds. This means you may get stopped out of a short sale several times on the same stock before you finally hit the "sweet spot" and catch a stock just before it cascades to the downside and gives you a quick 20–30% profit.

PART 3

MODELS
OF GREATEST
SHORT SALES

Armed with our short selling templates, we can now examine some of the greatest short selling opportunities in market history. In the first few examples we discuss some of the salient points and details of each short sale "model." This should help the reader identify important characteristics and features of the remaining examples. By studying each of these examples carefully, the reader should be able to gain a strong sense of what constitutes a "model" short selling candidate and be able to apply such knowledge to real-time trading.

Cisco Systems, Inc.

Cisco Systems came public in 1990 and was a big market leader in all three bull cycles during the "go-go" decade of the 1990s. Cisco Systems defined the term "market leader" by achieving an astounding total gain of 75,000% from its initial pivot point in October 1990 to its ultimate top in March of 2000. At its top in March 2000, Cisco Systems was the darling of many institutional portfolios.

But besides providing a shining historical model of a big, winning stock, Cisco, more importantly, also proves that there is a time to sell every stock, no matter how wonderful everyone thinks it is, and no matter how many Wall Street analysts think it is a "screaming buy" on the way down.

A basic leadership characteristic of Cisco during its entire run from 1991 to its top in 2000 was that it was always one of the last stocks to correct during a general market correction. When it did finally begin to break down during such a correction, this usually marked the end, or nearly the end, of the overall, general market correction. By closely studying the accompanying weekly CSCO chart, you can observe that this was true. Every time the market corrected, Cisco held up during the initial phases of the general market downturn (labeled A through D on the chart), and as the correction progressed and market psychology began to become more fearful, Cisco would inevitably begin a correction for a few days, bottom, and then turn to the upside and break out again, essentially leading the market back out of its correction and into a new bull phase.

With this in mind, when the general market began to get into some of its most serious trouble in nearly a century and Cisco began to correct, something very interesting occurred. Cisco broke this pattern for the first time! When it began to correct it continued to come down, and did not produce its usual pattern of correcting and then quickly coming out of it to lead the market out of its correction and start another upside move. This was very significant, and a major clue that it was now time to sell, even sell short, Cisco Systems.

Alert chart readers will notice that Cisco formed an easily recognizable head & shoulders top pattern right around its March 2000 peak. However, short sellers who tried to establish positions as the stock broke down through the neckline on the right shoulder quickly discovered that their short sales were premature. Since the breakdown through the neckline occurred only two and a half months after the March peak, bullish psychology in the stock in the form of Cisco "bargain-hunters" enabled it to rally sharply higher back above the 50-day moving average and into resistance at the $70 price level. This served to run in the premature short sellers.

As with most of the successful short selling examples we will look at, Cisco took another four months to completely wring out the remaining bullish psychology still in the stock and finally collapse. The principal we have discussed in prior chapters, whereby the optimal shorting point for a former leader occurs many months after the ultimate top, is quite evident in this example.

The accompanying CSCO daily chart shows in detail the four rally attempts back above the 50-day moving average that are also shown on the weekly chart. Normally, we will be alert to short selling signals in a stock after the third to fourth rally attempt. In Cisco's case, the fourth failed rally attempt proved to be its death knell, and the short selling bell rang loud and clear when the stock crashed through its 50-day and 200-day moving averages on heavy volume. Note that the fourth rally attempt back above the 50-day moving average showed stalling action as volume was picking up, a slight detail that distinguishes this final rally from the three previous ones, and gives a very subtle clue that the stock was likely to fail very soon thereafter.

If you missed the first short selling point, the stock provided one more opportunity just above the $50 price level when it briefly rallied above its 50-day moving average for two days before crashing back down through the moving average on heavy volume. This was a clear secondary shorting point. Cisco eventually dropped below $10 a share, leading to widespread shock among the stock's fans who just couldn't believe that the "investment grade" darling of the '90s bull market had lost over 90% of its value from its March 2000 peak!

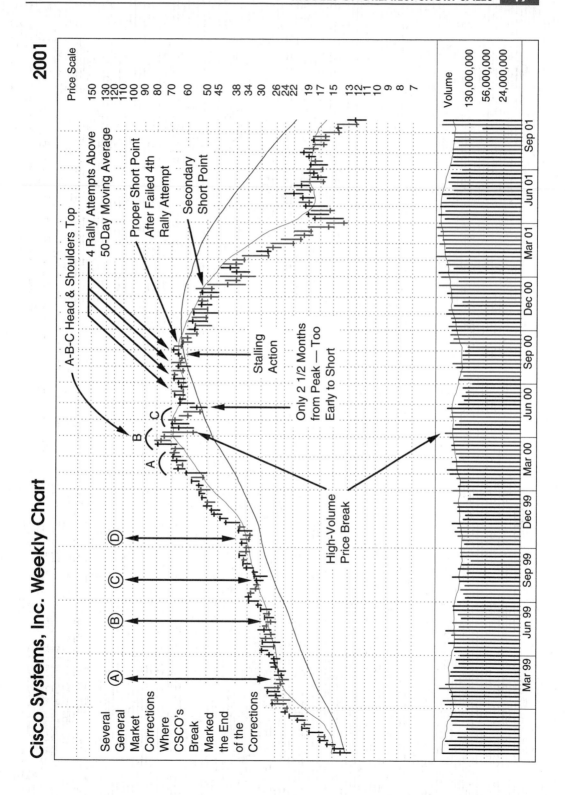

Cisco Systems, Inc. Weekly Chart

2001

Price Scale

A-B-C Head & Shoulders Top

4 Rally Attempts Above
50-Day Moving Average

Proper Short Point
After Failed 4th
Rally Attempt

Secondary
Short Point

Several
General
Market
Corrections
Where
CSCO's
Break
Marked
the End
of the
Corrections

Stalling
Action

Only 2 1/2 Months
from Peak — Too
Early to Short

High-Volume
Price Break

Volume

130,000,000
56,000,000
24,000,000

Cisco Systems, Inc. Daily Chart

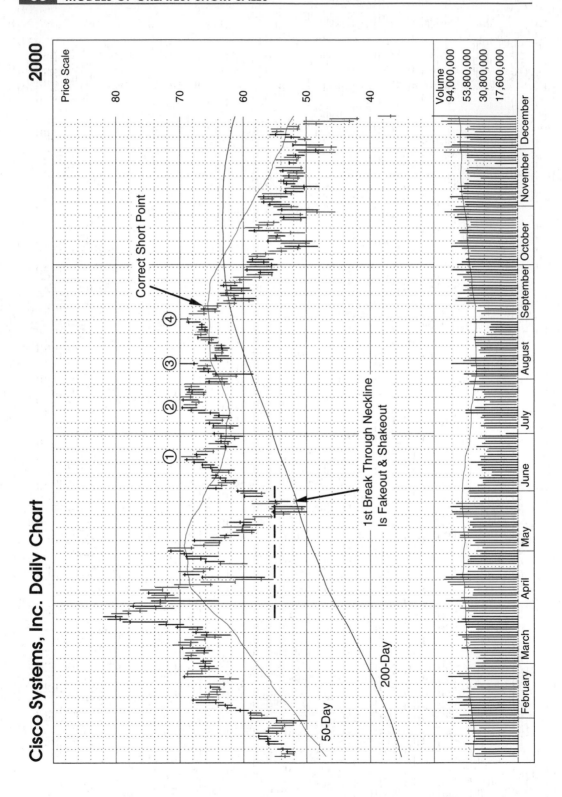

2000

Price Scale

Correct Short Point

50-Day

200-Day

1st Break Through Neckline
Is Fakeout & Shakeout

Volume
94,000,000
53,800,000
30,800,000
17,600,000

February | March | April | May | June | July | August | September | October | November | December

Lucent Technologies, Inc.

Lucent Technologies was another "investment grade" darling of late 1990's bull market, having been spun off from AT&T in April 1996. Lucent Technologies was engaged in the research and development of a number of cutting-edge telecommunications technologies at AT&T, and so was considered the "crown jewel" of AT&T's portfolio of subsidiaries. After the spin-off, LU shares were distributed to holders of AT&T stock, representing a juicy bone thrown out to "Telephone's" shareholders who could now realize the full value of Lucent's technology innovations in the shares of a separate company. And realize this value they did, as Lucent stock rocketed from $7 to just above $60 a share on a split-adjusted basis over the next 44 months. Lucent Technologies stock was at this point a favorite of many a Wall Street analyst, garnering "focus list" and "investment grade" buy recommendations from all of the major Wall Street brokerages.

But the beginning of the end for Lucent commenced with a massive, one-week price break that occurred during the week of January 7, 2000, as shown in the accompanying LU weekly chart. This price break represented the right side of what would become the "head" of what at that time was still an unfolding head & shoulders topping pattern.

However, short sellers trying to jump on this major downside price break were premature in trying to short Lucent only four weeks from its absolute price peak. Short sellers were immediately run in by the first of four rallies back over the 50-day moving average. Like Cisco in the previous example, Lucent finally failed after the fourth attempted rally above the 50-day failed, providing an optimal short point as the stock reversed back down through the 50-day on massive volume. In fact, close examination of the stock's daily chart reveals that there were actually three shorting points as the stock failed. The first occurred as the stock moved above the 200-day moving average and then failed to the downside, the second occurred as the stock knifed through its 50-day moving average, and the third occurred as the stock broke through the "neckline" of the right shoulder making up the overall head & shoulders top pattern.

From the absolute price peak, note that it took 33 weeks for Lucent to finally break loose to the downside, but when it began this major downside move the multiple failures through the 200-day moving average, 50-day moving average, and the "neckline" of the head & shoulders on tremendous volume provided a very clear short selling signal. It is clear in this example that once Lucent put in its absolute top in late 1999, the would-be short seller had to be both alert and patient with respect to the proper timing of a Lucent short sale, as a premature short seller would have surely been "run in" and forced to cover.

Lucent Technologies, Inc. Weekly Chart

2001

A-B-C Head & Shoulders Top

4 Rallies Back Above 50-Day Moving Average

Proper Short Point as Stock Breaks Moving Average on Huge Volume

33 Weeks from Absolute Top

Selling Short on the 1st Break of Neckline on Right Shoulder Is Premature!

High-Volume Price Break

Price Scale
110
100
90
80
70
60
50
45
38
34
30
26
24
22
19
17
15
13
12
11
10
9
8
7
6
5
4.5

A

B

C

Volume
74,000,000
38,000,000
20,000,000

Sep 98
Dec 98
Mar 99
Jun 99
Sep 99
Dec 99
Mar 00
Jun 00
Sep 00
Dec 00
Mar 01
Jun 01

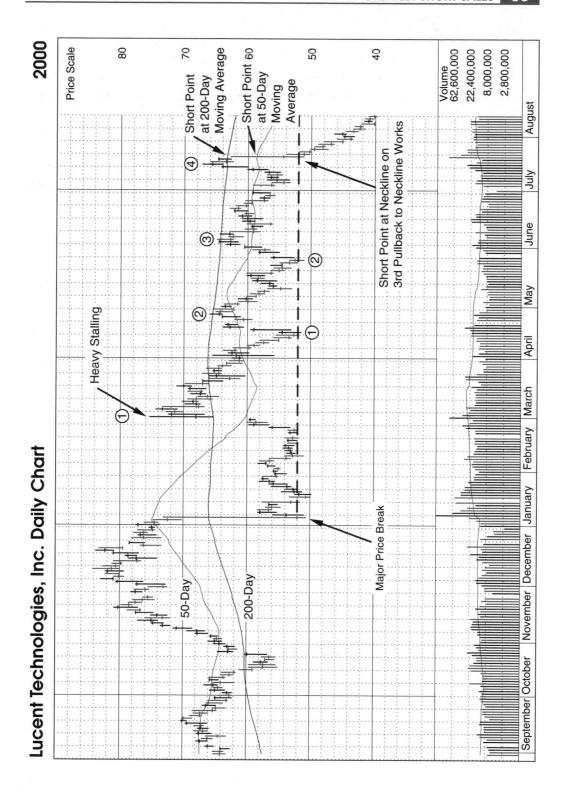

Lucent Technologies, Inc. Daily Chart

2000

Price Scale

Short Point at 200-Day Moving Average

Short Point at 50-Day Moving Average

Short Point at Neckline on 3rd Pullback to Neckline Works

Heavy Stalling

50-Day

200-Day

Major Price Break

Volume
62,600,000
22,400,000
8,000,000
2,800,000

Calpine Corp.

Power generator Calpine Corp. is a good example of a late-stage cup with handle chart base that failed, setting up a strong short selling opportunity several months from its absolute price peak. It is interesting and relevant to note that as Calpine approached its ultimate top in March 2001, power generation and fears of an impending electric energy crisis were being highlighted in the news. Rolling black-outs in California had attracted the public's attention and helped to create a crisis mentality at that time. Suddenly everyone knew that power generation was a "hot" sector, despite the fact that stocks like Calpine had been marching steadily higher over the past two-and-a-half years. Unfortunately, in the stock market, when every-body finally "knows" something, it's all over.

On its journey from an initial breakout at the $2.60 per share price level to over $58, Calpine formed six bases, the first five of which were all relatively well con-tained and proper. The sixth base showed the first signs of a change in Calpine's character. This last, late-stage base had the appearance of a large, loose cup with handle base with three distinct bottoms. As the stock attempted to emerge from this base, the first two weeks showed hints of stalling action as volume picked up on the breakout. Eight weeks later, the breakout failed as the stock plummeted through its 50-day moving average.

One typical phenomenon that occurs in stocks that are weakening and break-ing down can be observed on the accompanying daily chart. Note how the down-trend from the mid-$50 price area down to the $20 price level is characterized by small, short rallies that show declining volume as the stock moves up (wedging ral-lies) which are then followed by downside price breaks, which actually increase vol-ume as the stock moves lower. This sort of technical action is often seen in down trending situations, and often a stock that is acting this way can be shorted at points where such declining-volume, or wedging, rallies move into resistance at their 50-day or 200-day moving averages.

Once the stock had broken down, the optimal short point occurred nearly eight months from the stock's absolute price peak. A low-volume rally took the stock just above its 50-day moving average as the stock showed stalling action on the weekly chart. Volume then picked up as the stock broke through its 50-day moving aver-age and plummeted from $26 to down below $10 a share in three weeks.

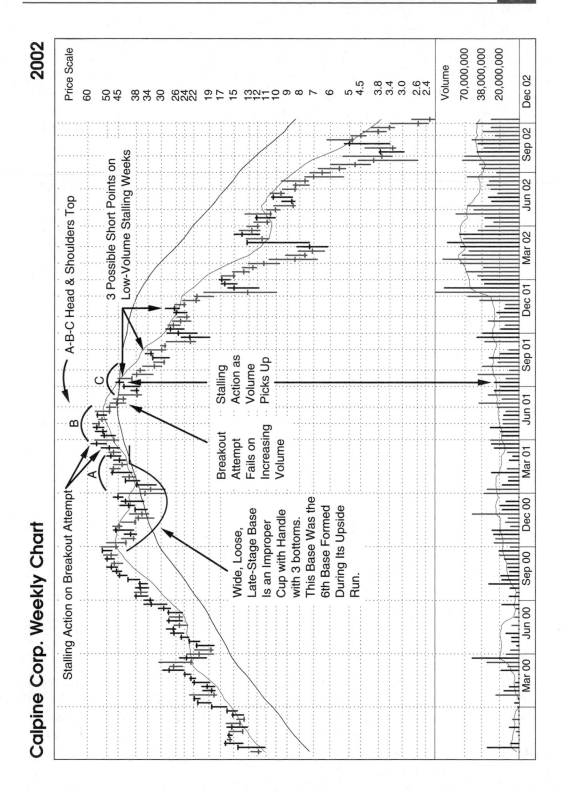

Calpine Corp. Weekly Chart

2002

Stalling Action on Breakout Attempt

A-B-C Head & Shoulders Top

3 Possible Short Points on
Low-Volume Stalling Weeks

B

C

A

Breakout
Attempt
Fails on
Increasing
Volume

Stalling
Action as
Volume
Picks Up

Wide, Loose,
Late-Stage Base
Is an Improper
Cup with Handle
with 3 bottoms.
This Base Was the
6th Base Formed
During Its Upside
Run.

Price Scale

60

50
45

38
34

30

26
24
22

19
17
15

13
12
11
10
9
8
7
6

5
4.5

3.8
3.4
3.0

2.6
2.4

Volume

70,000,000

38,000,000

20,000,000

Mar 00   Jun 00   Sep 00   Dec 00   Mar 01   Jun 01   Sep 01   Dec 01   Mar 02   Jun 02   Sep 02   Dec 02

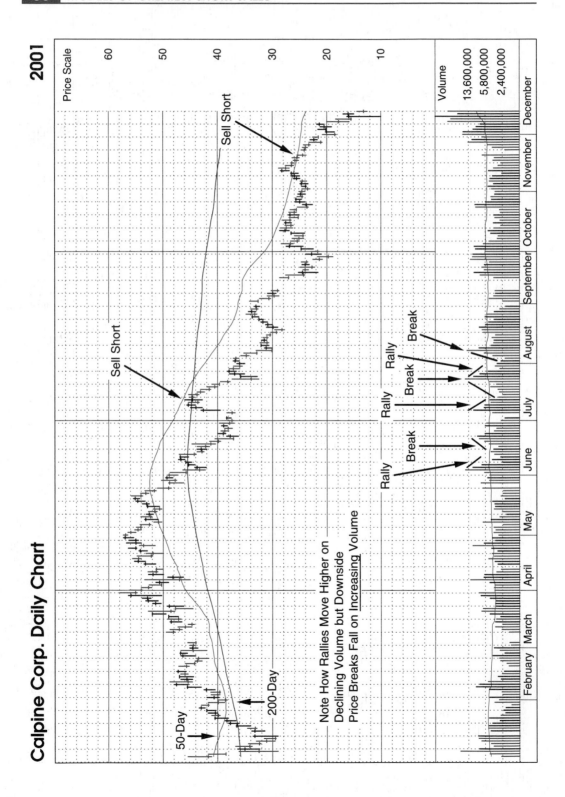

Calpine Corp. Daily Chart

2001

Price Scale

60

50

40

30

20

10

Sell Short

Sell Short

50-Day

200-Day

Note How Rallies Move Higher on
Declining Volume but Downside
Price Breaks Fall on Increasing Volume

Rally

Break

Rally

Break

Rally

Break

Rally

Break

Rally

Break

Volume

13,600,000

5,800,000

2,400,000

February March April May June July August September October November December

Yahoo!, Inc.

A big Internet winner in the 1998–1999 bull market, Yahoo! finally came apart in classic fashion. The final leg of the stock's move featured a massive streak to new highs at the $250 price level. Notice, however, that the final two up-weeks in Yahoo!'s run occurred on some of the lightest weekly volume in the entire move. This was followed by a massive, high-volume reversal right off the peak at $150.06, followed by another high-volume down week. The stock then back-and-filled for the next three months on light volume before breaking down again, this time below the 200-day moving average. Seven weeks later, the 50-day moving average crossed below the 200-day moving average. From here the stock made four attempts on the weekly chart to rally back above the 50-day moving average. After the fourth attempt, the stock gapped down beneath the 50-day moving average with a significant pick-up in volume. This was the optimal short sale point.

Yahoo! stock eventually bottomed at $8.02 per share, an astounding 96.8% decline from its peak at $250.06!

Broadcom Corp.

High-speed, broadband communications were all the rage during the 1998–1999 bull market, and Broadcom Corp. rode this wave to a 994% gain over 71 weeks from its initial pivot point in November 1998.

Initially Broadcom began to show signs that something was not quite right as it rallied into the $253 price level in March of 2000. As the stock moved towards these new highs, two things happened that offered the first clues to Broadcom's demise. First, as the stock rallied to new highs, upside volume was at an extreme low for two weeks at the top. Also, simultaneously, the stock began to form "railroad tracks," entirely retracing the prior week's move.

The stock then broke badly, getting cut in half in a mere two weeks. This set up a rally and the formation of a very wide, loose cup with handle pattern from which it then attempted to break out. However, this base was extremely faulty, and the stock failed on three rally attempts to the $260 price area. After the third attempt failed, the stock broke on a massive increase in downside volume, finally bottoming in October 2002 at $9.52 per share.

Certain-Teed Products Corp.

Certain-Teed Products scored huge gains during the 1960–1961 bull market, soaring 400% from December 1961 to December 1962. In fact, Certain-Teed was one of my first mistakes on the buy side. I originally bought the stock in the low $20s as it was emerging from a high, tight flag pattern and sold it for a 2- or 3-point gain, only to watch the stock soar to $80 a share! It was from the study of

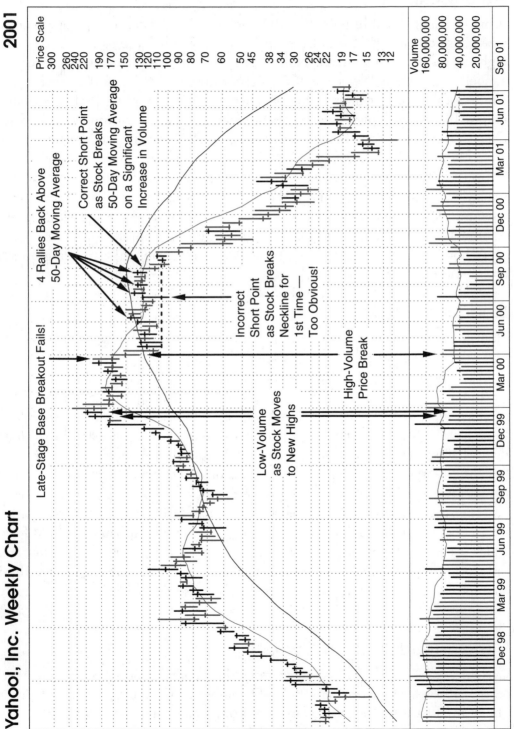

Yahoo!, Inc. Weekly Chart

2001

Price Scale
300
260
240
220
190
170
150
130
120
110
100
90
80
70
60
50
45
38
34
30
26
24
22
19
17
15
13
12

Volume
160,000,000
80,000,000
40,000,000
20,000,000

Late-Stage Base Breakout Fails!

4 Rallies Back Above
50-Day Moving Average

Correct Short Point
as Stock Breaks
50-Day Moving Average
on a Significant
Increase in Volume

Incorrect
Short Point
as Stock Breaks
Neckline for
1st Time —
Too Obvious!

Low-Volume
as Stock Moves
to New Highs

High-Volume
Price Break

Sep 98   Dec 98   Mar 99   Jun 99   Sep 99   Dec 99   Mar 00   Jun 00   Sep 00   Dec 00   Mar 01   Jun 01   Sep 01

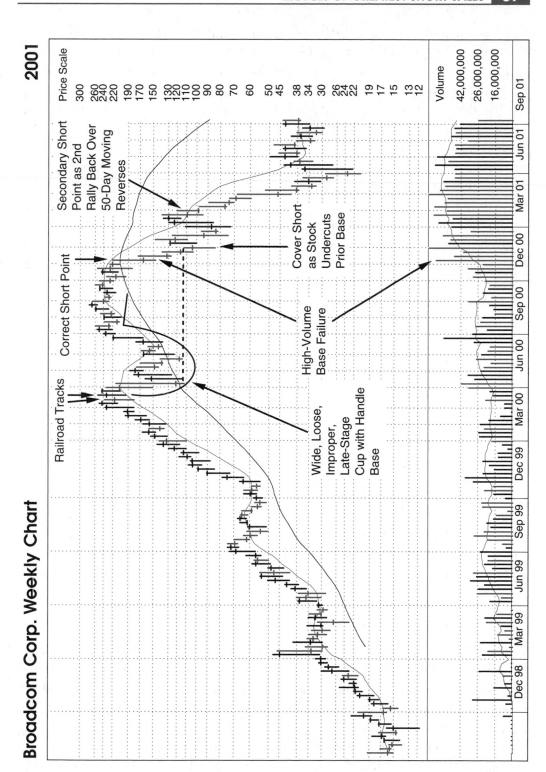

Broadcom Corp. Weekly Chart
2001

this mistake and others that I discovered many of the principals that later became the CAN SLIM system, as well the General Market System I use to determine the general direction of the market indices and which has saved my skin many times by getting me out of or short many a bear market.

My discovery of the General Market System led me to recommend Certain-Teed and other big winners from that period like Korvette Corp. as short sales. Back then, as a young stockbroker with Hayden Stone, a firm that was very prominent in those days but today no longer exists, I got in trouble with the home office in New York. Hayden Stone's analysts were recommending the stock as a buy at the same time I was going around telling my clients that the stock was a short. In fact, because at that time I was one of the biggest producers in the firm, I was asked to speak on a firm broadcast to the other Hayden Stone firms in our region. On this branch broadcast I stated that I believed Certain-Teed was a sell, even though Hayden Stone analysts had just recommended the stock as a buy the day before. I could hear the gasp coming back over the phone from all the brokers at the other Hayden Stone branches who were listening to the broadcast!

But market facts are market facts, and Certain-Teed was indeed a sell. I shorted the stock in the $44–45 area and made a quick 25–30% gain as the stock plummeted very sharply over the next five weeks. The chart of Certain-Teed shown here, which is from an old *Model Book of Greatest Stock Market Winners* that I marked up heavily, shows how I handled the stock during that period. It is simple to see on the chart that the stock formed a clear head & shoulders top, and collapsed on its second downside penetration through the neckline. Often, the first time a stock breaks its neckline on the right shoulder of a head & shoulders top formation, it will quickly rally back up through the neckline, running in short sellers who saw this obvious break the first time. The second break of the neckline was likely not as obvious, and short sellers who were licking their wounds from being run in on the first break of the neckline were probably not too eager to pounce on the stock the second time around, which did work. Again, what is obvious to many in the stock market seldom works.

Loews Corp.

In the 1960s, American consumers began to embrace the freedom that a new era of jet travel had ushered in, and consequently several airline stocks had big moves during this period. With consumers now able to reach far-flung regions of the country and the world in relatively short order, airline travel boomed. On the heels of this boom came the "follow-on" move in that group of stocks providing an essential component in the new era of travel: namely, hotel accommodations. Among several hotel stocks that had big moves in the 1960s, Loews Corp. was one of the big leaders.

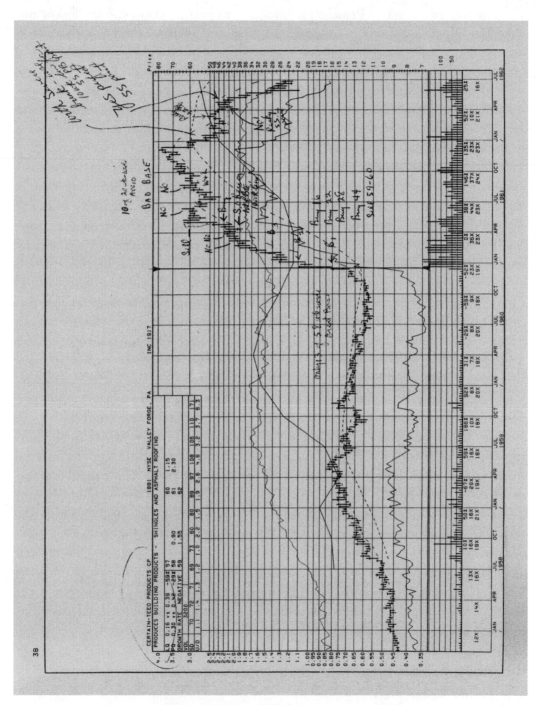

Annotated chart of Certain-Teed Products Corp. from
the 1971 *Model Book of Greatest Stock Market Winners.*

The move in the hotel stocks provides an interesting lesson in the "follow-on" concept. Often, a big move in one group of stocks (in this case, the airlines) will lead to a follow-on move by a group of stocks in an industry that is related to and benefiting from the same business trends and developments that caused the move in the first group. In this case, an increase in air travel led to an increase in demand for hotel accommodations. The difference in this case was that the airline stocks had their move in one bull cycle, the 1962–1965 bull market, and the hotel stocks in the ensuing 1966–1969 bull market.

After the airline stocks had topped in late 1965 along with the rest of the market, they all came back down to earth, finally bottoming and attempting to rally with the market as it began the next bull move in 1966. Unfortunately, many of these airline stocks were over-owned by institutions and their rally off their lows eventually fizzled out. But the broader concept of increased travel by American consumers was sound, and alert investors would have noticed that the concept was, by 1967, being manifested in the hotel stocks.

Loews Corp. had a tremendous move, rocketing over 1,230% in 24 months, finally topping in March of 1969 as it broke down from its peak for three weeks in a row with volume increasing sharply, forming the head of what was to become a head & shoulders top formation. The right shoulder consisted of two rallies back above the 50-day, and the correct short point occurred right after the second rally as the stock was rolling down and forming the right side of the right shoulder and breaking down through the 50-day moving average on increasing volume.

The stock then broke and headed lower over the next eight weeks, finally bottoming at a point that undercut the low point of a prior base formed in June–August 1968. This was a clear cover point, as the stock then turned and rallied from $25 a share to just over $40. This rally into the $40 area actually produced three separate rallies back above the 200-day moving average, and after the third rally the stock logged two weeks that were up a tiny amount on very weak upside volume. The next week the stock broke down through both the 50-day and 200-day moving averages, a secondary short sell point. The stock then plummeted into the 'teens and the Loews Corporation went on to move away from their focus on the hotel business and diversify into a variety of operations, including interests in tobacco, insurance, and oil & gas production, among others.

Redman Industries, Inc. & Skyline Corp.

The mobile home today doesn't do much to get investors' blood boiling with excitement. But in the 1960s the mobile home industry was booming, and mobile home manufacturers like Redman Industries and Skyline Corporation boomed right along with it.

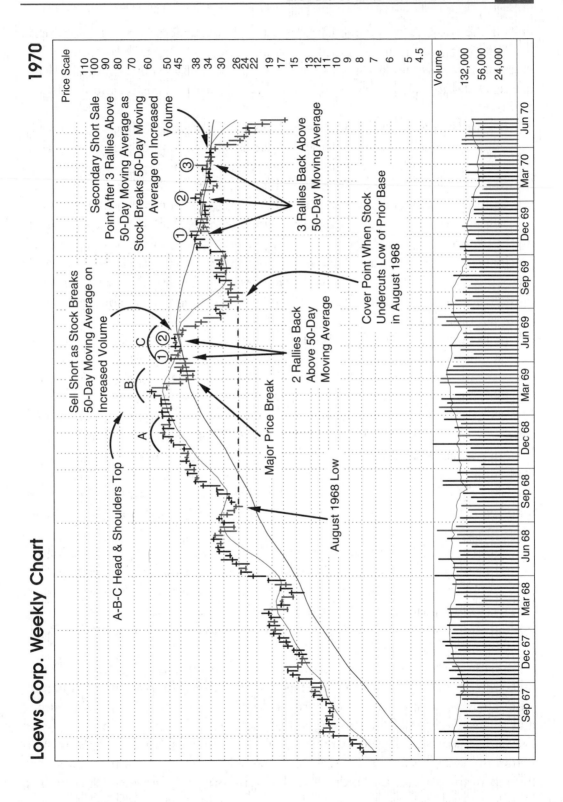

Loews Corp. Weekly Chart 1970

Of the two stocks, Skyline Corp. was the first to emerge from its initial base and had the bigger move, logging a gain of 1,233% over 28 months, while Redman Industries broke out six months later to be up 837% in 17 months. Being the less powerful of the two, Redman Industries also topped five months before Skyline Corp.

It is instructive to study the moves of Skyline Corp. and Redman Industries in the 1966–1968 bull market because it demonstrates how stocks move in groups. They break out within a few months of each other, and they top within a few months of each other. Once Redman Industries had topped in May of 1969, that was a clue to investors in Skyline Corp. that it might soon top as well.

You can tell from the charts that both stocks had very well contained up trends as they moved higher, forming several tight, little bases on the way up. As the stocks neared their eventual tops, it becomes evident that the character of their chart price action began to change as well. After long runs, the stocks began to correct, with each forming what appear to be a pair of cup with handle bases near their ultimate peaks.

In Redman's case, the failed breakout from the first wide, loose, late-stage cup with handle base marked its final top, while Skyline's failed breakout from its second, late-stage cup with handle base was the beginning of the end for its upside run.

Redman's final peak and price break off the top formed the right side of the head of what became a clear head & shoulders top formation. As the stock came down the right side of the head it undercut the low of the first late-stage cup with handle base and set off on a rally that carried it above the 50-day moving average. Remember, breaches of so-called "major support levels" such as that marked by the low of the first cup with handle base in Redman's chart often fool short sellers who see the break as a short selling point. But this is too obvious, and they are soon run in.

Redman put in two more rallies above the 50-day moving average, making for a total of three rallies above the 50-day moving average and completing the right shoulder of its head & shoulders top formation. After the third rally, which showed two weeks of churning on lighter volume, trading volume picked up and the stock broke through its 50-day moving average for the last time, falling into the 'teens over the next several months.

Skyline Corp., on the other hand, did not top until October 1969 when it failed after breaking out of what appears at first to be a late-stage cup with handle base but is actually a late-stage, improper double bottom with handle formation, and this is also true of the first cup with handle base. Closer study of these bases shows that each is actually an improper double bottom with handle formation. The reason this is so is that in the first pattern, the first three weeks down form the first bottom in the pattern, and in the second pattern, the first two weeks form the first

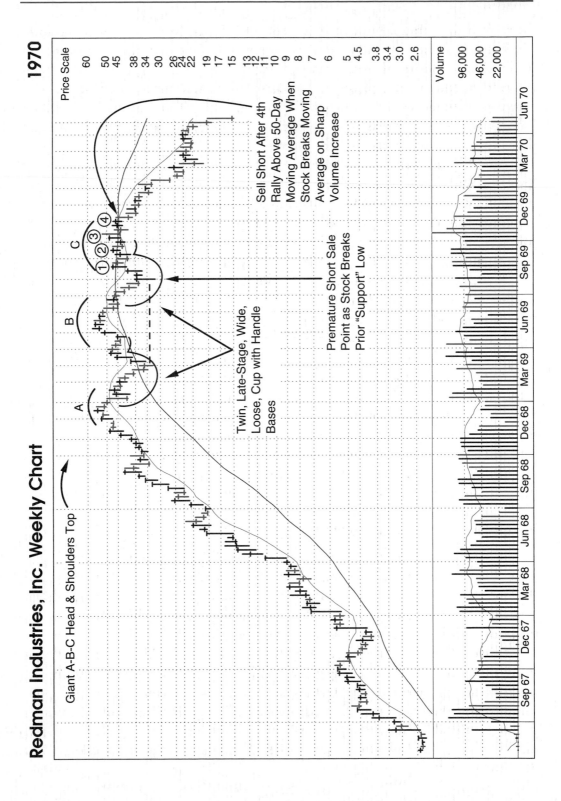

Redman Industries, Inc. Weekly Chart

1970

Giant A-B-C Head & Shoulders Top

Twin, Late-Stage, Wide,
Loose, Cup with Handle
Bases

Premature Short Sale
Point as Stock Breaks
Prior "Support" Low

Sell Short After 4th
Rally Above 50-Day
Moving Average When
Stock Breaks Moving
Average on Sharp
Volume Increase

Price Scale

60

50
45

38
34

30

26
24
22

19
17
15

13
12
11
10
9
8
7

6

5
4.5

3.8
3.4
3.0

2.6

Volume

96,000

46,000

22,000

Sep 67 Dec 67 Mar 68 Jun 68 Sep 68 Dec 68 Mar 69 Jun 69 Sep 69 Dec 69 Mar 70 Jun 70

bottom in the pattern. Either case is incorrect, because in proper double bottoms the left side of the base leading to the first bottom in most cases should form over the course of four to six weeks, not two or three. The reason for this is that bases in general, and late-stage bases in particular, need more time as they are coming down on their left sides to clean out all the weak hands that are in the stock. A drop of only two or three weeks is not enough time to push out all the weak hands and leads to a faulty base structure that is prone to failure.

After Skyline put in its final price high in October 1969, the stock broke badly over the next three months, finally mustering two rallies back above the 50-day moving average. The second rally consisted of three weeks trading below-average volume, and the first two weeks of the rally showed severe stalling action. Two weeks after the second rally, volume picked up and the stock crashed through its 50-day moving average, breaking sharply lower over the next several weeks.

If you compare the two stocks, take note that Skyline was actually the stronger of the two based on the fact that it was the first to break out when it began its upside price run, had the bigger percentage move by the time it finally topped, and topped later than Redman. This relative strength also shows up in their downside moves as well. From the correct short point on each chart, identified by the point on the right side of the right shoulder as each stock drops through its 50-day moving average, Redman Industries was actually the better short sale play!

The moral of the story is that when several stocks in the same leading group have big bull market runs, when they finally top you should pick on the weakest one as your primary short sale candidate. Generally, this will be the one that may have broken out later at the beginning of the move, or the one that topped first at the end—this can improve your odds of being successful in your short sales.

C-Cube Microsystems, Inc.

During the 1995–1997 bull market, the Internet was just beginning to take off, and one of several reasons for this was the ability to transmit and view video over the Internet via a new type of multimedia format known as MPEG, which stands for "Moving Picture Experts Group." MPEG technology allowed for the compression of video and audio files so that they could easily be transmitted over the Internet.

One of the big players in video compression was C-Cube Microsystems, a company that produced the first single-chip MPEG decoder for consumer electronics and computer applications, the first single-chip decoder for communications applications, and the first single-chip video encoder. The company's ground-breaking technology enabled one to put a one-hour video program on a single CD-ROM disc. In its uncompressed form, such a video program would normally take up 100 CD-ROM discs.

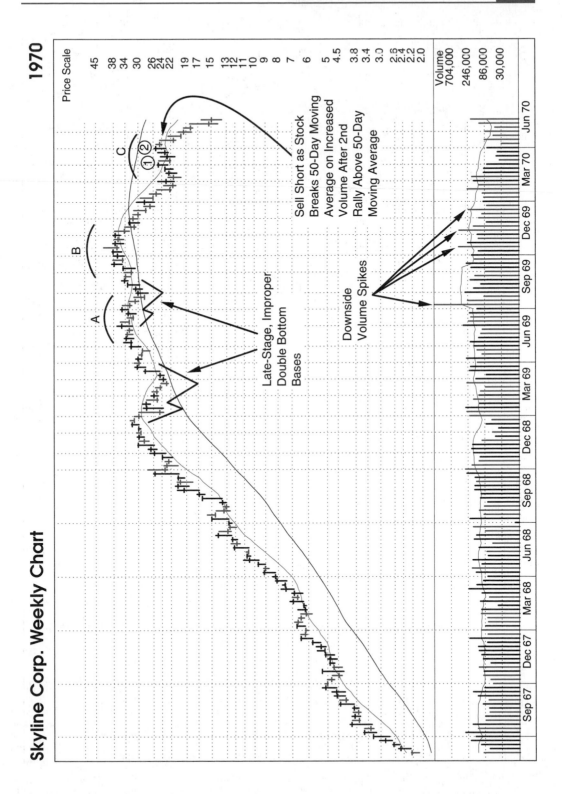

Skyline Corp. Weekly Chart

1970

Price Scale

Sell Short as Stock
Breaks 50-Day Moving
Average on Increased
Volume After 2nd
Rally Above 50-Day
Moving Average

Late-Stage, Improper:
Double Bottom
Bases

Downside
Volume Spikes

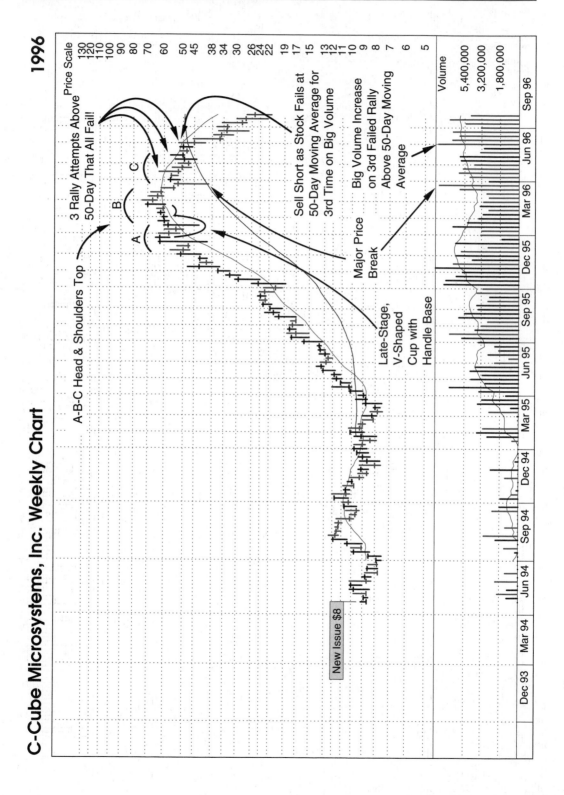

C-Cube Microsystems, Inc. Weekly Chart

1996

A-B-C Head & Shoulders Top

3 Rally Attempts Above
50-Day That All Fail!

Price Scale

Sell Short as Stock Fails at
50-Day Moving Average for
3rd Time on Big Volume

Big Volume Increase
on 3rd Failed Rally
Above 50-Day Moving
Average

Major Price
Break

Late-Stage,
V-Shaped
Cup with
Handle Base

New Issue $8

Volume

5,400,000
3,200,000
1,800,000

New products like these led to strong earnings growth that propelled C-Cube Microsystems 494% above its initial pivot point in May 1995 by the time it topped 41 weeks later. Just before its final top, C-Cube formed a wide, loose, v-shaped cup with handle base from which it broke out and promptly failed.

Following this failed breakout, the stock fell very sharply over the next five weeks, nearly getting cut in half. The fifth week down had the appearance of strong support as the stock undercut the low of the prior v-shaped cup with handle base and rallied to close very near to the peak of the weekly range on huge volume. In this particular case, C-Cube was a little different than some of our other examples in that the stock then logged three successive rallies, each lower than the prior, that traded above the 50-day moving average but failed to close above it on a weekly basis each time. The third rally above the 50-day moving average did not get up as far above the moving average as the prior two, providing a clue that these already weak rallies were losing whatever upside strength they had. Volume picked up very sharply as the third rally failed and reversed back down through the 50-day moving average, plummeting into the low $20s over the next seven weeks.

The main point to take away from this example is that rallies after the initial price break off the peak can take many forms, but the main idea is that you will see one, two, three, or more rallies that carry the stock up to or over the 50-day moving average as the stock runs in premature short sellers and sucks in "bargain hunters" who see a once hot stock as being "cheap." Once all the premature short sellers have been run in, and once all the bargain hunters have been sucked in, these rallies should normally show signs of weakening. These rallies can either close above the 50-day moving average, rally above but close below the 50-day on a weekly basis, or simply run into resistance right at the moving average. However these rallies take shape, the astute short seller must be able to assess which rally is the stock's last and be decisive enough to take action at the correct time as the stock fails and downside volume picks up sharply.

Additional Models of Greatest Short Sales

Selling stocks short is considerably more difficult than just buying stocks and requires a higher skill level that can only be attained through careful study and practice. The examples that follow should provide the reader with sufficient study material to reinforce and illustrate the short-selling concepts discussed in the main text of this book. By reviewing and studying the detailed characteristics of these real-world, short-selling examples from the past, the reader can develop a strong understanding of what constitutes an ideal short-selling candidate.

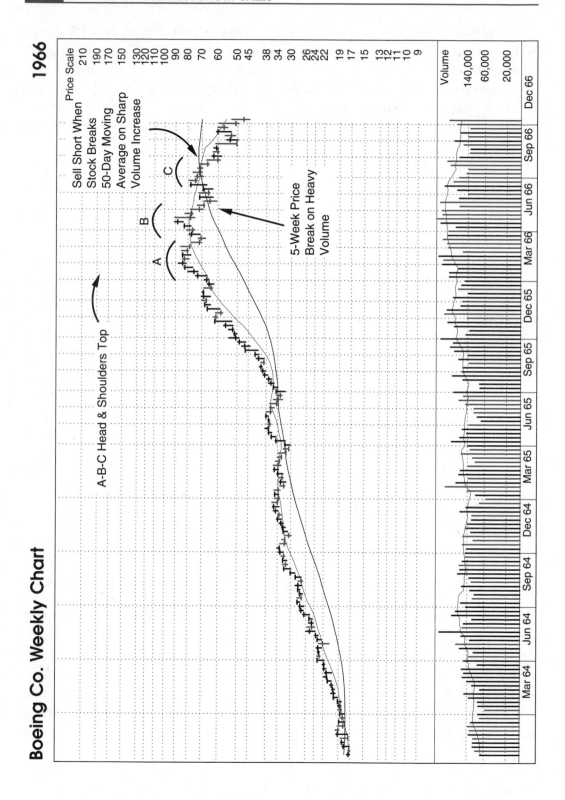

Boeing Co. Weekly Chart

1966

Price Scale

Sell Short When
Stock Breaks
50-Day Moving
Average on Sharp
Volume Increase

A-B-C Head & Shoulders Top

A   B   C

5-Week Price
Break on Heavy
Volume

Volume

Motorola, Inc. Weekly Chart

1966

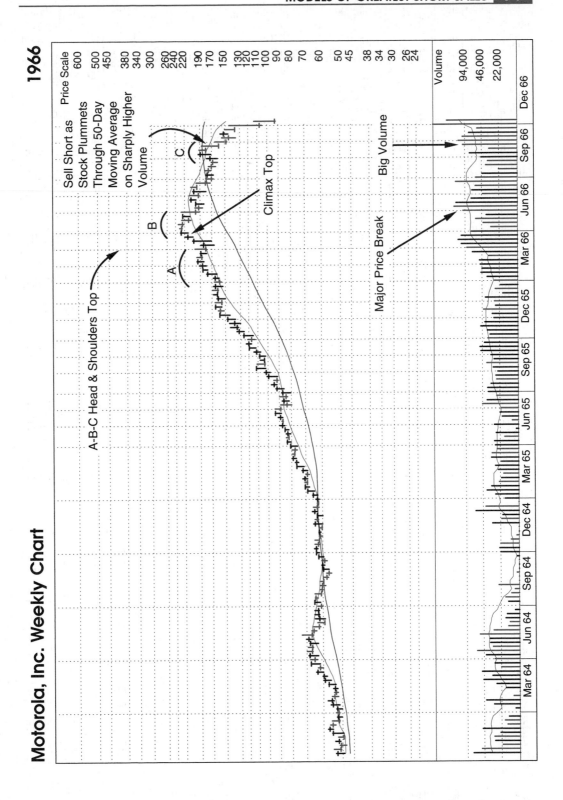

Price Scale
600
500
450
380
340
300
260
240
220
190
170
150
130
120
110
100
90
80
70
60
50
45
38
34
30
26
24

A-B-C Head & Shoulders Top

Sell Short as
Stock Plummets
Through 50-Day
Moving Average
on Sharply Higher
Volume

A

B

C

Climax Top

Major Price Break

Big Volume

Volume

94,000
46,000
22,000

Mar 64   Jun 64   Sep 64   Dec 64   Mar 65   Jun 65   Sep 65   Dec 65   Mar 66   Jun 66   Sep 66   Dec 66

Solitron Devices, Inc. Weekly Chart

1966

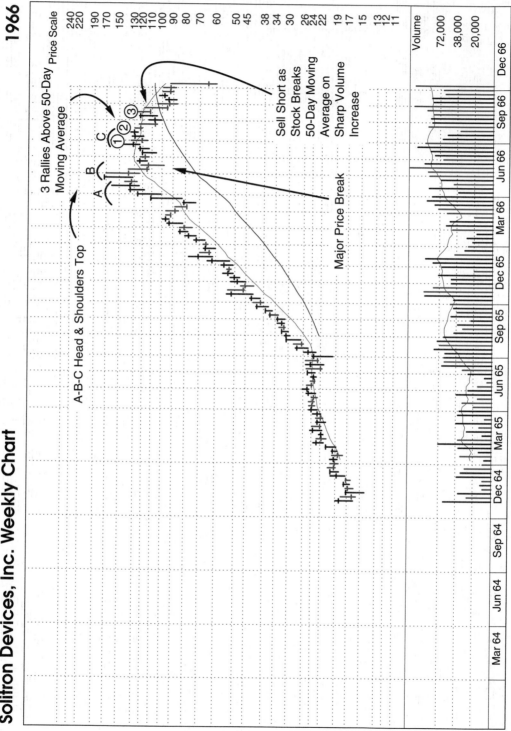

3 Rallies Above 50-Day Price Scale
Moving Average

A-B-C Head & Shoulders Top

C
A B

① ② ③

Sell Short as
Stock Breaks
50-Day Moving
Average on
Sharp Volume
Increase

Major Price Break

Volume

72,000

38,000

20,000

240
220
190
170
150
130
120
110
100
90
80
70
60
50
45
38
34
30
26
24
22
19
17
15
13
12
11

Mar 64 Jun 64 Sep 64 Dec 64 Mar 65 Jun 65 Sep 65 Dec 65 Mar 66 Jun 66 Sep 66 Dec 66

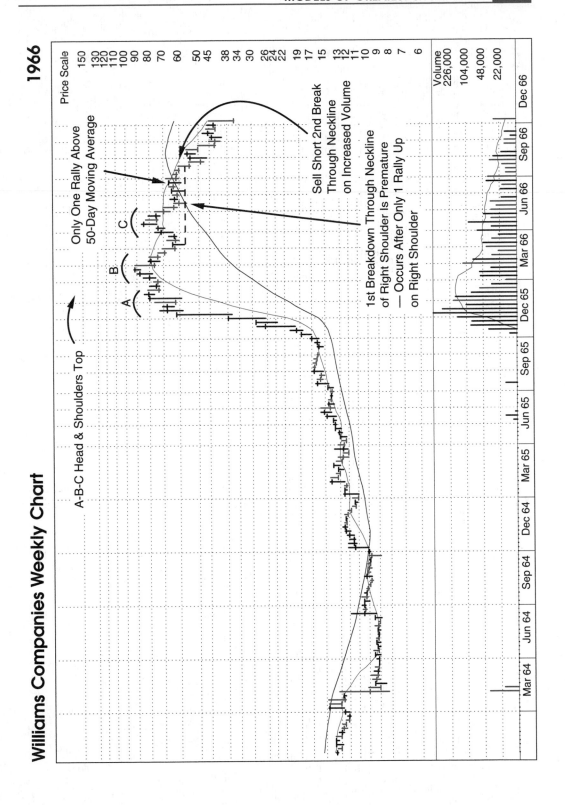

Williams Companies Weekly Chart

1966

A-B-C Head & Shoulders Top

Only One Rally Above 50-Day Moving Average

Sell Short 2nd Break Through Neckline on Increased Volume

1st Breakdown Through Neckline of Right Shoulder Is Premature — Occurs After Only 1 Rally Up on Right Shoulder

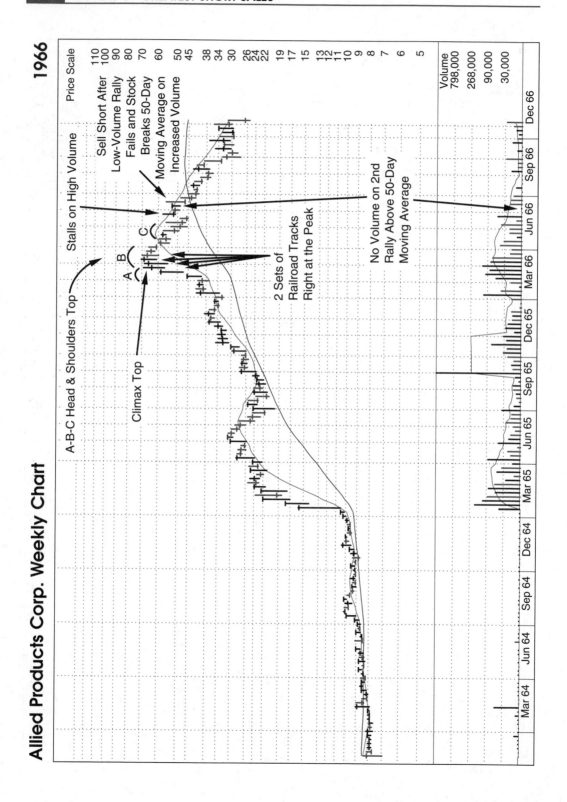

Allied Products Corp. Weekly Chart

1966

A-B-C Head & Shoulders Top

Stalls on High Volume

Price Scale

Sell Short After Low-Volume Rally Fails and Stock Breaks 50-Day Moving Average on Increased Volume

Climax Top

A B C

2 Sets of Railroad Tracks Right at the Peak

No Volume on 2nd Rally Above 50-Day Moving Average

Volume
798,000
268,000
90,000
30,000

DynCorp Weekly Chart

1969

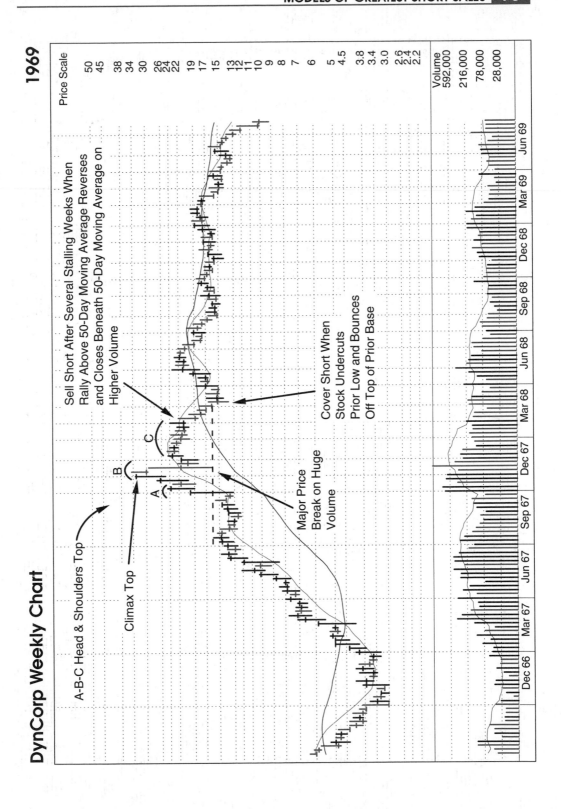

A-B-C Head & Shoulders Top

Climax Top

B

A

C

Sell Short After Several Stalling Weeks When Rally Above 50-Day Moving Average Reverses and Closes Beneath 50-Day Moving Average on Higher Volume

Cover Short When Stock Undercuts Prior Low and Bounces Off Top of Prior Base

Major Price Break on Huge Volume

Price Scale
50
45
38
34
30
26
24
22
19
17
15
13
12
11
10
9
8
7
6
5
4.5
3.8
3.4
3.0
2.6
2.4
2.2

Volume
592,000
216,000
78,000
28,000

Dec 66 Mar 67 Jun 67 Sep 67 Dec 67 Mar 68 Jun 68 Sep 68 Dec 68 Mar 69 Jun 69

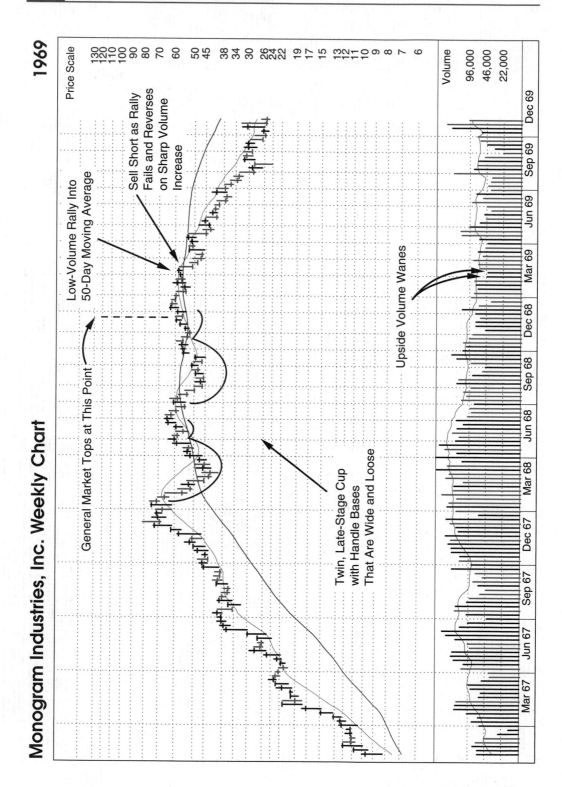

Monogram Industries, Inc. Weekly Chart

1969

Price Scale

General Market Tops at This Point

Low-Volume Rally Into
50-Day Moving Average

Sell Short as Rally
Fails and Reverses
on Sharp Volume
Increase

Twin, Late-Stage Cup
with Handle Bases
That Are Wide and Loose

Upside Volume Wanes

Volume

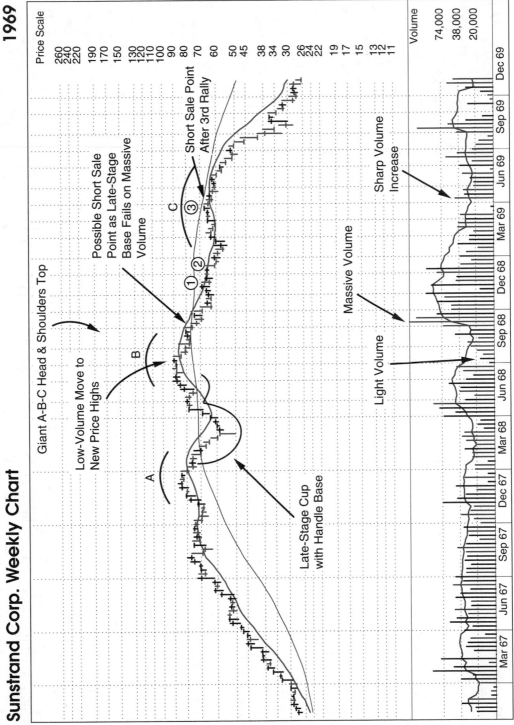

Sunstrand Corp. Weekly Chart   **1969**

Price Scale

Giant A-B-C Head & Shoulders Top

Low-Volume Move to New Price Highs

Possible Short Sale Point as Late-Stage Base Fails on Massive Volume

Short Sale Point After 3rd Rally

Late-Stage Cup with Handle Base

Light Volume

Massive Volume

Sharp Volume Increase

Volume
74,000
38,000
20,000

Aileen, Inc. Weekly Chart

1970

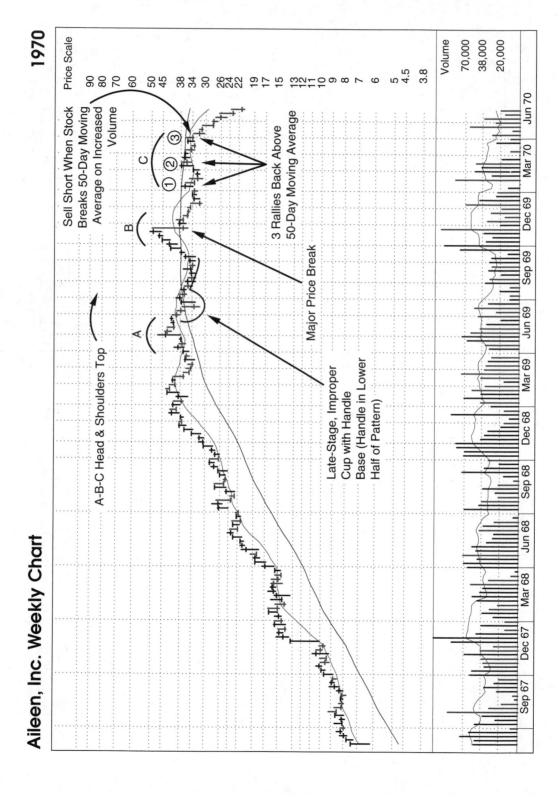

Sell Short When Stock
Breaks 50-Day Moving
Average on Increased
Volume

A-B-C Head & Shoulders Top

3 Rallies Back Above
50-Day Moving Average

Major Price Break

Late-Stage, Improper
Cup with Handle
Base (Handle in Lower
Half of Pattern)

Price Scale

90
80
70

60

50
45

38
34

30

26
24
22

19
17

15

13
12
11

10

9

8

7

6

5
4.5

3.8

Volume

70,000

38,000

20,000

Sep 67 · Dec 67 · Mar 68 · Jun 68 · Sep 68 · Dec 68 · Mar 69 · Jun 69 · Sep 69 · Dec 69 · Mar 70 · Jun 70

Radioshack Corp. Weekly Chart

1970

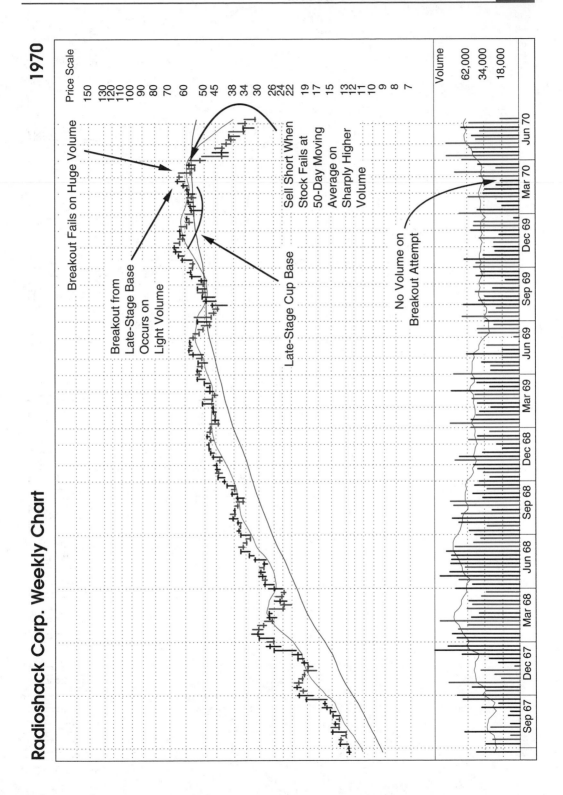

Price Scale

Breakout Fails on Huge Volume

Breakout from
Late-Stage Base
Occurs on
Light Volume

Late-Stage Cup Base

Sell Short When
Stock Fails at
50-Day Moving
Average on
Sharply Higher
Volume

No Volume on
Breakout Attempt

Volume

62,000
34,000
18,000

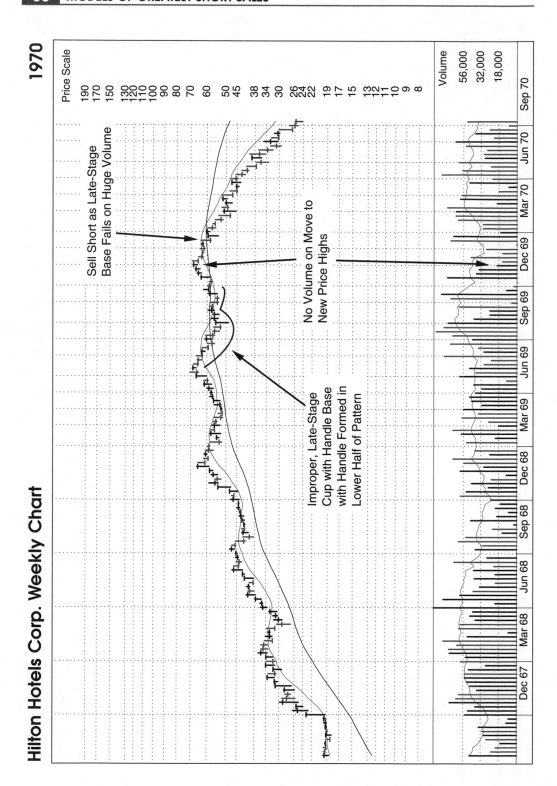

Hilton Hotels Corp. Weekly Chart

1970

Price Scale

Sell Short as Late-Stage
Base Fails on Huge Volume

No Volume on Move to
New Price Highs

Improper, Late-Stage
Cup with Handle Base
with Handle Formed in
Lower Half of Pattern

Volume
56,000
32,000
18,000

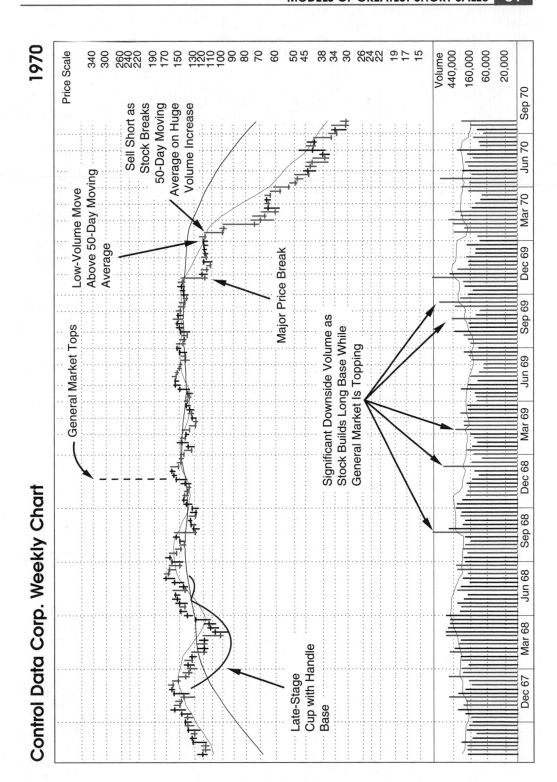

Control Data Corp. Weekly Chart
1970

Unisys Corp. Weekly Chart

1970

Price Scale

600

500
450

380
340
300

260
240
220

190
170
150

130
120
110
100
90
80
70

60

50
45

38
34
30

26
24

A-B-C Head & Shoulders Top

2-Week Rally
Stalls at 50-Day
Moving Average

Sell Short When
Stock Breaks 50-Day
on Increased Volume

A

B

C

Late-Stage
Cup with Handle

Low-Volume
Breakout to
New Price Highs

Volume

128,000

56,000

24,000

Dec 67   Mar 68   Jun 68   Sep 68   Dec 68   Mar 69   Jun 69   Sep 69   Dec 69   Mar 70   Jun 70   Sep 70

Computer Sciences Corp. Weekly Chart

1970

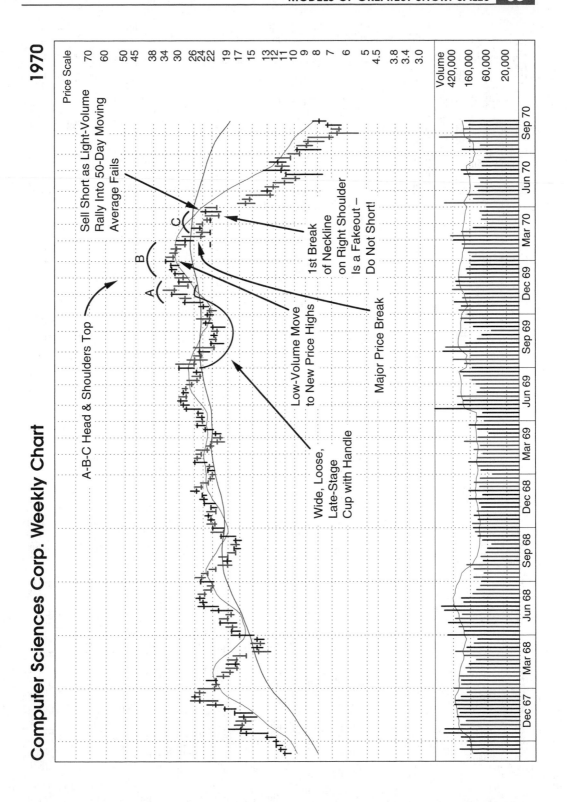

A-B-C Head & Shoulders Top

Sell Short as Light-Volume
Rally Into 50-Day Moving
Average Fails

1st Break
of Neckline
on Right Shoulder –
Is a Fakeout –
Do Not Short!

Low-Volume Move
to New Price Highs

Major Price Break

Wide, Loose,
Late-Stage
Cup with Handle

Price Scale

70
60
50
45
38
34
30
26
24
22
19
17
15
13
12
11
10
9
8
7
6
5
4.5
3.8
3.4
3.0

Volume
420,000
160,000
60,000
20,000

Dec 67 | Mar 68 | Jun 68 | Sep 68 | Dec 68 | Mar 69 | Jun 69 | Sep 69 | Dec 69 | Mar 70 | Jun 70 | Sep 70

Plant Industries, Inc. Weekly Chart

1970

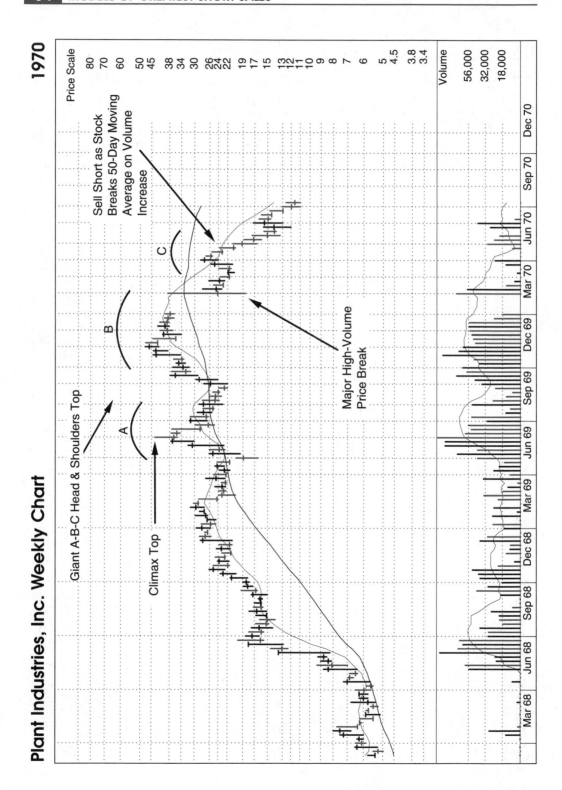

Giant A-B-C Head & Shoulders Top.

Climax Top

A

B

C

Sell Short as Stock Breaks 50-Day Moving Average on Volume Increase

Major High-Volume Price Break

Price Scale 80 70 60 50 45 38 34 30 26 24 22 19 17 15 13 12 11 10 9 8 7 6 5 4.5 3.8 3.4

Volume 56,000 32,000 18,000

Mar 68 Jun 68 Sep 68 Dec 68 Mar 69 Jun 69 Sep 69 Dec 69 Mar 70 Jun 70 Sep 70 Dec 70

Bausch & Lomb, Inc. Weekly Chart

1972

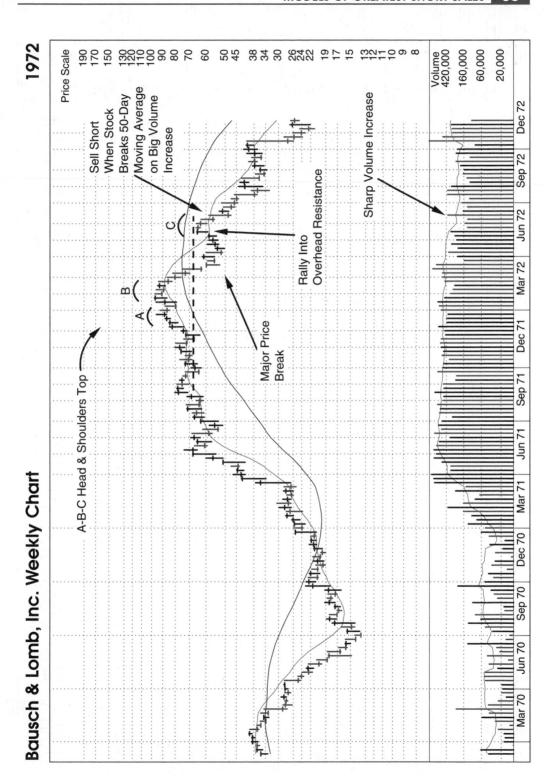

A-B-C Head & Shoulders Top

Sell Short
When Stock
Breaks 50-Day
Moving Average
on Big Volume
Increase

Rally Into
Overhead Resistance

Major Price
Break

Sharp Volume Increase

Price Scale

190
170
150
130
120
110
100
90
80
70
60
50
45
38
34
30
26
24
22
19
17
15
13
12
11
10
9
8

Volume
420,000
160,000
60,000
20,000

Mar 70   Jun 70   Sep 70   Dec 70   Mar 71   Jun 71   Sep 71   Dec 71   Mar 72   Jun 72   Sep 72   Dec 72

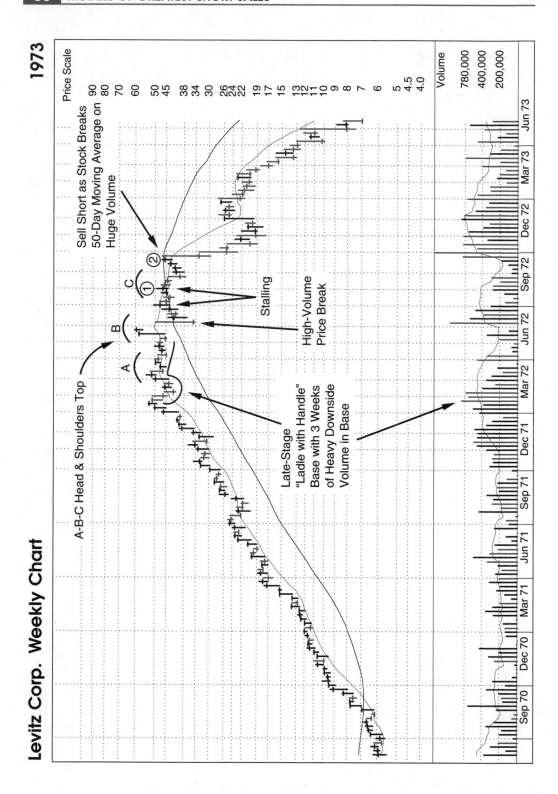

Levitz Corp. Weekly Chart

1973

Price Scale

A-B-C Head & Shoulders Top

Sell Short as Stock Breaks
50-Day Moving Average on
Huge Volume

Stalling

High-Volume
Price Break

Late-Stage
"Ladle with Handle"
Base with 3 Weeks
of Heavy Downside
Volume in Base

Volume

Winnebago Industries, Inc. Weekly Chart

1973

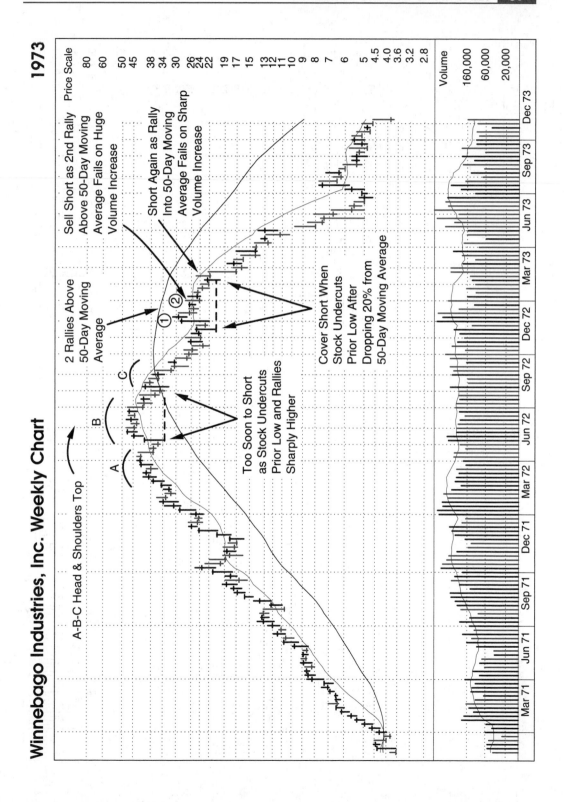

A-B-C Head & Shoulders Top

2 Rallies Above
50-Day Moving
Average

Sell Short as 2nd Rally
Above 50-Day Moving
Average Fails on Huge
Volume Increase

Short Again as Rally
Into 50-Day Moving
Average Fails on Sharp
Volume Increase

Too Soon to Short
as Stock Undercuts
Prior Low and Rallies
Sharply Higher

Cover Short When
Stock Undercuts
Prior Low After
Dropping 20% from
50-Day Moving Average

Price Scale
80
60
50
45
38
34
30
26
24
22
19
17
15
13
12
11
10
9
8
7
6
5
4.5
4.0
3.6
3.2
2.8

Volume
160,000
60,000
20,000

Mar 71 Jun 71 Sep 71 Dec 71 Mar 72 Jun 72 Sep 72 Dec 72 Mar 73 Jun 73 Sep 73 Dec 73

Knight-Ridder, Inc. Weekly Chart

1973

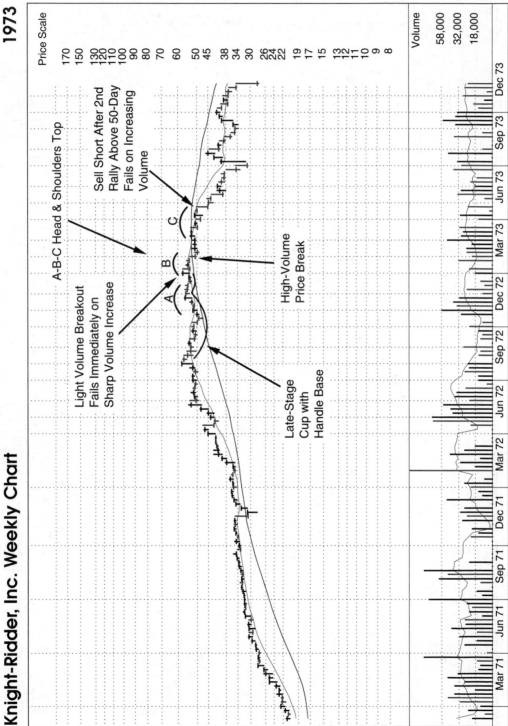

A-B-C Head & Shoulders Top

Sell Short After 2nd
Rally Above 50-Day
Fails on Increasing
Volume

Light Volume Breakout
Fails Immediately on
Sharp Volume Increase

High-Volume
Price Break

Late-Stage
Cup with
Handle Base

Price Scale

170
150
130
120
110
100
90
80
70
60
50
45
38
34
30
26
24
22
19
17
15
13
12
11
10
9
8

Volume

58,000
32,000
18,000

Walt Disney Company Weekly Chart

1973

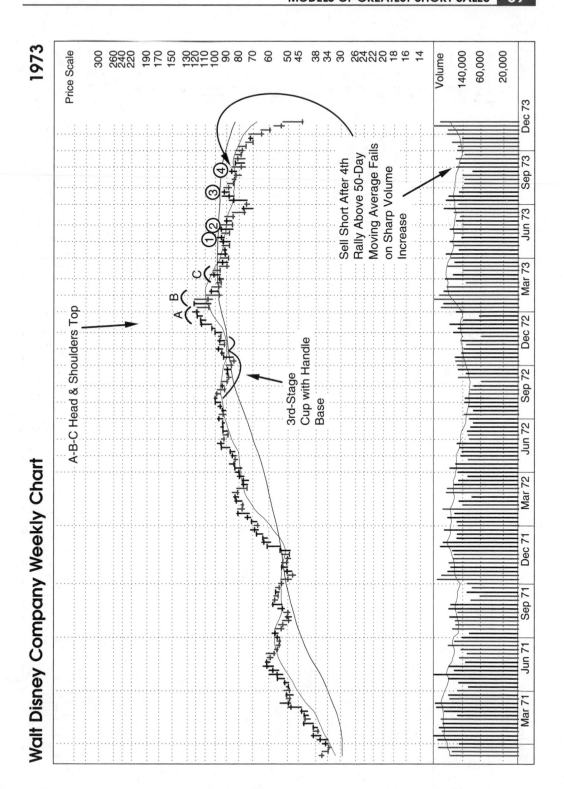

A-B-C Head & Shoulders Top

3rd-Stage Cup with Handle Base

Sell Short After 4th Rally Above 50-Day Moving Average Fails on Sharp Volume Increase

Price Scale

300
260
240
220
190
170
150
130
120
110
100
90
80
70
60
50
45
38
34
30
26
24
22
20
18
16
14

Volume

140,000
60,000
20,000

Mar 71 Jun 71 Sep 71 Dec 71 Mar 72 Jun 72 Sep 72 Dec 72 Mar 73 Jun 73 Sep 73 Dec 73

Brunswick Corp. Weekly Chart

1973

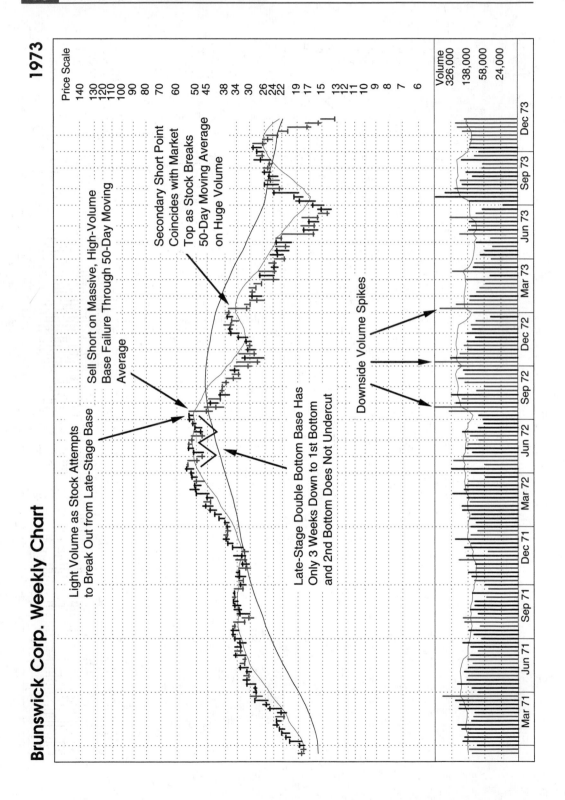

Price Scale
140
130
120
110
100
90
80
70
60
50
45
38
34
30
26
24
22
19
17
15
13
12
11
10
9
8
7
6

Light Volume as Stock Attempts to Break Out from Late-Stage Base

Sell Short on Massive, High-Volume Base Failure Through 50-Day Moving Average

Secondary Short Point Coincides with Market Top as Stock Breaks 50-Day Moving Average on Huge Volume

Late-Stage Double Bottom Base Has Only 3 Weeks Down to 1st Bottom and 2nd Bottom Does Not Undercut

Downside Volume Spikes

Volume
326,000
138,000
58,000
24,000

Mar 71 Jun 71 Sep 71 Dec 71 Mar 72 Jun 72 Sep 72 Dec 72 Mar 73 Jun 73 Sep 73 Dec 73

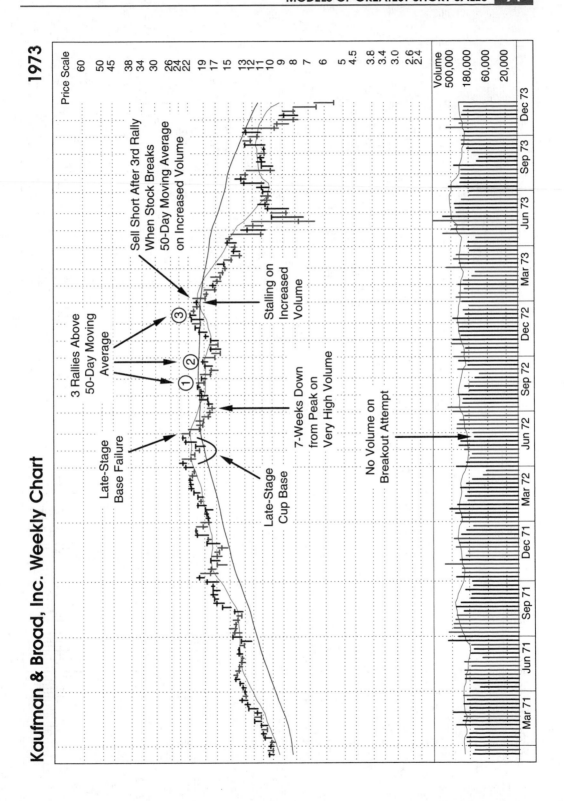

Kaufman & Broad, Inc. Weekly Chart

1973

Rite Aid Corp. Weekly Chart

1974

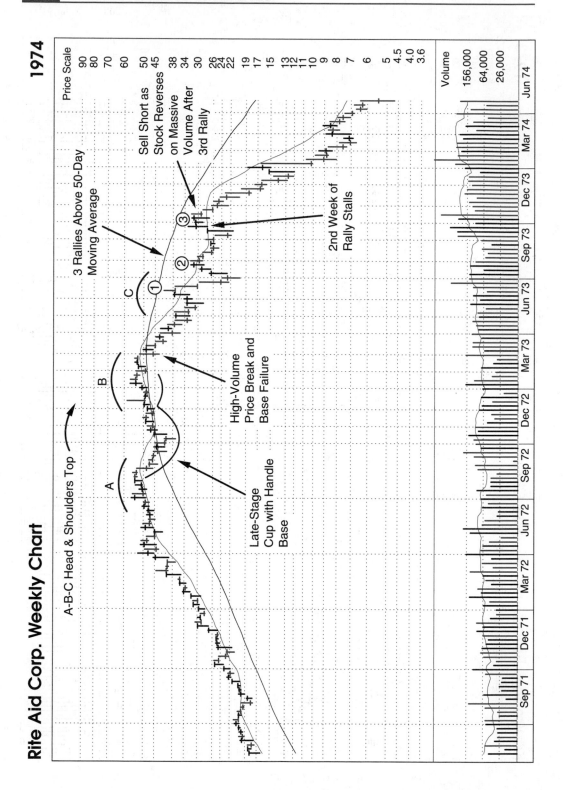

A-B-C Head & Shoulders Top

3 Rallies Above 50-Day
Moving Average

Sell Short as
Stock Reverses
on Massive
Volume After
3rd Rally

C

B

A

High-Volume
Price Break and
Base Failure

Late-Stage
Cup with Handle
Base

2nd Week of
Rally Stalls

Price Scale
90
80
70
60
50
45
38
34
30
26
24
22
19
17
15
13
12
11
10
9
8
7
6
5
4.5
4.0
3.6

Volume
156,000
64,000
26,000

Sep 71 Dec 71 Mar 72 Jun 72 Sep 72 Dec 72 Mar 73 Jun 73 Sep 73 Dec 73 Mar 74 Jun 74

Transworld Airlines, Inc. Weekly Chart

1974

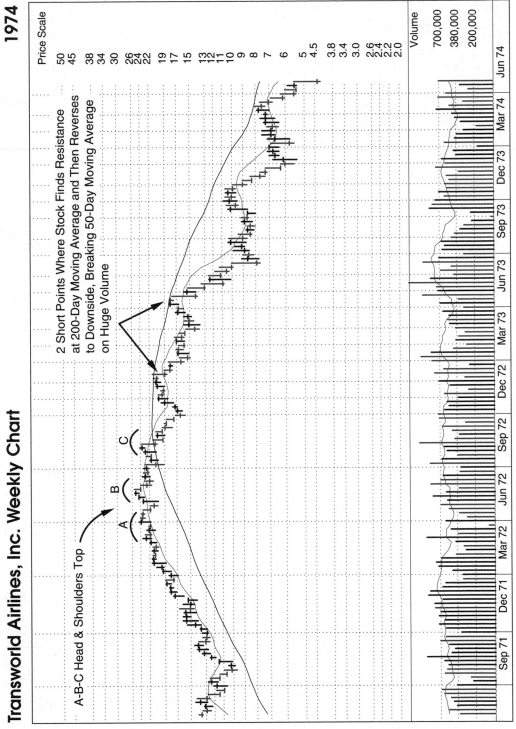

A-B-C Head & Shoulders Top

2 Short Points Where Stock Finds Resistance at 200-Day Moving Average and Then Reverses to Downside, Breaking 50-Day Moving Average on Huge Volume

Price Scale

| 50 |
| 45 |
| 38 |
| 34 |
| 30 |
| 26 |
| 24 |
| 22 |
| 19 |
| 17 |
| 15 |
| 13 |
| 12 |
| 11 |
| 10 |
| 9 |
| 8 |
| 7 |
| 6 |
| 5 |
| 4.5 |
| 3.8 |
| 3.4 |
| 3.0 |
| 2.6 |
| 2.4 |
| 2.2 |
| 2.0 |

Volume

700,000
380,000
200,000

Sep 71 Dec 71 Mar 72 Jun 72 Sep 72 Dec 72 Mar 73 Jun 73 Sep 73 Dec 73 Mar 74 Jun 74

Bank of America Corp. Weekly Chart

1974

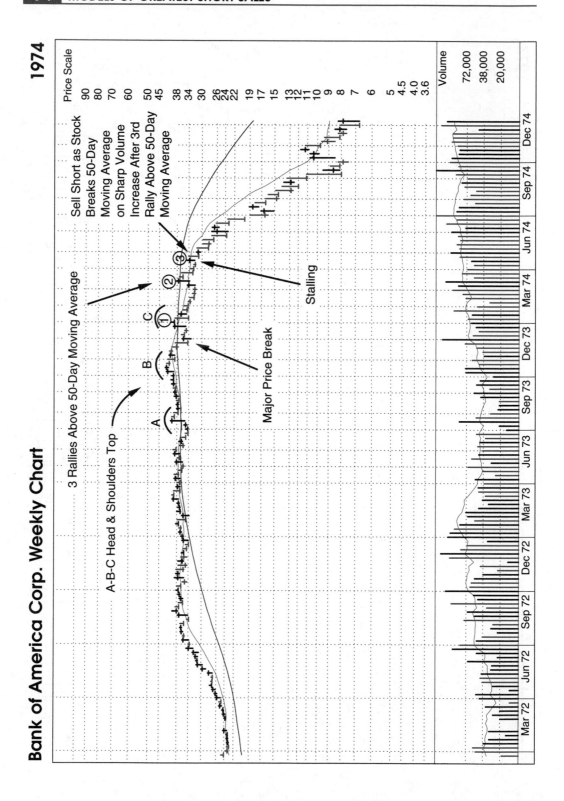

3 Rallies Above 50-Day Moving Average

A-B-C Head & Shoulders Top

Sell Short as Stock
Breaks 50-Day
Moving Average
on Sharp Volume
Increase After 3rd
Rally Above 50-Day
Moving Average

Stalling

Major Price Break

Price Scale

90
80
70
60
50
45
38
34
30
26
24
22
19
17
15
13
12
11
10
9
8
7
6
5
4.5
4.0
3.6

Volume

72,000
38,000
20,000

Mar 72 Jun 72 Sep 72 Dec 72 Mar 73 Jun 73 Sep 73 Dec 73 Mar 74 Jun 74 Sep 74 Dec 74

Coca Cola Co. Weekly Chart

1974

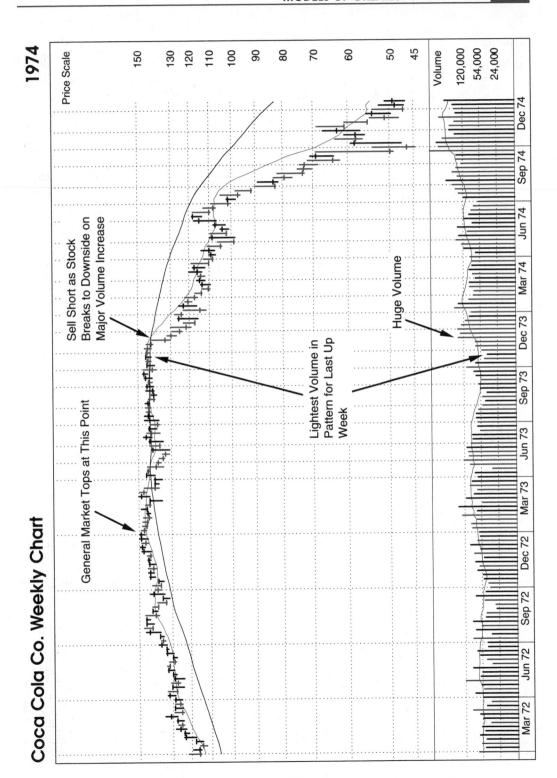

Price Scale

General Market Tops at This Point

Sell Short as Stock
Breaks to Downside on
Major Volume Increase

Lightest Volume in
Pattern for Last Up
Week

Huge Volume

Volume

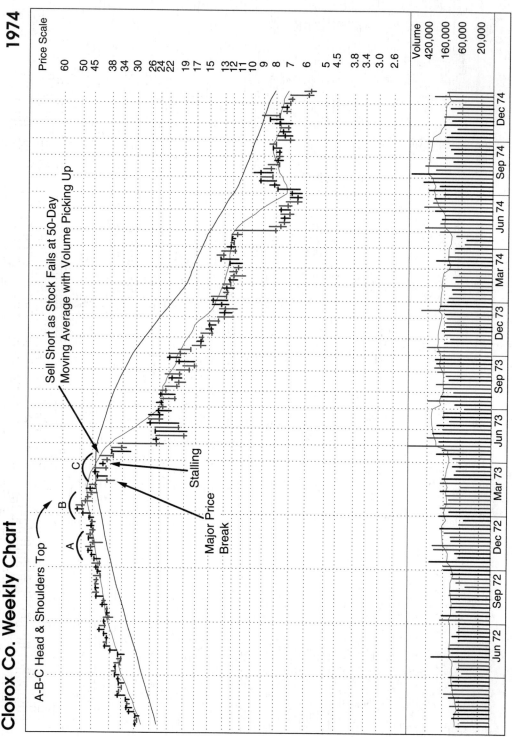

Clorox Co. Weekly Chart 1974

Price Scale

A-B-C Head & Shoulders Top

Sell Short as Stock Fails at 50-Day
Moving Average with Volume Picking Up

Stalling

Major Price
Break

Volume

Medtronic, Inc. Weekly Chart

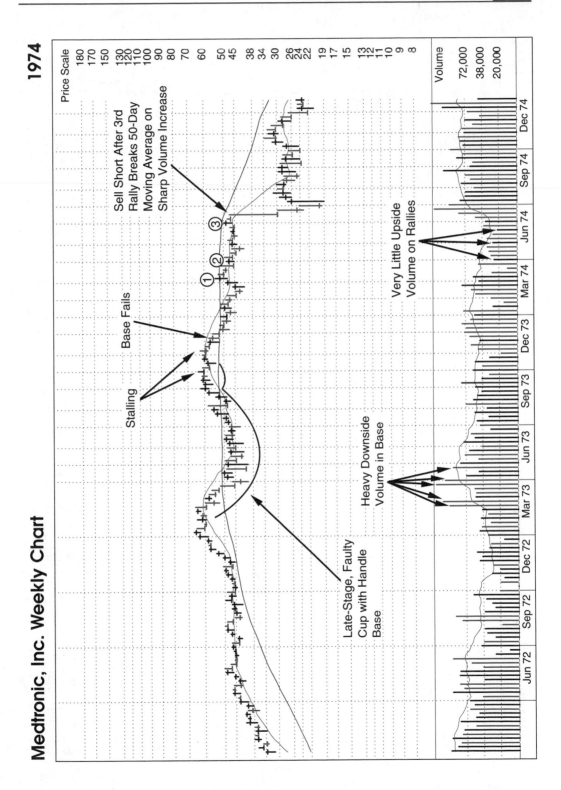

1974

Price Scale

Sell Short After 3rd
Rally Breaks 50-Day
Moving Average on
Sharp Volume Increase

Base Fails

Stalling

Late-Stage, Faulty
Cup with Handle
Base

Heavy Downside
Volume in Base

Very Little Upside
Volume on Rallies

Volume

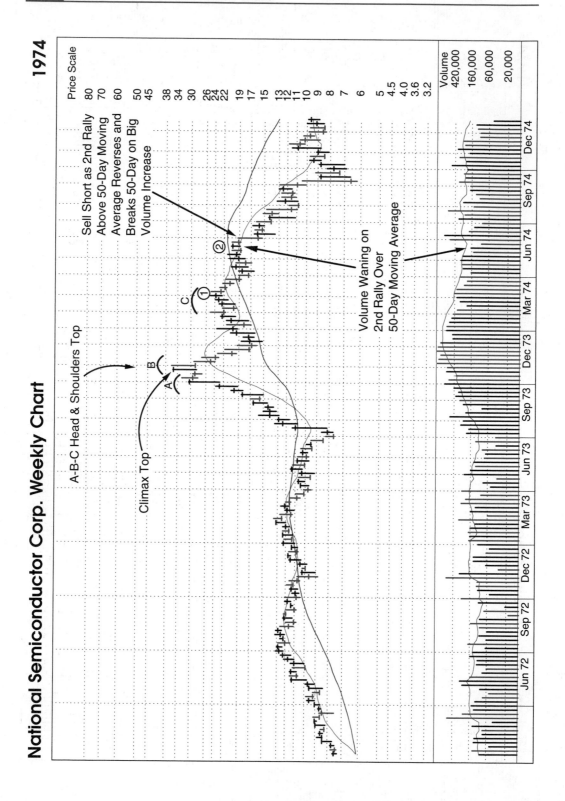

National Semiconductor Corp. Weekly Chart

1974

A-B-C Head & Shoulders Top

Climax Top

Sell Short as 2nd Rally
Above 50-Day Moving
Average Reverses and
Breaks 50-Day on Big
Volume Increase

Volume Waning on
2nd Rally Over
50-Day Moving Average

Price Scale
80
70
60
50
45
38
34
30
26
24
22
19
17
15
13
12
11
10
9
8
7
6
5
4.5
4.0
3.6
3.2

Volume
420,000
160,000
60,000
20,000

Jun 72 Sep 72 Dec 72 Mar 73 Jun 73 Sep 73 Dec 73 Mar 74 Jun 74 Sep 74 Dec 74

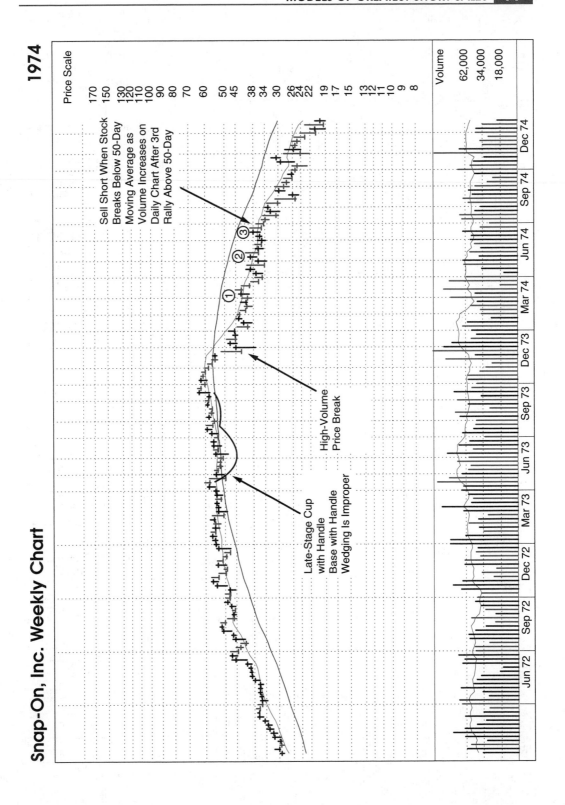

Snap-On, Inc. Weekly Chart

1974

Price Scale

170
150
130
120
110
100
90
80
70
60
50
45
38
34
30
26
24
22
19
17
15
13
12
11
10
9
8

Sell Short When Stock
Breaks Below 50-Day
Moving Average as
Volume Increases on
Daily Chart After 3rd
Rally Above 50-Day

① ② ③

High-Volume
Price Break

Late-Stage Cup
with Handle
Base with Handle
Wedging Is Improper

Volume

62,000
34,000
18,000

Jun 72   Sep 72   Dec 72   Mar 73   Jun 73   Sep 73   Dec 73   Mar 74   Jun 74   Sep 74   Dec 74

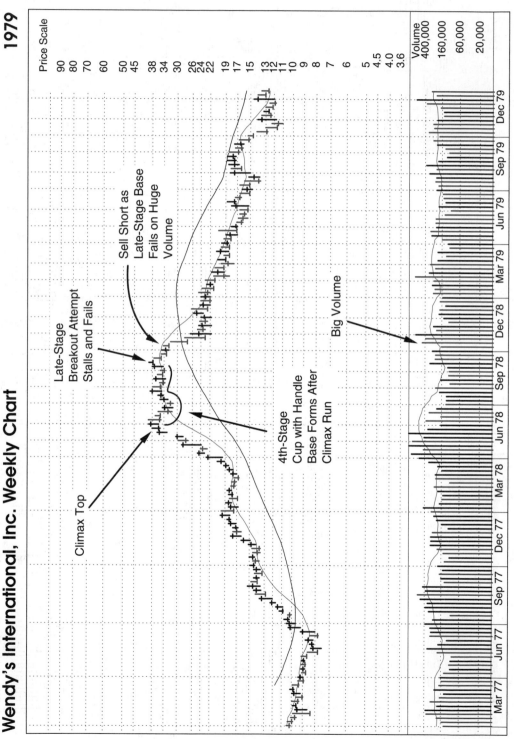

Wendy's International, Inc. Weekly Chart

1979

Price Scale

Climax Top

Late-Stage
Breakout Attempt
Stalls and Fails

Sell Short as
Late-Stage Base
Fails on Huge
Volume

4th-Stage
Cup with Handle
Base Forms After
Climax Run

Big Volume

Volume
400,000
160,000
60,000
20,000

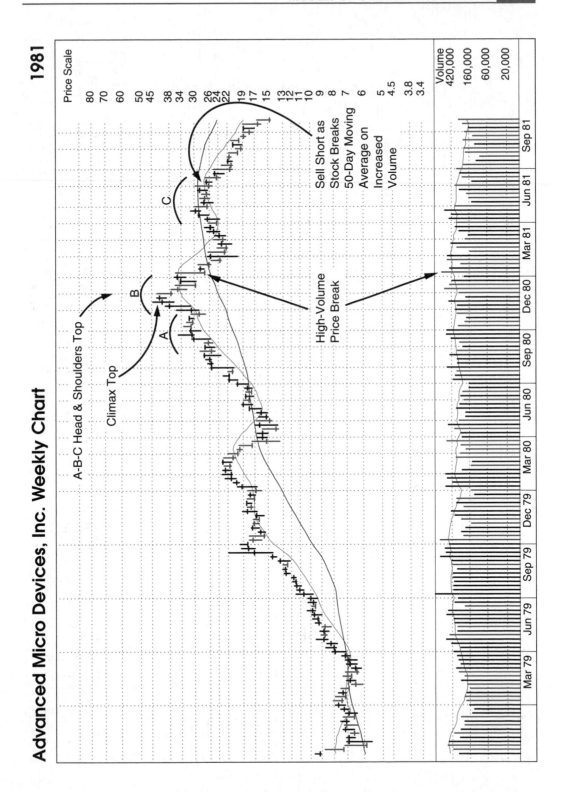

Advanced Micro Devices, Inc. Weekly Chart

1981

A-B-C Head & Shoulders Top

Climax Top

High-Volume
Price Break

Sell Short as
Stock Breaks
50-Day Moving
Average on
Increased
Volume

Price Scale

80
70
60

50
45

38
34

30

26
24
22

19
17

15

13
12
11
10

9
8
7

6

5
4.5

3.8
3.4

Volume
420,000

160,000

60,000

20,000

Mar 79 Jun 79 Sep 79 Dec 79 Mar 80 Jun 80 Sep 80 Dec 80 Mar 81 Jun 81 Sep 81

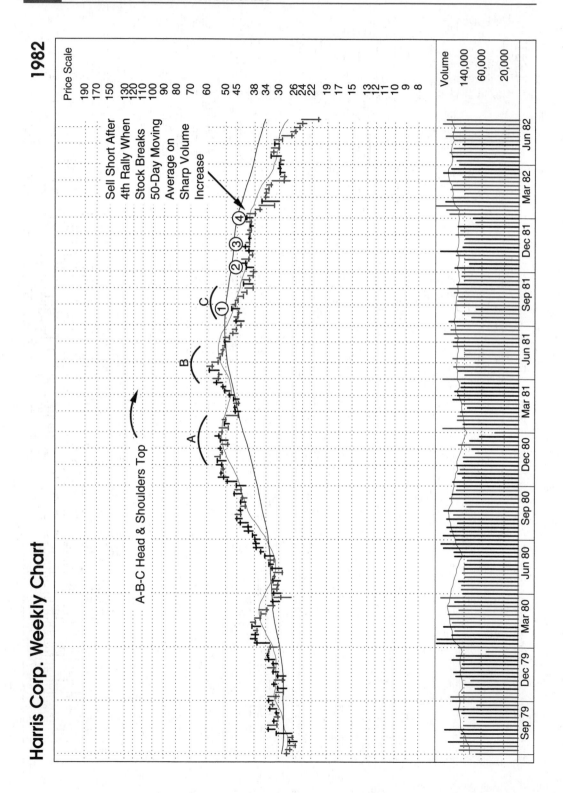

Harris Corp. Weekly Chart   1982

Price Scale

A-B-C Head & Shoulders Top

Sell Short After
4th Rally When
Stock Breaks
50-Day Moving
Average on
Sharp Volume
Increase

Volume

140,000
60,000
20,000

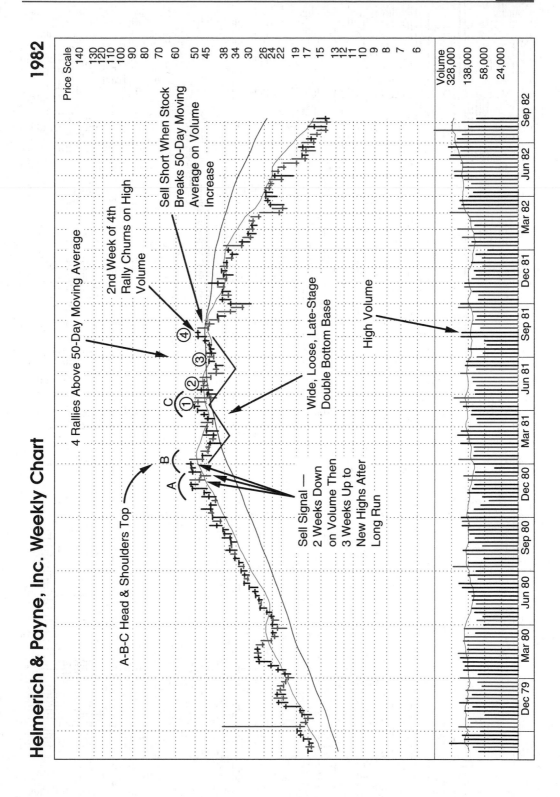

Helmerich & Payne, Inc. Weekly Chart

1982

4 Rallies Above 50-Day Moving Average

A-B-C Head & Shoulders Top

2nd Week of 4th
Rally Churns on High
Volume

Sell Short When Stock
Breaks 50-Day Moving
Average on Volume
Increase

Wide, Loose, Late-Stage
Double Bottom Base

Sell Signal —
2 Weeks Down
on Volume Then
3 Weeks Up to
New Highs After
Long Run

High Volume

Price Scale
140
130
120
110
100
90
80
70
60
50
45
38
34
30
26
24
22
19
17
15
13
12
11
10
9
8
7
6

Volume
328,000
138,000
58,000
24,000

Dec 79 Mar 80 Jun 80 Sep 80 Dec 80 Mar 81 Jun 81 Sep 81 Dec 81 Mar 82 Jun 82 Sep 82

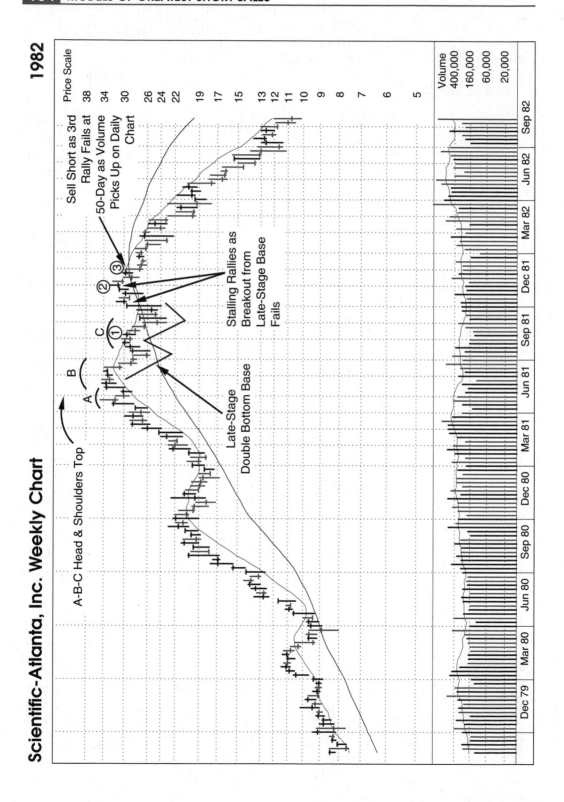

Scientific-Atlanta, Inc. Weekly Chart

1982

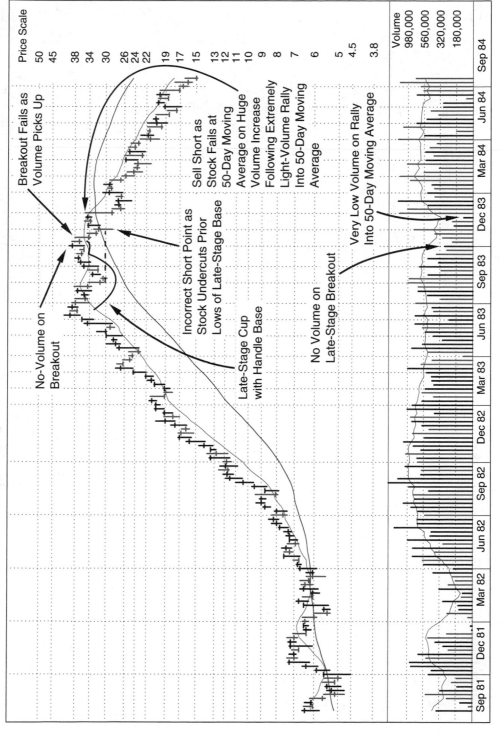

Fleetwood Enterprises, Inc. Weekly Chart

1984

Price Scale

Breakout Fails as
Volume Picks Up

No-Volume on
Breakout

Sell Short as
Stock Fails at
50-Day Moving
Average on Huge
Volume Increase
Following Extremely
Light-Volume Rally
Into 50-Day Moving
Average

Incorrect Short Point as
Stock Undercuts Prior
Lows of Late-Stage Base

Late-Stage Cup
with Handle Base

No Volume on
Late-Stage Breakout

Very Low Volume on Rally
Into 50-Day Moving Average

Volume

Home Depot, Inc. Weekly Chart

1984

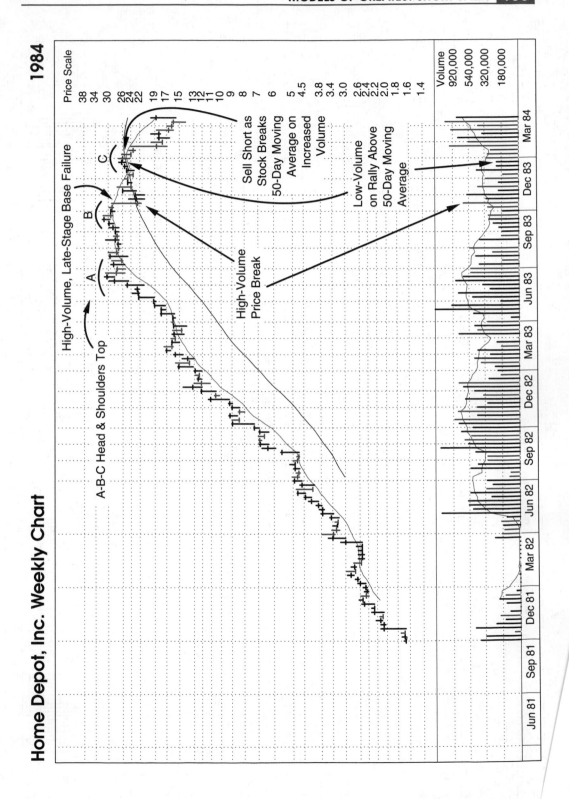

High-Volume, Late-Stage Base Failure

A-B-C Head & Shoulders Top

A

B

C

Sell Short as
Stock Breaks
50-Day Moving
Average on
Increased
Volume

Low-Volume
on Rally Above
50-Day Moving
Average

High-Volume
Price Break

Price Scale
38
34
30
26
24
22
19
17
15
13
12
11
10
9
8
7
6
5
4.5
3.8
3.4
3.0
2.6
2.4
2.2
2.0
1.8
1.6
1.4

Volume
920,000
540,000
320,000
180,000

Jun 81 Sep 81 Dec 81 Mar 82 Jun 82 Sep 82 Dec 82 Mar 83 Jun 83 Sep 83 Dec 83 Mar 84

Pulte Homes, Inc. Weekly Chart

1984

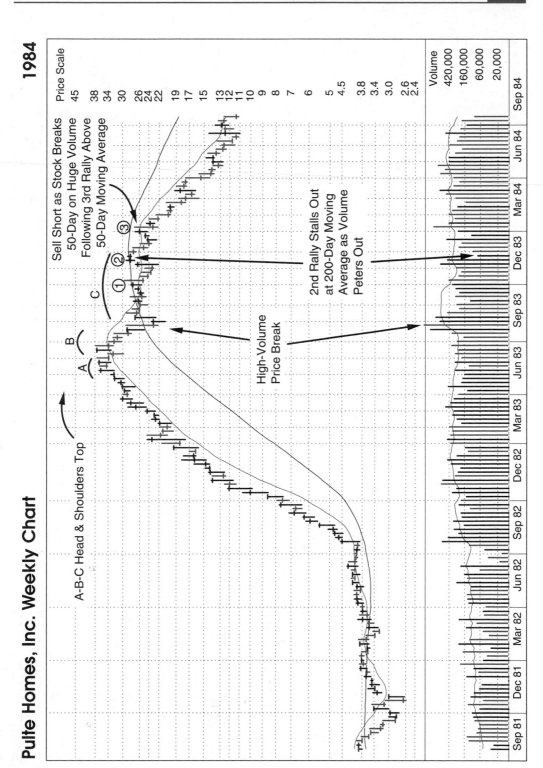

Price Scale

A-B-C Head & Shoulders Top

Sell Short as Stock Breaks
50-Day on Huge Volume
Following 3rd Rally Above
50-Day Moving Average

2nd Rally Stalls Out
at 200-Day Moving
Average as Volume
Peters Out

High-Volume
Price Break

A B C ①②③

Volume
420,000
160,000
60,000
20,000

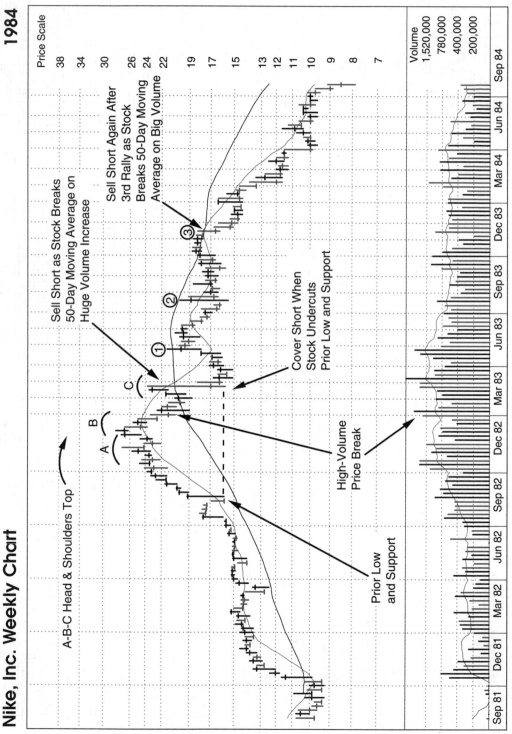

Nike, Inc. Weekly Chart

1984

Price Scale

A-B-C Head & Shoulders Top

Sell Short as Stock Breaks
50-Day Moving Average on
Huge Volume Increase

Sell Short Again After
3rd Rally as Stock
Breaks 50-Day Moving
Average on Big Volume

Cover Short When
Stock Undercuts
Prior Low and Support

High-Volume
Price Break

Prior Low
and Support

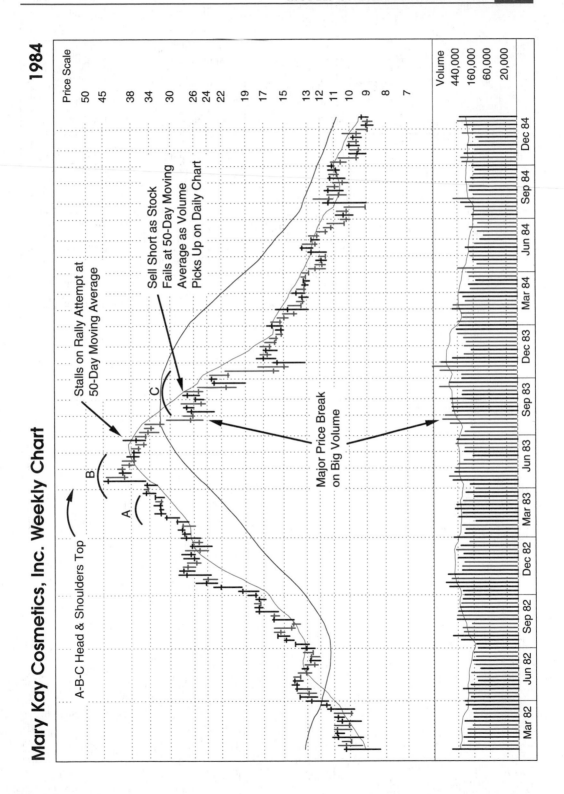

Mary Kay Cosmetics, Inc. Weekly Chart

1984

A-B-C Head & Shoulders Top

Stalls on Rally Attempt at
50-Day Moving Average

Sell Short as Stock
Fails at 50-Day Moving
Average as Volume
Picks Up on Daily Chart

Major Price Break
on Big Volume

Price Scale

50
45
38
34
30
26
24
22
19
17
15
13
12
11
10
9
8
7

Volume
440,000
160,000
60,000
20,000

Mar 82 Jun 82 Sep 82 Dec 82 Mar 83 Jun 83 Sep 83 Dec 83 Mar 84 Jun 84 Sep 84 Dec 84

Adobe Systems, Inc. Weekly Chart

1987

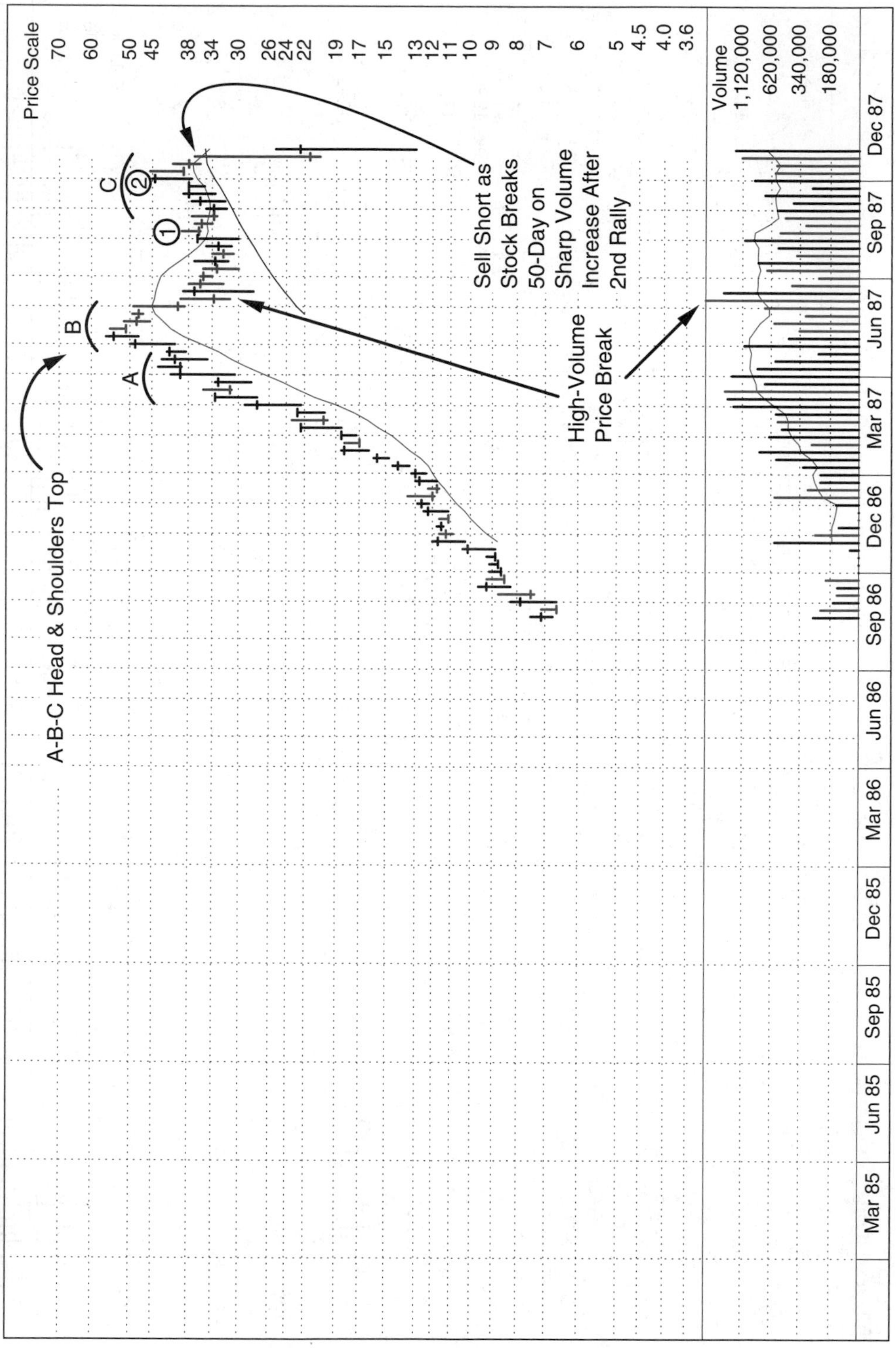

Price Scale
70
60
50
45
38
34
30
26
24
22
19
17
15
13
12
11
10
9
8
7
6
5
4.5
4.0
3.6

A-B-C Head & Shoulders Top

C
② ①
B
A

Sell Short as
Stock Breaks
50-Day on
Sharp Volume
Increase After
2nd Rally

High-Volume
Price Break

Volume
1,120,000
620,000
340,000
180,000

Mar 85 Jun 85 Sep 85 Dec 85 Mar 86 Jun 86 Sep 86 Dec 86 Mar 87 Jun 87 Sep 87 Dec 87

Chiron Corp. Weekly Chart

1987

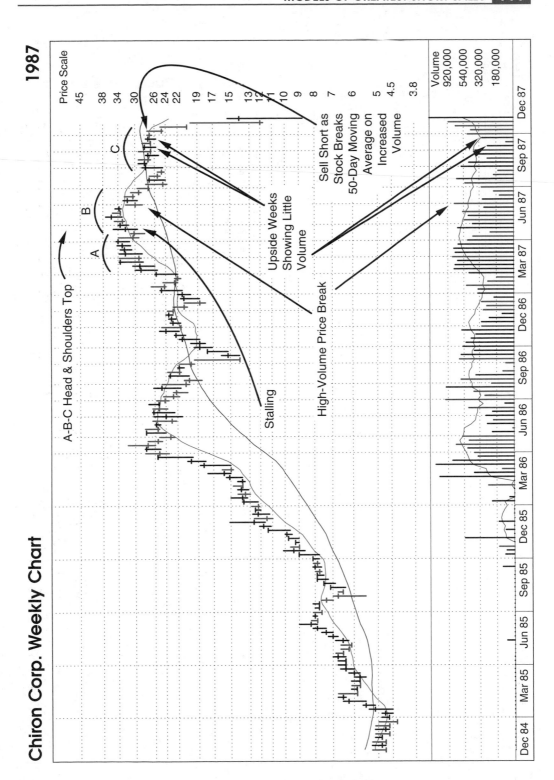

A-B-C Head & Shoulders Top

A

B

C

Price Scale

45

38

34

30

26
24
22

19

17

15

13
12
11
10

9

8

7

6

5

4.5

3.8

Sell Short as
Stock Breaks
50-Day Moving
Average on
Increased
Volume

Upside Weeks
Showing Little
Volume

High-Volume Price Break

Stalling

Volume
920,000
540,000
320,000
180,000

Dec 84   Mar 85   Jun 85   Sep 85   Dec 85   Mar 86   Jun 86   Sep 86   Dec 86   Mar 87   Jun 87   Sep 87   Dec 87

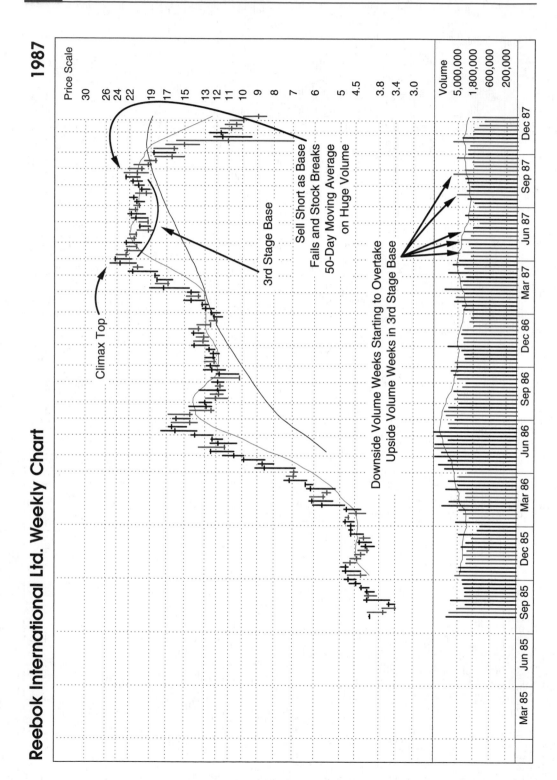

Reebok International Ltd. Weekly Chart

1987

Price Scale

Climax Top.

3rd Stage Base

Sell Short as Base
Fails and Stock Breaks
50-Day Moving Average
on Huge Volume

Downside Volume Weeks Starting to Overtake
Upside Volume Weeks in 3rd Stage Base

Volume

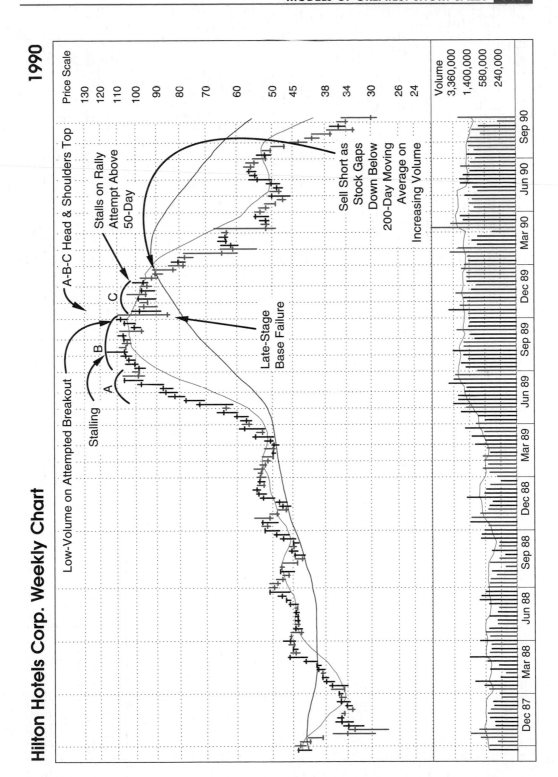

Hilton Hotels Corp. Weekly Chart

1990

Price Scale

A-B-C Head & Shoulders Top

Low-Volume on Attempted Breakout

Stalls on Rally
Attempt Above
50-Day

Stalling

Sell Short as
Stock Gaps
Down Below
200-Day Moving
Average on
Increasing Volume

Late-Stage
Base Failure

A

B

C

Price Scale: 130 120 110 100 90 80 70 60 50 45 38 34 30 26 24

Volume: 3,360,000 1,400,000 580,000 240,000

Dec 87 Mar 88 Jun 88 Sep 88 Dec 88 Mar 89 Jun 89 Sep 89 Dec 89 Mar 90 Jun 90 Sep 90

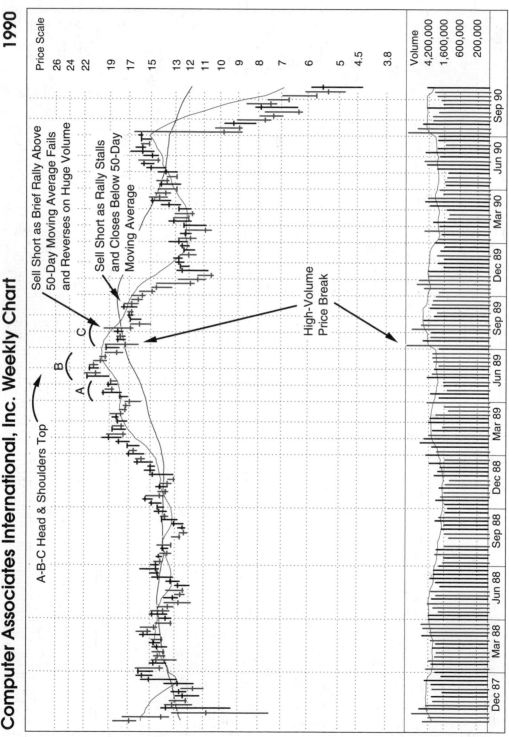

Computer Associates International, Inc. Weekly Chart

1990

Price Scale

A-B-C Head & Shoulders Top

Sell Short as Brief Rally Above
50-Day Moving Average Fails
and Reverses on Huge Volume

Sell Short as Rally Stalls
and Closes Below 50-Day
Moving Average

High-Volume
Price Break

Volume
4,200,000
1,600,000
600,000
200,000

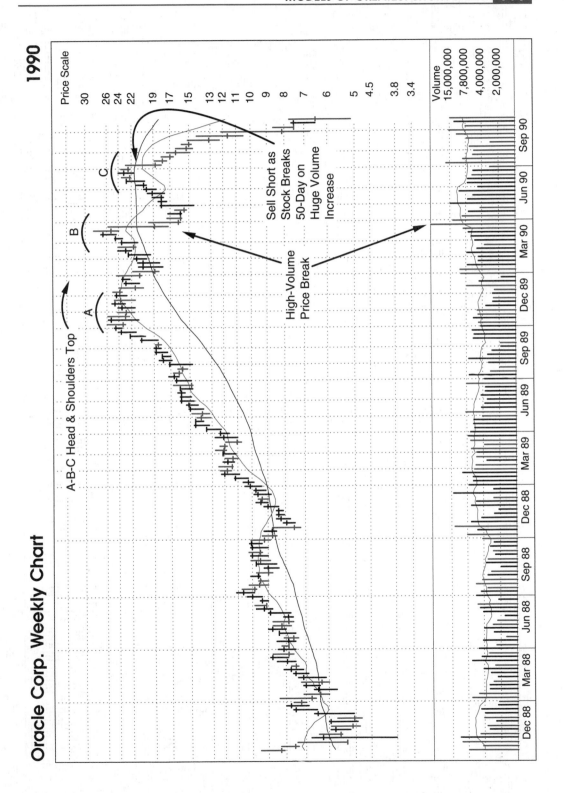

Oracle Corp. Weekly Chart

1990

A-B-C Head & Shoulders Top

A

B

C

Sell Short as
Stock Breaks
50-Day on
Huge Volume
Increase

High-Volume
Price Break

Price Scale

30
26
24
22
19
17
15
13
12
11
10
9
8
7
6
5
4.5
3.8
3.4

Volume
15,000,000
7,800,000
4,000,000
2,000,000

Dec 88 Mar 88 Jun 88 Sep 88 Dec 88 Mar 89 Jun 89 Sep 89 Dec 89 Mar 90 Jun 90 Sep 90

Rogers Communications, Inc. Weekly Chart

1990

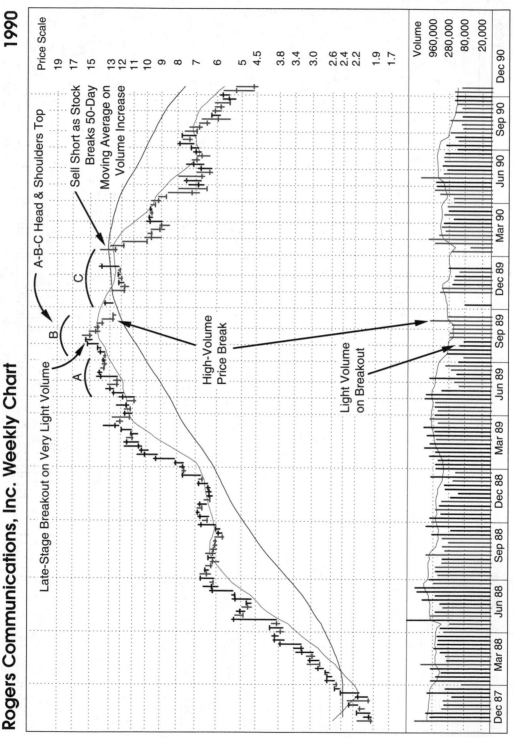

Late-Stage Breakout on Very Light Volume

A-B-C Head & Shoulders Top

Sell Short as Stock
Breaks 50-Day
Moving Average on
Volume Increase

A

B

C

High-Volume
Price Break

Light Volume
on Breakout

Price Scale

19
17
15
13
12
11
10
9
8
7
6
5
4.5
3.8
3.4
3.0
2.6
2.4
2.2
1.9
1.7

Volume
960,000
280,000
80,000
20,000

Dec 87   Mar 88   Jun 88   Sep 88   Dec 88   Mar 89   Jun 89   Sep 89   Dec 89   Mar 90   Jun 90   Sep 90   Dec 90

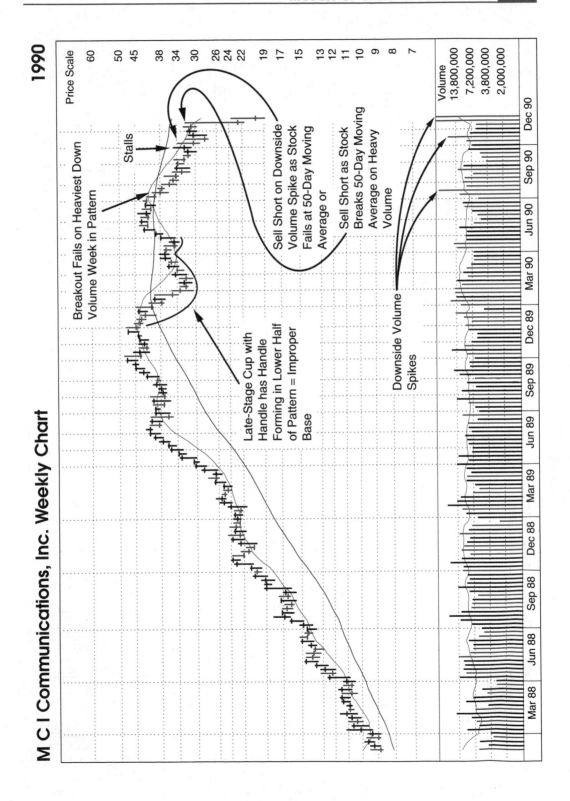

M C I Communications, Inc. Weekly Chart

1990

Price Scale

Breakout Fails on Heaviest Down Volume Week in Pattern

Stalls

Late-Stage Cup with Handle has Handle Forming in Lower Half of Pattern = Improper Base

Sell Short on Downside Volume Spike as Stock Fails at 50-Day Moving Average or

Sell Short as Stock Breaks 50-Day Moving Average on Heavy Volume

Downside Volume Spikes

Volume
13,800,000
7,200,000
3,800,000
2,000,000

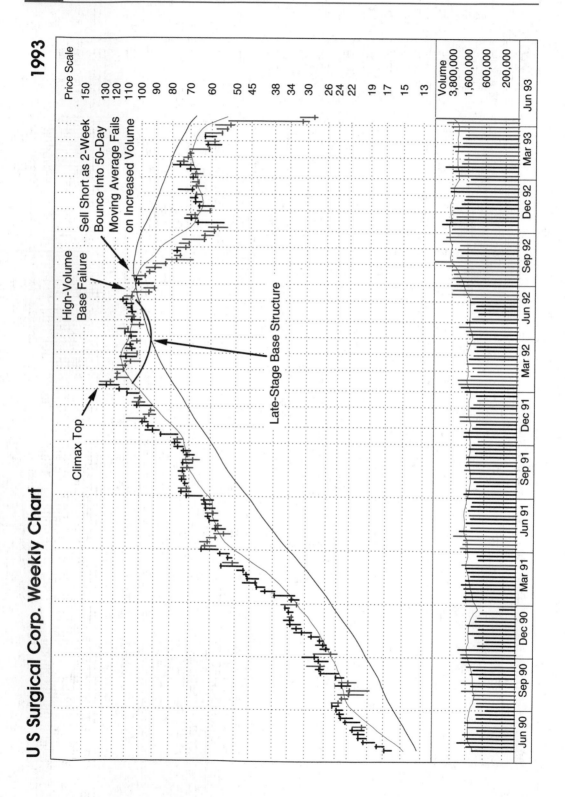

U S Surgical Corp. Weekly Chart

1993

Climax Top

High-Volume
Base Failure

Sell Short as 2-Week
Bounce Into 50-Day
Moving Average Fails
on Increased Volume

Late-Stage Base Structure

Price Scale

150
130
120
110
100
90
80
70
60
50
45
38
34
30
26
24
22
19
17
15
13

Volume
3,800,000
1,600,000
600,000
200,000

Jun 90 · Sep 90 · Dec 90 · Mar 91 · Jun 91 · Sep 91 · Dec 91 · Mar 92 · Jun 92 · Sep 92 · Dec 92 · Mar 93 · Jun 93

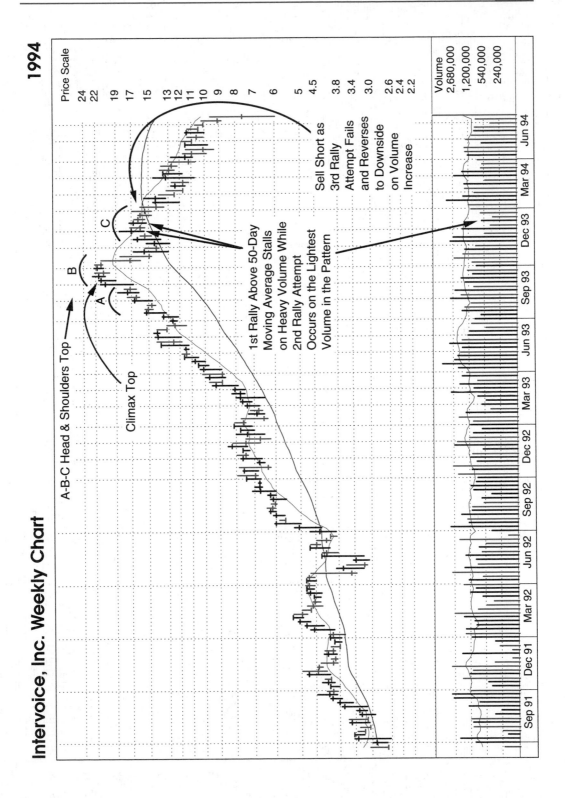

Intervoice, Inc. Weekly Chart

1994

A-B-C Head & Shoulders Top

Climax Top

1st Rally Above 50-Day Moving Average Stalls on Heavy Volume While 2nd Rally Attempt Occurs on the Lightest Volume in the Pattern

Sell Short as 3rd Rally Attempt Fails and Reverses to Downside on Volume Increase

Price Scale
24
22
19
17
15
13
12
11
10
9
8
7
6
5
4.5
3.8
3.4
3.0
2.6
2.4
2.2

Volume
2,680,000
1,200,000
540,000
240,000

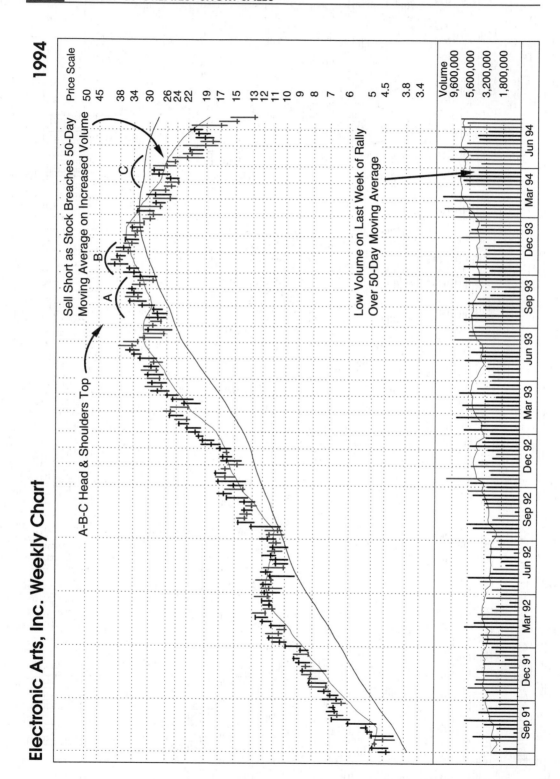

Electronic Arts, Inc. Weekly Chart   1994

A-B-C Head & Shoulders Top

Sell Short as Stock Breaches 50-Day
Moving Average on Increased Volume

Low Volume on Last Week of Rally
Over 50-Day Moving Average

A   B   C

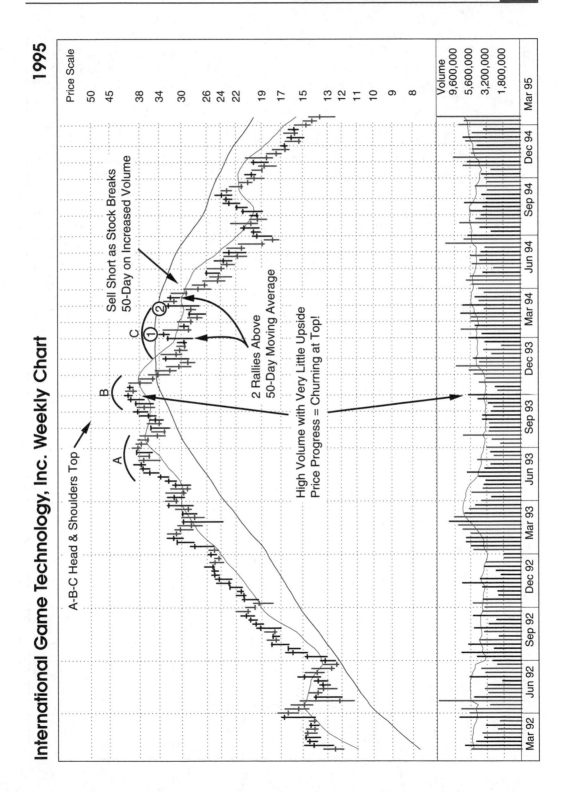

International Game Technology, Inc. Weekly Chart   1995

A-B-C Head & Shoulders Top

Sell Short as Stock Breaks
50-Day on Increased Volume

2 Rallies Above
50-Day Moving Average

High Volume with Very Little Upside
Price Progress = Churning at Top!

Price Scale
50
45
38
34
30
26
24
22
19
17
15
13
12
11
10
9
8

Volume
9,600,000
5,600,000
3,200,000
1,800,000

Mar 92   Jun 92   Sep 92   Dec 92   Mar 93   Jun 93   Sep 93   Dec 93   Mar 94   Jun 94   Sep 94   Dec 94   Mar 95

Integrated Silicon Solution, Inc. Weekly Chart

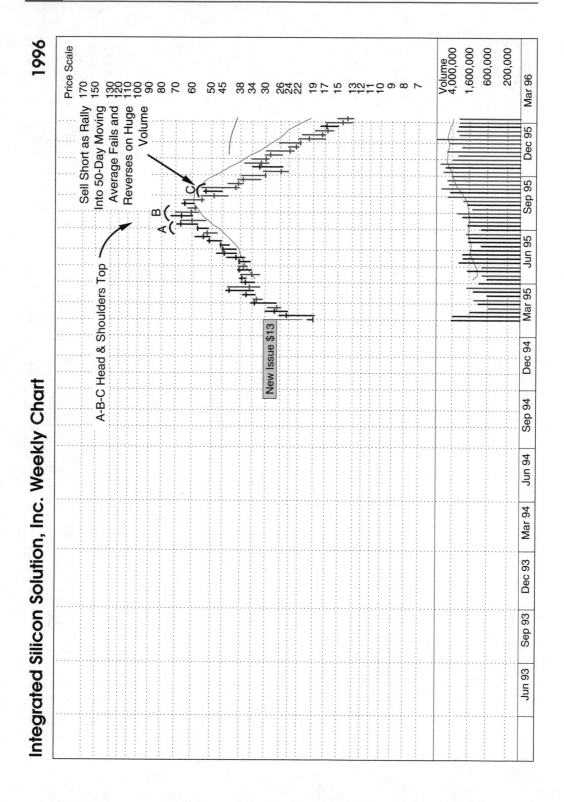

Best Buy Co., Inc. Weekly Chart

1996

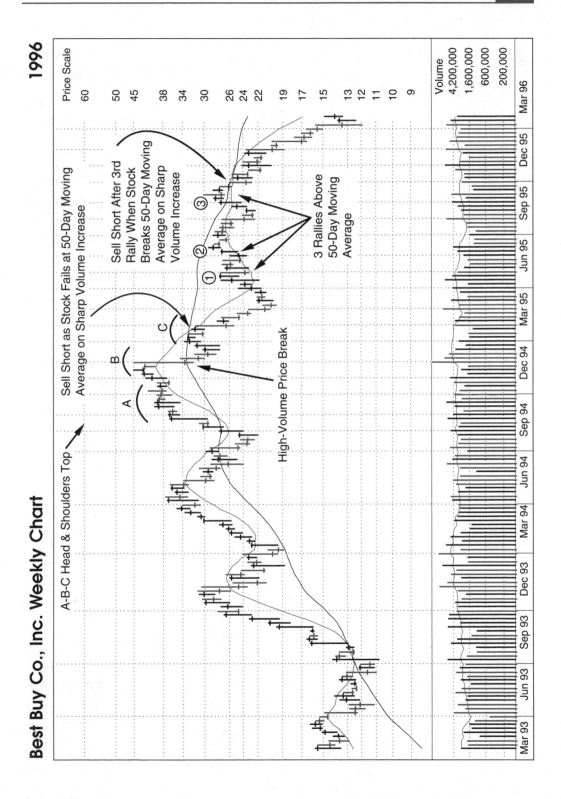

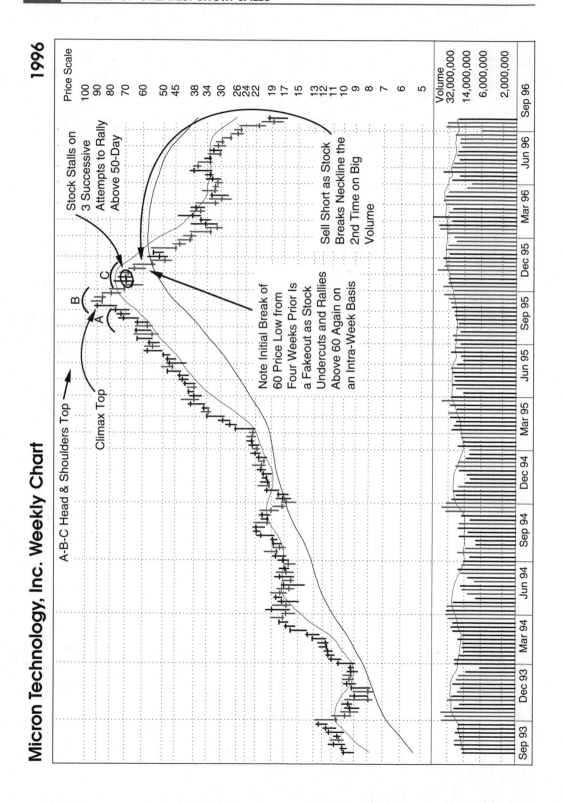

Micron Technology, Inc. Weekly Chart

1996

A-B-C Head & Shoulders Top

Climax Top

Stock Stalls on 3 Successive Attempts to Rally Above 50-Day

Note Initial Break of 60 Price Low from Four Weeks Prior Is a Fakeout as Stock Undercuts and Rallies Above 60 Again on an Intra-Week Basis

Sell Short as Stock Breaks Neckline the 2nd Time on Big Volume

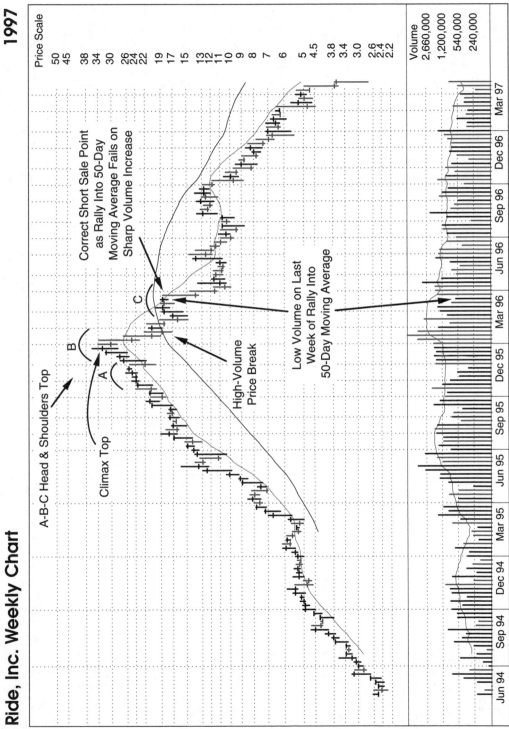

Ride, Inc. Weekly Chart

1997

A-B-C Head & Shoulders Top

Climax Top

Correct Short Sale Point as Rally Into 50-Day Moving Average Fails on Sharp Volume Increase

High-Volume Price Break

Low Volume on Last Week of Rally Into 50-Day Moving Average

Price Scale

Volume

Clarify, Inc. Weekly Chart

1997

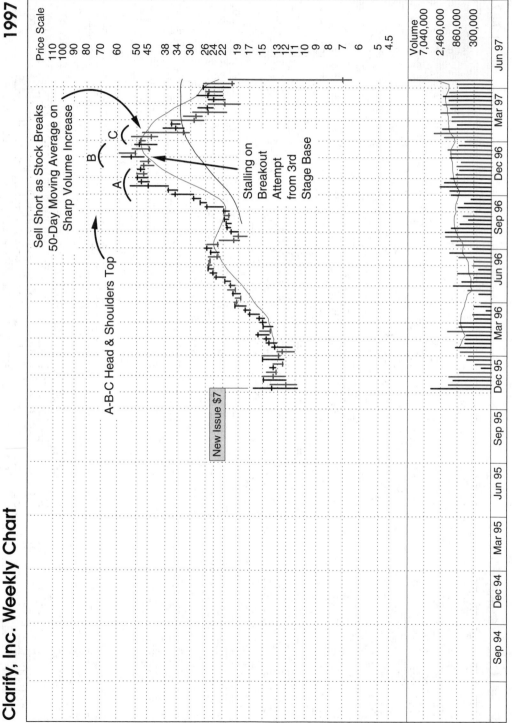

Price Scale
110
100
90
80
70
60
50
45
38
34
30
26
24
22
19
17
15
13
12
11
10
9
8
7
6
5
4.5

Sell Short as Stock Breaks
50-Day Moving Average on
Sharp Volume Increase

A-B-C Head & Shoulders Top

C

B

A

Stalling on
Breakout
Attempt
from 3rd
Stage Base

New Issue $7

Volume
7,040,000
2,460,000
860,000
300,000

Sep 94 | Dec 94 | Mar 95 | Jun 95 | Sep 95 | Dec 95 | Mar 96 | Jun 96 | Sep 96 | Dec 96 | Mar 97 | Jun 97

Glenayre Technologies, Inc. Weekly Chart 1997

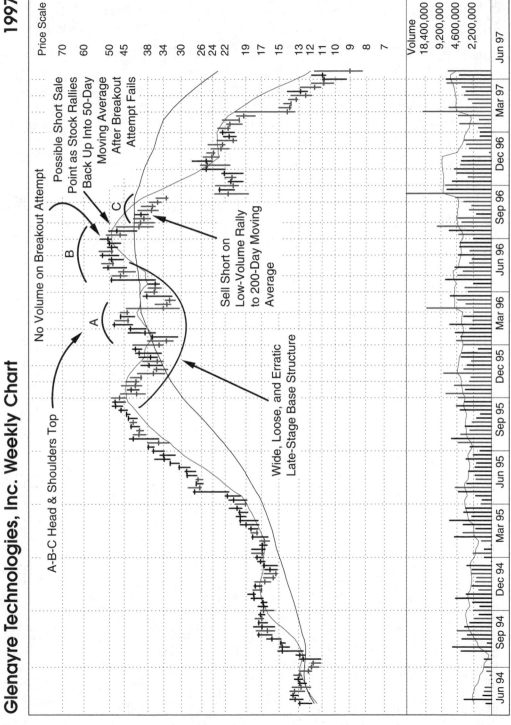

Price Scale

A-B-C Head & Shoulders Top

No Volume on Breakout Attempt

Possible Short Sale
Point as Stock Rallies
Back Up Into 50-Day
Moving Average
After Breakout
Attempt Fails

Sell Short on
Low-Volume Rally
to 200-Day Moving
Average

Wide, Loose, and Erratic
Late-Stage Base Structure

Volume
18,400,000
9,200,000
4,600,000
2,200,000

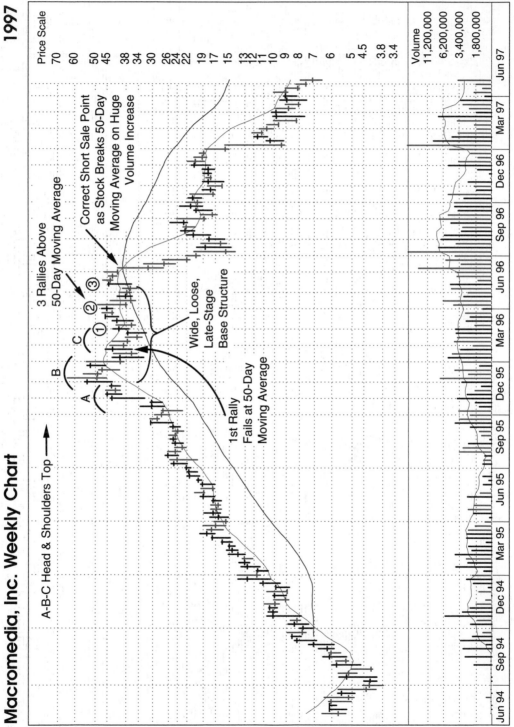

Macromedia, Inc. Weekly Chart

1997

A-B-C Head & Shoulders Top →

3 Rallies Above
50-Day Moving Average

Correct Short Sale Point
as Stock Breaks 50-Day
Moving Average on Huge
Volume Increase

Wide, Loose,
Late-Stage
Base Structure

1st Rally
Fails at 50-Day
Moving Average

Price Scale

70
60
50
45
38
34
30
26
24
22
19
17
15
13
12
11
10
9
8
7
6
5
4.5
3.8
3.4

Volume
11,200,000
6,200,000
3,400,000
1,800,000

Jun 94   Sep 94   Dec 94   Mar 95   Jun 95   Sep 95   Dec 95   Mar 96   Jun 96   Sep 96   Dec 96   Mar 97   Jun 97

Paigain Technologies, Inc. Weekly Chart

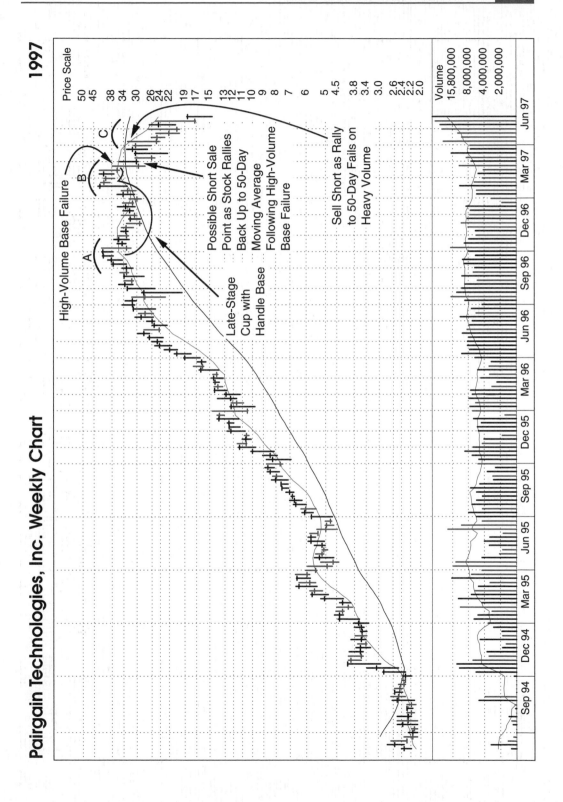

1997

Price Scale
50
45
38
34
30
26
24
22
19
17
15
13
12
11
10
9
8
7
6
5
4.5
3.8
3.4
3.0
2.6
2.4
2.2
2.0

High-Volume Base Failure

C

B

A

Possible Short Sale
Point as Stock Rallies
Back Up to 50-Day
Moving Average
Following High-Volume
Base Failure

Late-Stage
Cup with
Handle Base

Sell Short as Rally
to 50-Day Fails on
Heavy Volume

Volume
15,800,000
8,000,000
4,000,000
2,000,000

Sep 94 Dec 94 Mar 95 Jun 95 Sep 95 Dec 95 Mar 96 Jun 96 Sep 96 Dec 96 Mar 97 Jun 97

Aames Financial Corp. Weekly Chart

1997

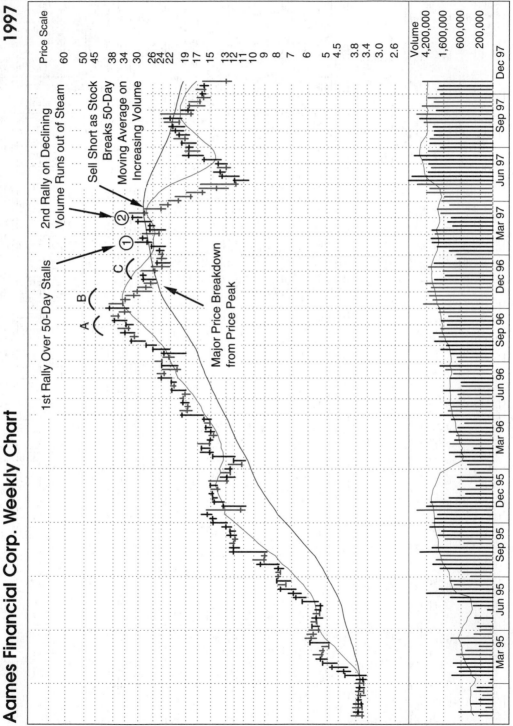

Price Scale

1st Rally Over 50-Day Stalls

2nd Rally on Declining
Volume Runs out of Steam

Sell Short as Stock
Breaks 50-Day
Moving Average on
Increasing Volume

Major Price Breakdown
from Price Peak

A B

C

① ②

Ascend Communications, Inc. Weekly Chart

1997

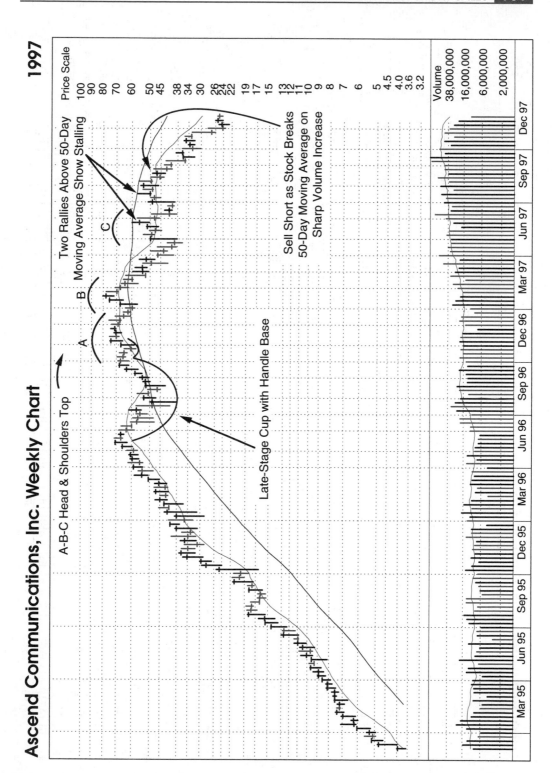

A-B-C Head & Shoulders Top

Two Rallies Above 50-Day
Moving Average Show Stalling

C

B

A

Sell Short as Stock Breaks
50-Day Moving Average on
Sharp Volume Increase

Late-Stage Cup with Handle Base

Price Scale
100
90
80
70
60
50
45
38
34
30
26
24
22
19
17
15
13
12
11
10
9
8
7
6
5
4.5
4.0
3.6
3.2

Volume
38,000,000
16,000,000
6,000,000
2,000,000

Mar 95 Jun 95 Sep 95 Dec 95 Mar 96 Jun 96 Sep 96 Dec 96 Mar 97 Jun 97 Sep 97 Dec 97

Miller Industries, Inc. Weekly Chart

1998

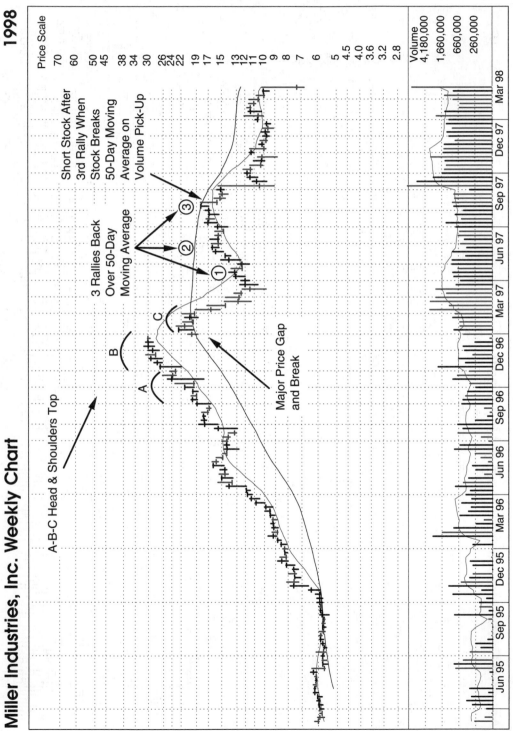

A-B-C Head & Shoulders Top

3 Rallies Back Over 50-Day Moving Average

Short Stock After 3rd Rally When Stock Breaks 50-Day Moving Average on Volume Pick-Up

Major Price Gap and Break

Price Scale
70
60
50
45
38
34
30
26
24
22
19
17
15
13
12
11
10
9
8
7
6
5
4.5
4.0
3.6
3.2
2.8

Volume
4,180,000
1,660,000
660,000
260,000

Chesapeake Energy Corp. Weekly Chart

1998

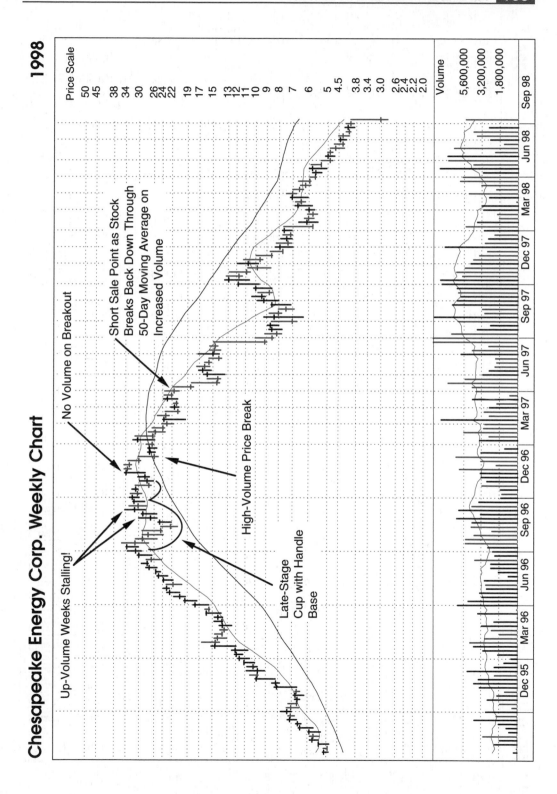

Price Scale

50
45
38
34
30
26
24
22
19
17
15
13
12
11
10
9
8
7
6
5
4.5
3.8
3.4
3.0
2.6
2.4
2.2
2.0

No Volume on Breakout

Short Sale Point as Stock
Breaks Back Down Through
50-Day Moving Average on
Increased Volume

Up-Volume Weeks Stalling!

High-Volume Price Break

Late-Stage
Cup with Handle
Base

Volume

5,600,000
3,200,000
1,800,000

Dec 95 Mar 96 Jun 96 Sep 96 Dec 96 Mar 97 Jun 97 Sep 97 Dec 97 Mar 98 Jun 98 Sep 98

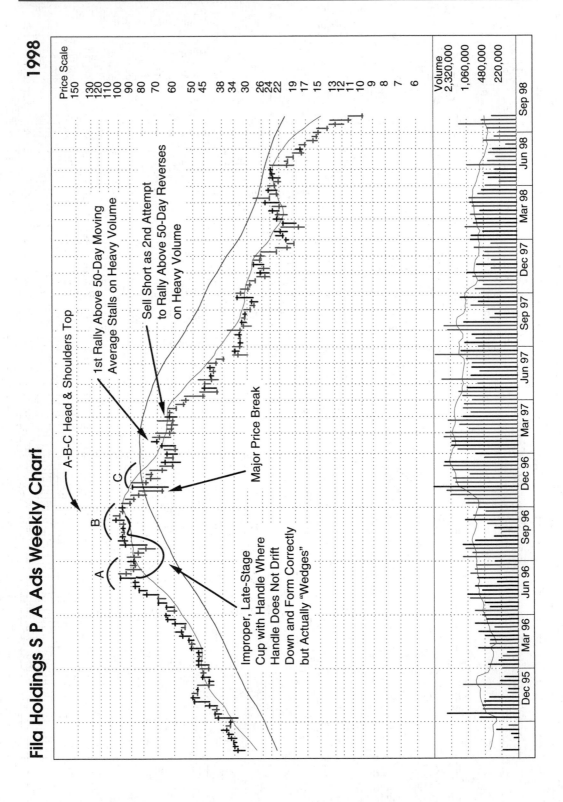

Fila Holdings S P A Ads Weekly Chart   1998

A-B-C Head & Shoulders Top

1st Rally Above 50-Day Moving
Average Stalls on Heavy Volume

Sell Short as 2nd Attempt
to Rally Above 50-Day Reverses
on Heavy Volume

Major Price Break

Improper, Late-Stage
Cup with Handle Where
Handle Does Not Drift
Down and Form Correctly
but Actually "Wedges"

Shiva Corp. Weekly Chart

1998

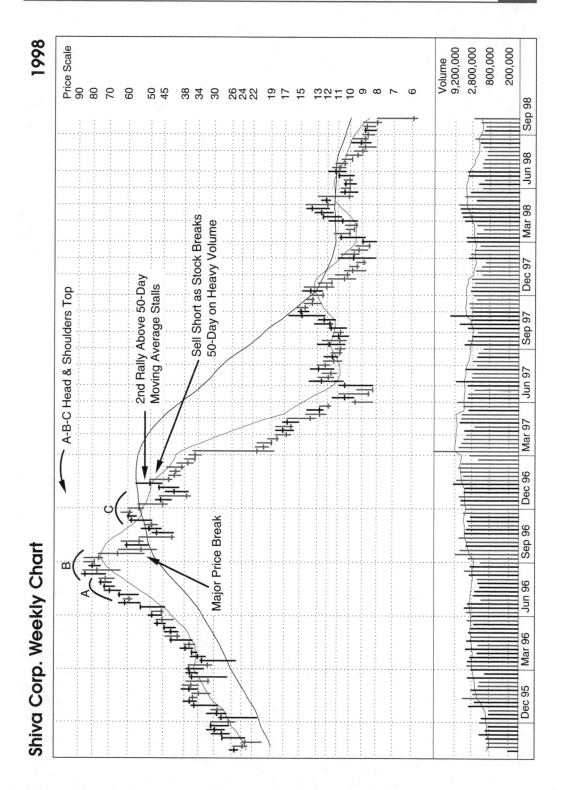

Price Scale

A-B-C Head & Shoulders Top

2nd Rally Above 50-Day
Moving Average Stalls

Sell Short as Stock Breaks
50-Day on Heavy Volume

Major Price Break

B

C

A

Volume

A P A C Customer Services, Inc. Weekly Chart

1998

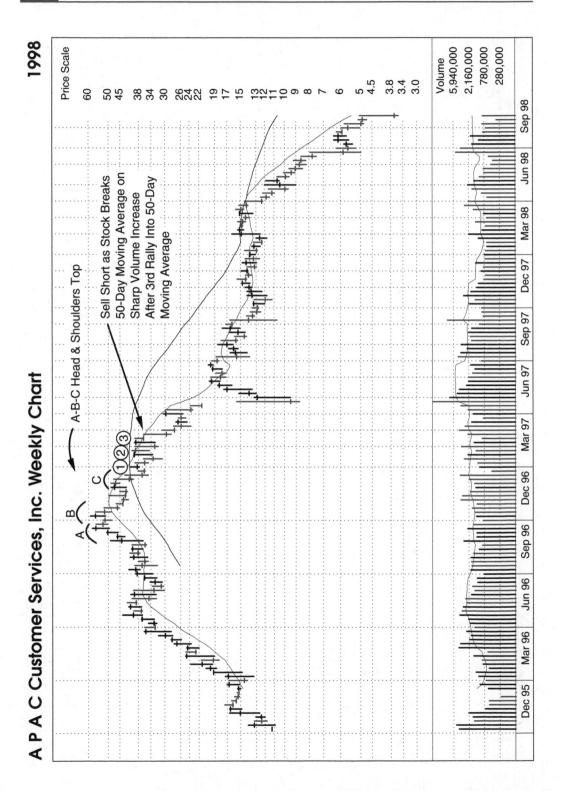

A-B-C Head & Shoulders Top

Sell Short as Stock Breaks
50-Day Moving Average on
Sharp Volume Increase
After 3rd Rally Into 50-Day
Moving Average

Price Scale

60

50
45

38
34

30

26
24
22

19
17

15

13
12
11
10

9

8

7

6

5
4.5

3.8
3.4

3.0

Volume
5,940,000

2,160,000

780,000

280,000

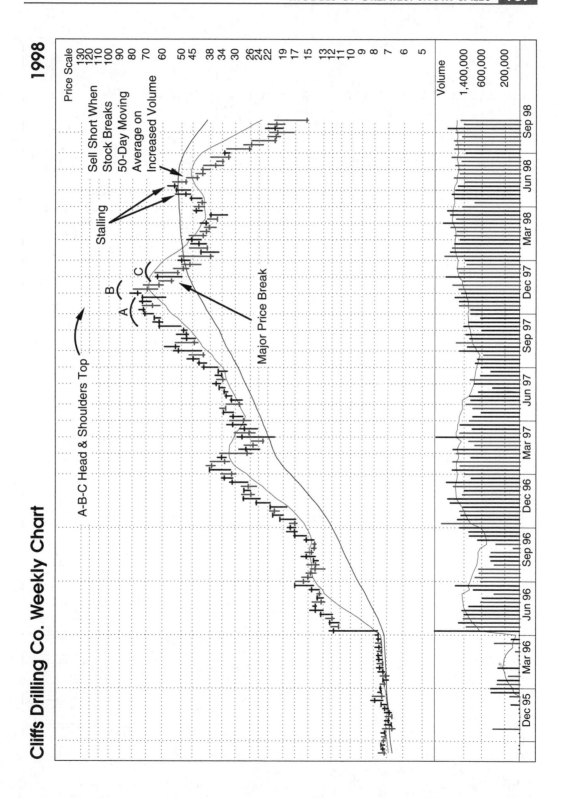

Cliffs Drilling Co. Weekly Chart

1998

A-B-C Head & Shoulders Top

Sell Short When
Stock Breaks
50-Day Moving
Average on
Increased Volume

Stalling

Major Price Break

Price Scale

Volume

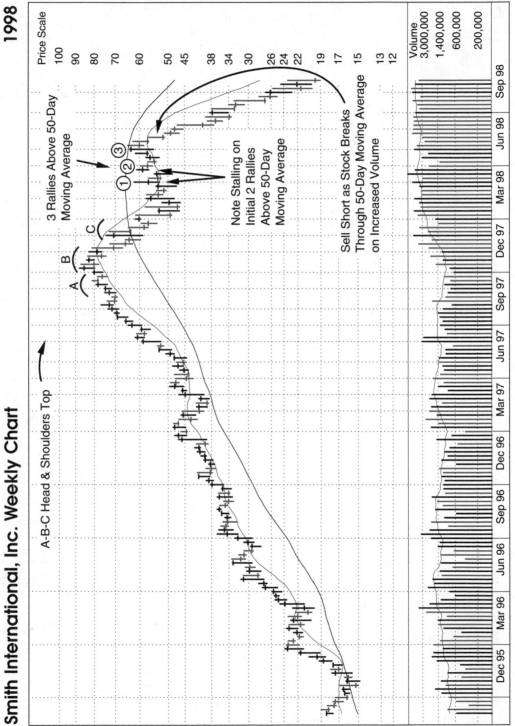

Smith International, Inc. Weekly Chart

1998

A-B-C Head & Shoulders Top

3 Rallies Above 50-Day Moving Average

Note Stalling on Initial 2 Rallies Above 50-Day Moving Average

Sell Short as Stock Breaks Through 50-Day Moving Average on Increased Volume

Price Scale
100
90
80
70
60
50
45
38
34
30
26
24
22
19
17
15
13
12

Volume
3,000,000
1,400,000
600,000
200,000

Dec 95 Mar 96 Jun 96 Sep 96 Dec 96 Mar 97 Jun 97 Sep 97 Dec 97 Mar 98 Jun 98 Sep 98

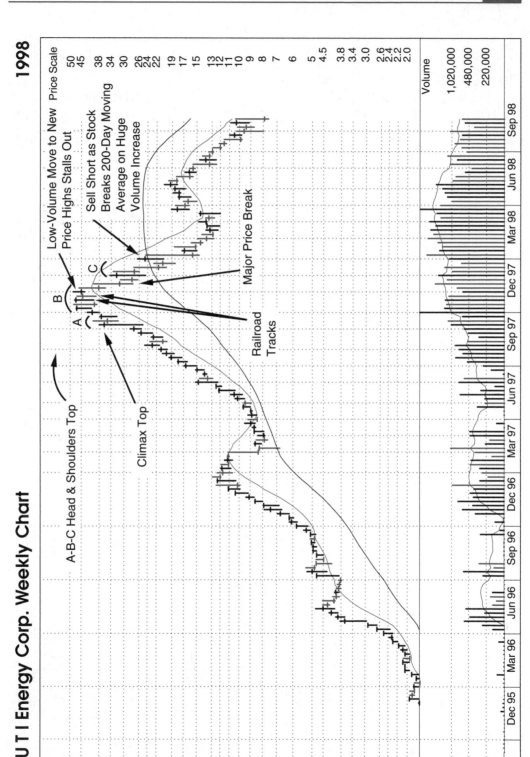

U T I Energy Corp. Weekly Chart 1998

A-B-C Head & Shoulders Top

Low-Volume Move to New Price Highs Stalls Out

Sell Short as Stock Breaks 200-Day Moving Average on Huge Volume Increase

Climax Top

Major Price Break

Railroad Tracks

Price Scale

50
45
38
34
30
26
24
22
19
17
15
13
12
11
10
9
8
7
6
5
4.5
3.8
3.4
3.0
2.6
2.4
2.2
2.0

Volume

1,020,000
480,000
220,000

Dec 95   Mar 96   Jun 96   Sep 96   Dec 96   Mar 97   Jun 97   Sep 97   Dec 97   Mar 98   Jun 98   Sep 98

Saville Systems PLC ADR, Weekly Chart

1998

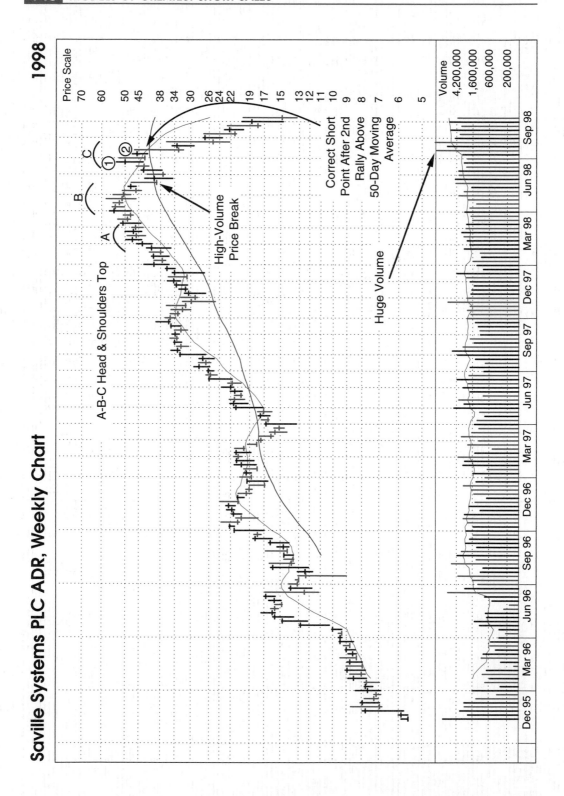

Price Scale
70
60
50
45
38
34
30
26
24
22
19
17
15
13
12
11
10
9
8
7
6
5

A-B-C Head & Shoulders Top

A
B
C

High-Volume
Price Break

Correct Short
Point After 2nd
Rally Above
50-Day Moving
Average

Huge Volume

Volume
4,200,000
1,600,000
600,000
200,000

Dec 95 Mar 96 Jun 96 Sep 96 Dec 96 Mar 97 Jun 97 Sep 97 Dec 97 Mar 98 Jun 98 Sep 98

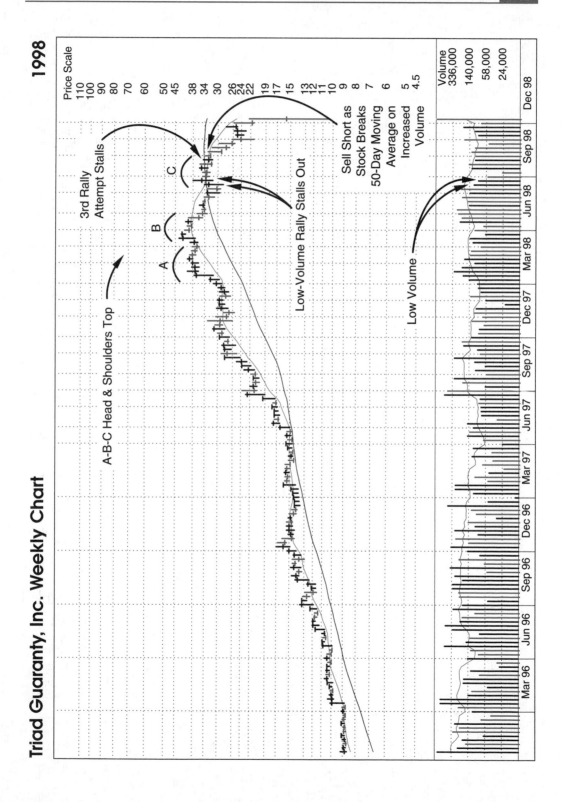

Triad Guaranty, Inc. Weekly Chart

1998

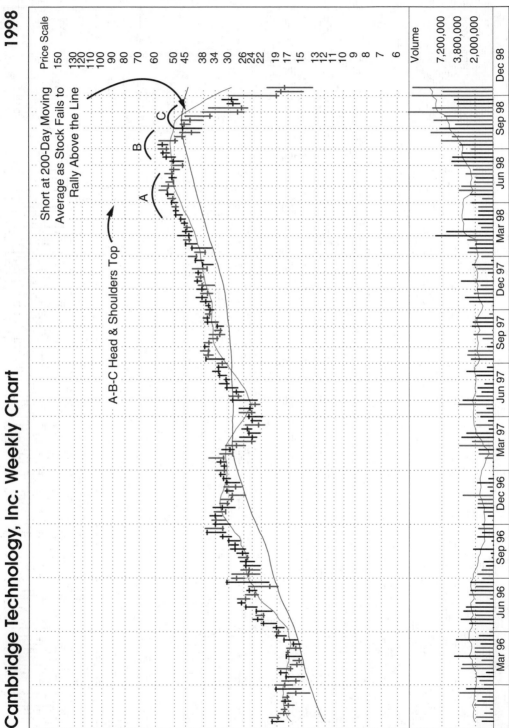

Cambridge Technology, Inc. Weekly Chart

1998

Price Scale

Short at 200-Day Moving
Average as Stock Fails to
Rally Above the Line

A-B-C Head & Shoulders Top

Volume
7,200,000
3,800,000
2,000,000

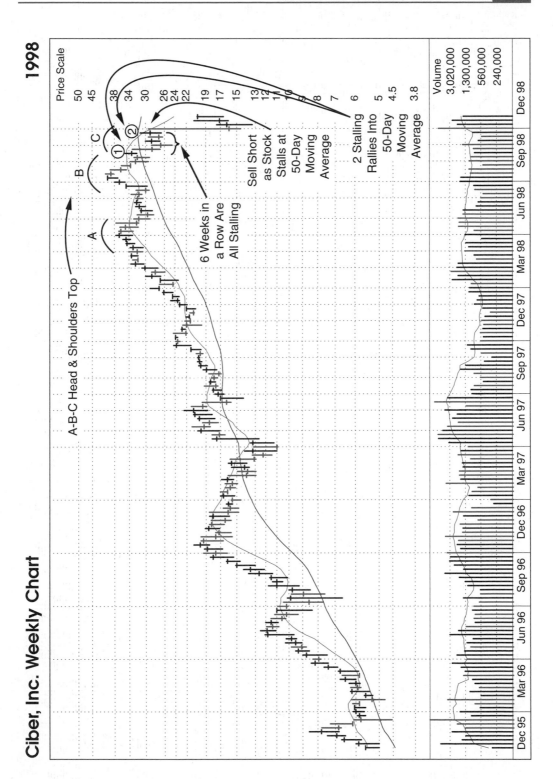

Ciber, Inc. Weekly Chart

1998

A-B-C Head & Shoulders Top

A
B
C

① ②

6 Weeks in
a Row Are
All Stalling

Sell Short
as Stock
Stalls at
50-Day
Moving
Average

2 Stalling
Rallies Into
50-Day
Moving
Average

Price Scale

50
45
38
34
30
26
24
22
19
17
15
13
12
11
10
9
8
7
6
5
4.5
3.8

Volume
3,020,000
1,300,000
560,000
240,000

Dec 95 Mar 96 Jun 96 Sep 96 Dec 96 Mar 97 Jun 97 Sep 97 Dec 97 Mar 98 Jun 98 Sep 98 Dec 98

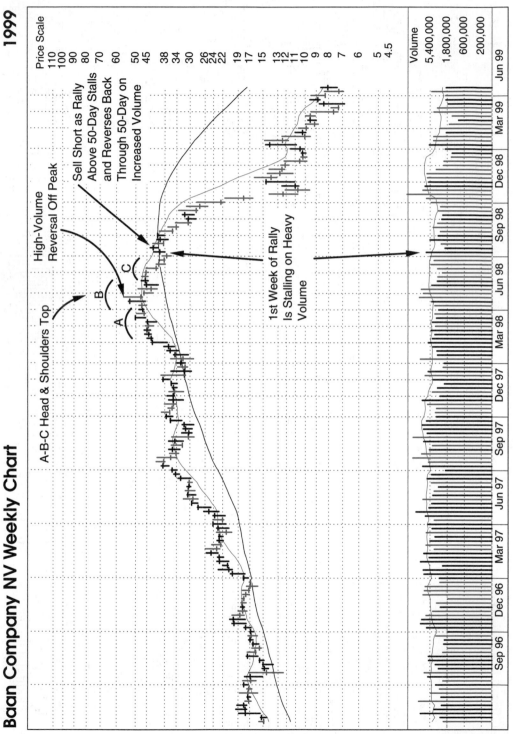

Baan Company NV Weekly Chart   1999

Price Scale
110
100
90
80
70
60
50
45
38
34
30
26
24
22
19
17
15
13
12
11
10
9
8
7
6
5
4.5

A-B-C Head & Shoulders Top

High-Volume
Reversal Off Peak

Sell Short as Rally
Above 50-Day Stalls
and Reverses Back
Through 50-Day on
Increased Volume

A   B   C

1st Week of Rally
Is Stalling on Heavy
Volume

Volume
5,400,000
1,800,000
600,000
200,000

Sep 96   Dec 96   Mar 97   Jun 97   Sep 97   Dec 97   Mar 98   Jun 98   Sep 98   Dec 98   Mar 99   Jun 99

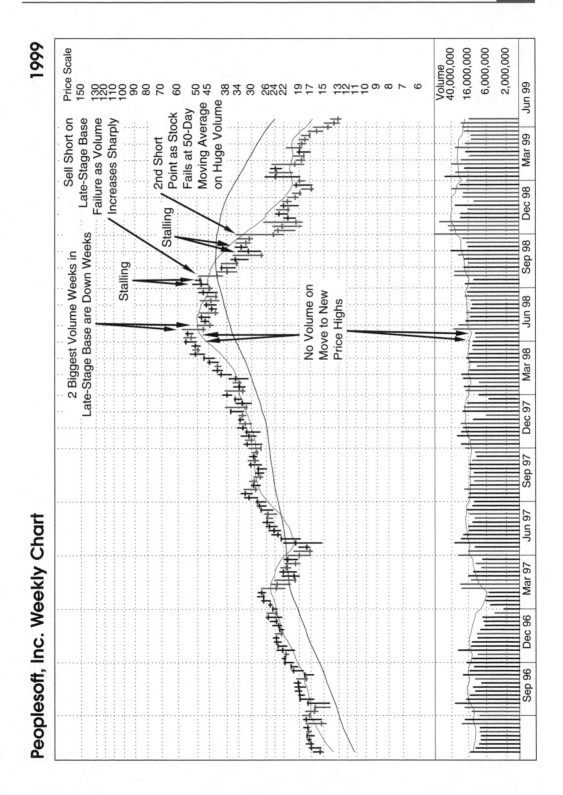

Peoplesoft, Inc. Weekly Chart   1999

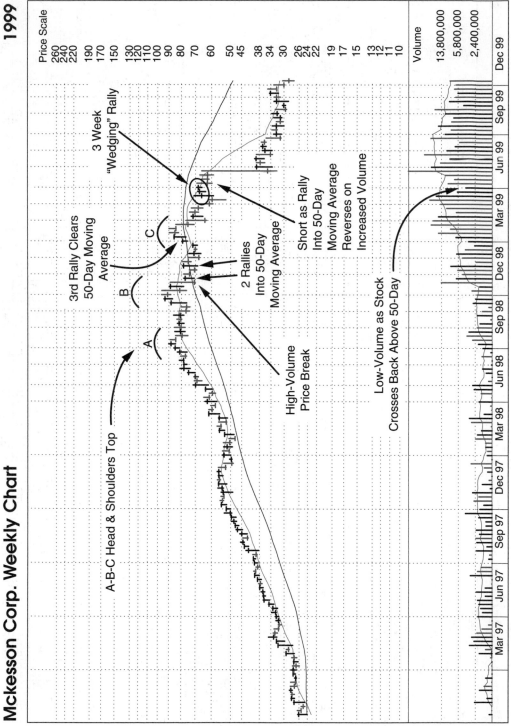

Mckesson Corp. Weekly Chart

1999

Price Scale

A-B-C Head & Shoulders Top

3rd Rally Clears
50-Day Moving
Average

3 Week
"Wedging" Rally

2 Rallies
Into 50-Day
Moving Average

High-Volume
Price Break

Short as Rally
Into 50-Day
Moving Average
Reverses on
Increased Volume

Low-Volume as Stock
Crosses Back Above 50-Day

Volume

13,800,000

5,800,000

2,400,000

Gap, Inc. Del Weekly Chart

2000

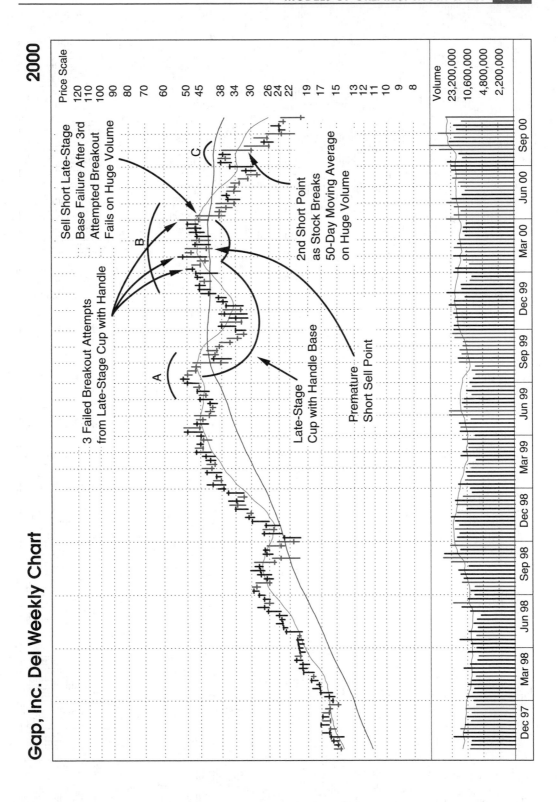

3 Failed Breakout Attempts
from Late-Stage Cup with Handle

Sell Short Late-Stage
Base Failure After 3rd
Attempted Breakout
Fails on Huge Volume

2nd Short Point
as Stock Breaks
50-Day Moving Average
on Huge Volume

Late-Stage
Cup with Handle Base

Premature
Short Sell Point

A

B

C

Price Scale
120
110
100
90
80
70
60
50
45
38
34
30
26
24
22
19
17
15
13
12
11
10
9
8

Volume
23,200,000
10,600,000
4,800,000
2,200,000

Dec 97   Mar 98   Jun 98   Sep 98   Dec 98   Mar 99   Jun 99   Sep 99   Dec 99   Mar 00   Jun 00   Sep 00

Teradyne, Inc. Weekly Chart

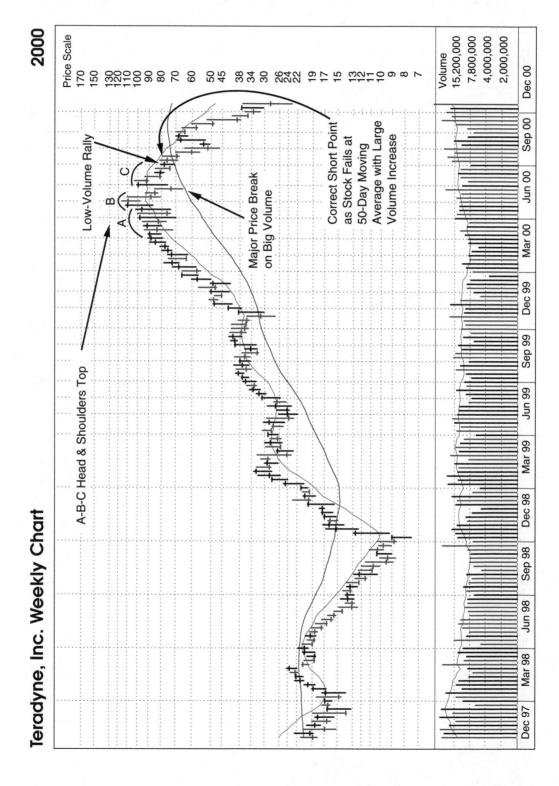

A-B-C Head & Shoulders Top

Low-Volume Rally

A B C

Major Price Break
on Big Volume

Correct Short Point
as Stock Fails at
50-Day Moving
Average with Large
Volume Increase

Price Scale
170
150
130
120
110
100
90
80
70
60
50
45
38
34
30
26
24
22
19
17
15
13
12
11
10
9
8
7

Volume
15,200,000
7,800,000
4,000,000
2,000,000

Dec 97   Mar 98   Jun 98   Sep 98   Dec 98   Mar 99   Jun 99   Sep 99   Dec 99   Mar 00   Jun 00   Sep 00   Dec 00

2000

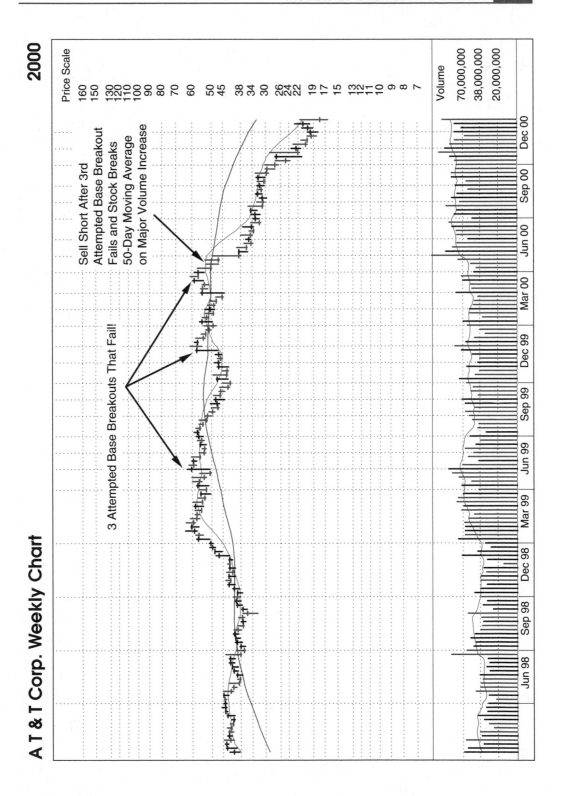

AT & T Corp. Weekly Chart

2000

Price Scale

Sell Short After 3rd
Attempted Base Breakout
Fails and Stock Breaks
50-Day Moving Average
on Major Volume Increase

3 Attempted Base Breakouts That Fail!

Volume

Sprint FON Group Weekly Chart

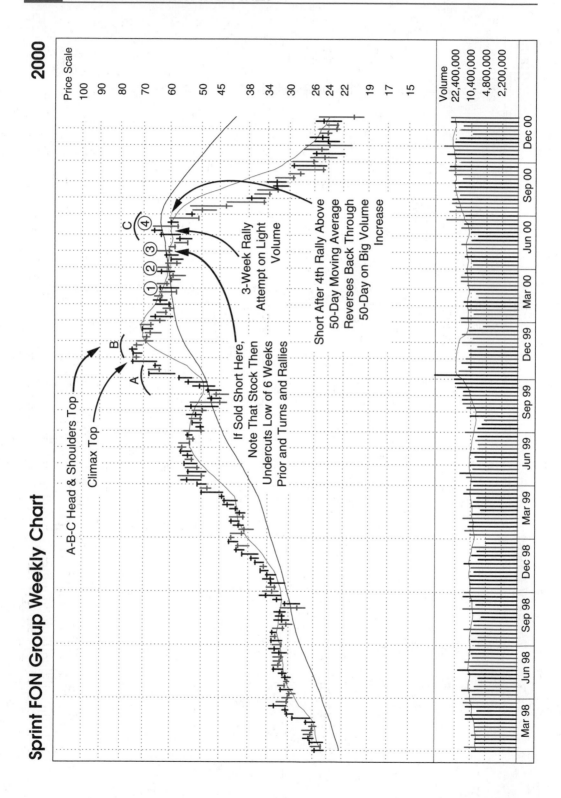

2000

Price Scale

100
90
80
70
60
50
45
38
34
30
26
24
22
19
17
15

A-B-C Head & Shoulders Top

Climax Top

C
A
B

① ② ③ ④

3-Week Rally
Attempt on Light
Volume

If Sold Short Here,
Note That Stock Then
Undercuts Low of 6 Weeks
Prior and Turns and Rallies

Short After 4th Rally Above
50-Day Moving Average
Reverses Back Through
50-Day on Big Volume
Increase

Volume
22,400,000
10,400,000
4,800,000
2,200,000

Mar 98 Jun 98 Sep 98 Dec 98 Mar 99 Jun 99 Sep 99 Dec 99 Mar 00 Jun 00 Sep 00 Dec 00

Compuware Corp. Weekly Chart

2000

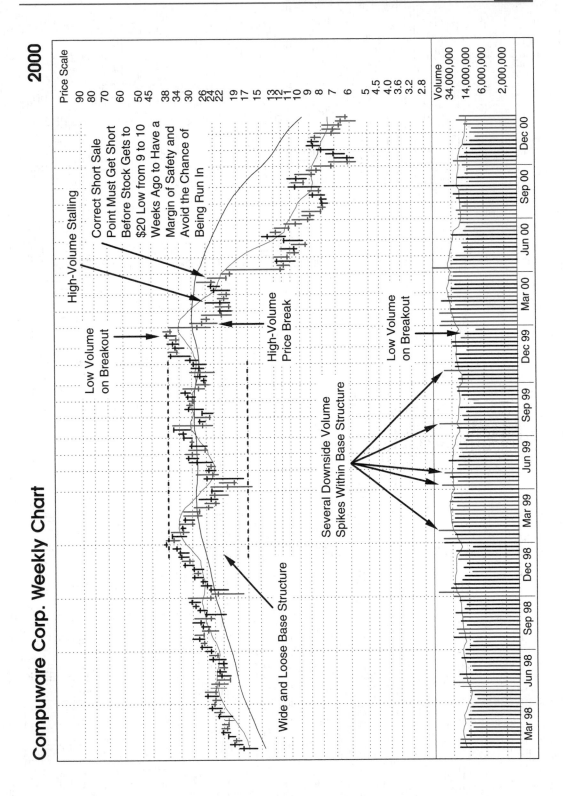

Price Scale
90
80
70
60
50
45
38
34
30
26
24
22
19
17
15
13
12
11
10
9
8
7
6
5
4.5
4.0
3.6
3.2
2.8

High-Volume Stalling

Low Volume
on Breakout

Correct Short Sale
Point Must Get Short
Before Stock Gets to
$20 Low from 9 to 10
Weeks Ago to Have a
Margin of Safety and
Avoid the Chance of
Being Run In

High-Volume
Price Break

Wide and Loose Base Structure

Several Downside Volume
Spikes Within Base Structure

Low Volume
on Breakout

Volume
34,000,000
14,000,000
6,000,000
2,000,000

Mar 98   Jun 98   Sep 98   Dec 98   Mar 99   Jun 99   Sep 99   Dec 99   Mar 00   Jun 00   Sep 00   Dec 00

B M C Software, Inc. Weekly Chart

2001

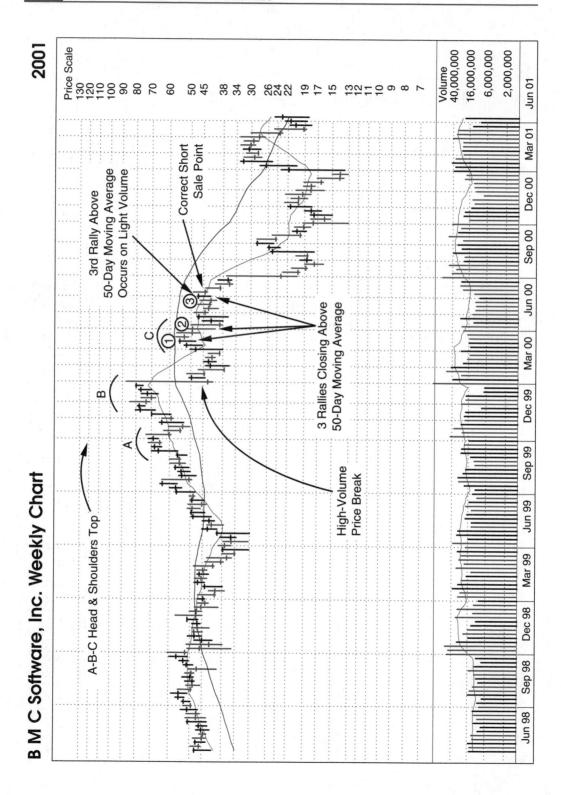

A-B-C Head & Shoulders Top

3rd Rally Above
50-Day Moving Average
Occurs on Light Volume

Correct Short
Sale Point

3 Rallies Closing Above
50-Day Moving Average

High-Volume
Price Break

Price Scale
130
120
110
100
90
80
70
60
50
45
38
34
30
26
24
22
19
17
15
13
12
11
10
9
8
7

Volume
40,000,000
16,000,000
6,000,000
2,000,000

Jun 98   Sep 98   Dec 98   Mar 99   Jun 99   Sep 99   Dec 99   Mar 00   Jun 00   Sep 00   Dec 00   Mar 01   Jun 01

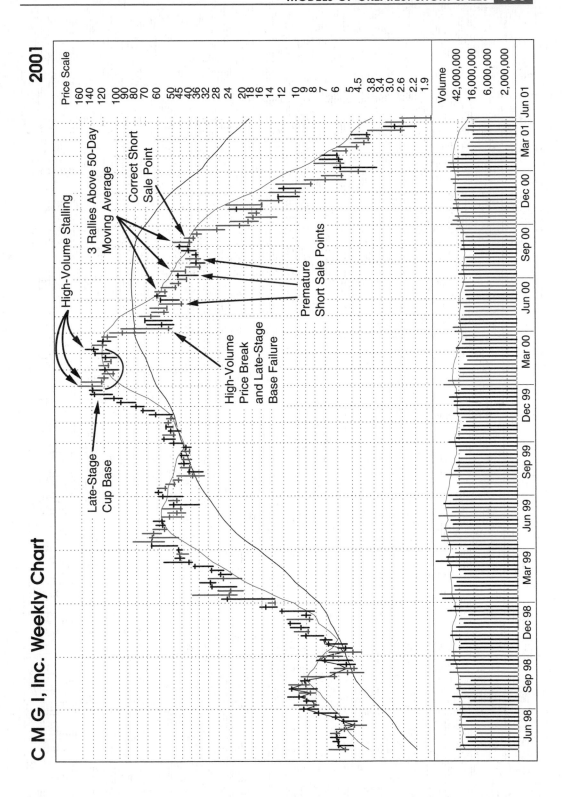

CMGI, Inc. Weekly Chart

2001

High-Volume Stalling

3 Rallies Above 50-Day
Moving Average

Correct Short
Sale Point

Premature
Short Sale Points

Late-Stage
Cup Base

High-Volume
Price Break
and Late-Stage
Base Failure

Price Scale
160
140
120
100
90
80
70
60
50
45
40
36
32
28
24
20
18
16
14
12
10
9
8
7
6
5
4.5
3.8
3.4
3.0
2.6
2.2
1.9

Volume
42,000,000
16,000,000
6,000,000
2,000,000

Jun 98 Sep 98 Dec 98 Mar 99 Jun 99 Sep 99 Dec 99 Mar 00 Jun 00 Sep 00 Dec 00 Mar 01 Jun 01

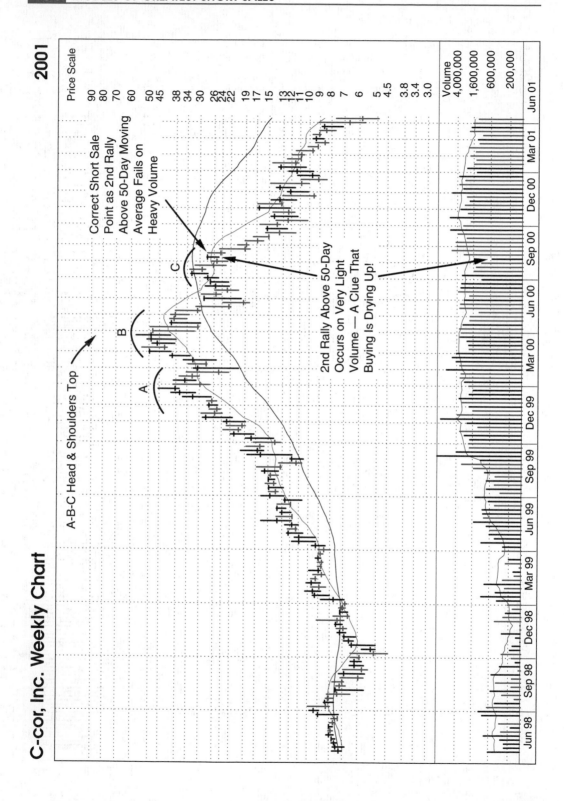

C-cor, Inc. Weekly Chart

2001

A-B-C Head & Shoulders Top

Correct Short Sale
Point as 2nd Rally
Above 50-Day Moving
Average Fails on
Heavy Volume

2nd Rally Above 50-Day
Occurs on Very Light
Volume — A Clue That
Buying Is Drying Up!

Price Scale

90
80
70
60
50
45
38
34
30
26
24
22
19
17
15
13
12
11
10
9
8
7
6
5
4.5
3.8
3.4
3.0

Volume
4,000,000
1,600,000
600,000
200,000

Jun 98 Sep 98 Dec 98 Mar 99 Jun 99 Sep 99 Dec 99 Mar 00 Jun 00 Sep 00 Dec 00 Mar 01 Jun 01

Network Appliance, Inc. Weekly Chart

2001

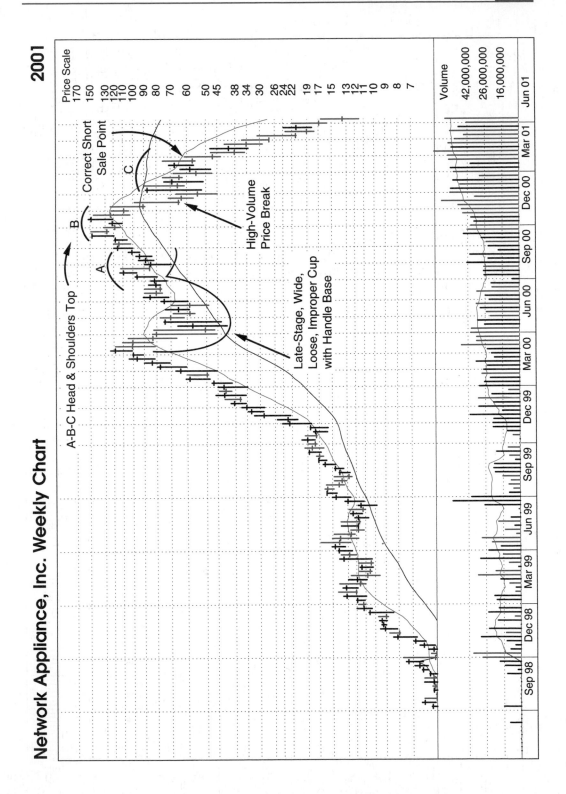

A-B-C Head & Shoulders Top

B

A

C

Correct Short
Sale Point

High-Volume
Price Break

Late-Stage, Wide,
Loose, Improper Cup
with Handle Base

Price Scale
170
150
130
120
110
100
90
80
70
60
50
45
38
34
30
26
24
22
19
17
15
13
12
11
10
9
8
7

Volume
42,000,000
26,000,000
16,000,000

Sep 98   Dec 98   Mar 99   Jun 99   Sep 99   Dec 99   Mar 00   Jun 00   Sep 00   Dec 00   Mar 01   Jun 01

Verisign, Inc. Weekly Chart

2001

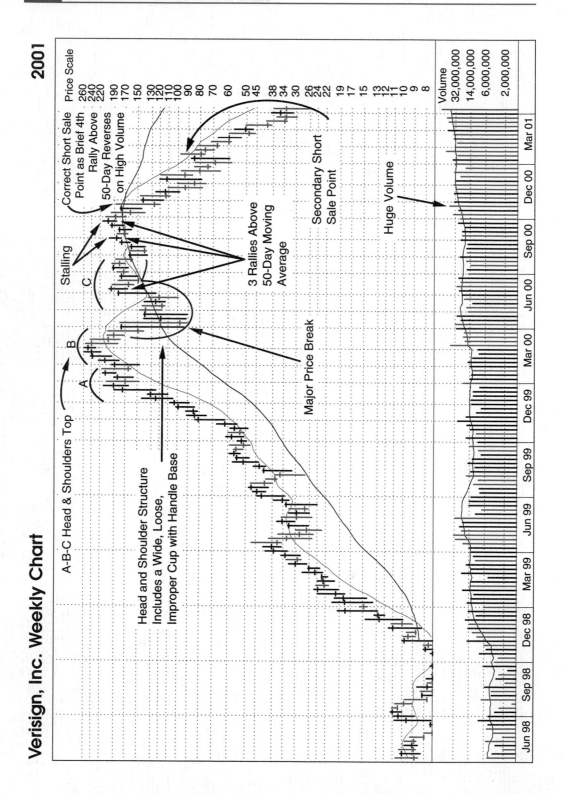

A-B-C Head & Shoulders Top

Head and Shoulder Structure
Includes a Wide, Loose,
Improper Cup with Handle Base

Correct Short Sale
Point as Brief 4th
Rally Above
50-Day Reverses
on High Volume

Stalling

3 Rallies Above
50-Day Moving
Average

Secondary Short
Sale Point

Major Price Break

Huge Volume

Price Scale
260
240
220
190
170
150
130
120
110
100
90
80
70
60
50
45
38
34
30
26
24
22
19
17
15
13
12
11
10
9
8

Volume
32,000,000
14,000,000
6,000,000
2,000,000

Jun 98 Sep 98 Dec 98 Mar 99 Jun 99 Sep 99 Dec 99 Mar 00 Jun 00 Sep 00 Dec 00 Mar 01

Applied Materials, Inc. Weekly Chart

2001

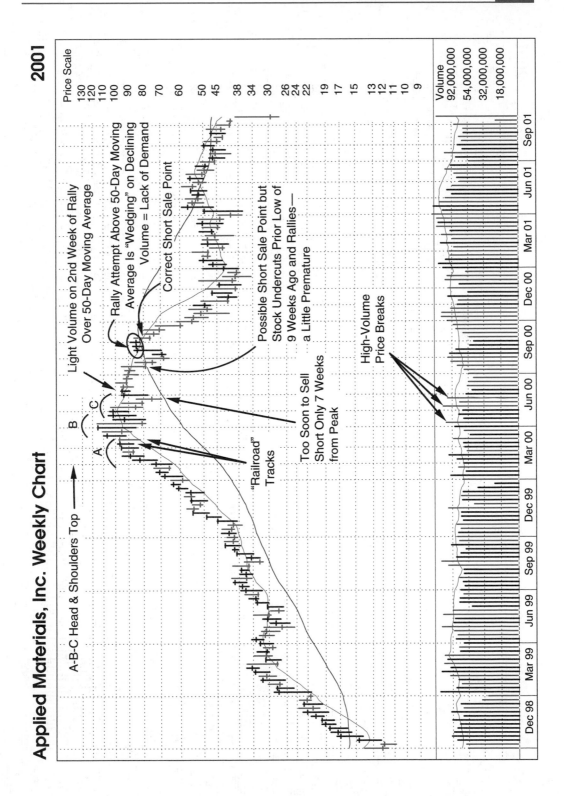

A-B-C Head & Shoulders Top ➡

Light Volume on 2nd Week of Rally
Over 50-Day Moving Average

Rally Attempt Above 50-Day Moving
Average Is "Wedging" on Declining
Volume = Lack of Demand

Correct Short Sale Point

Possible Short Sale Point but
Stock Undercuts Prior Low of
9 Weeks Ago and Rallies—
a Little Premature

Too Soon to Sell
Short Only 7 Weeks
from Peak

"Railroad"
Tracks

High-Volume
Price Breaks

B

A   C

Price Scale

130
120
110
100
90
80

70

60

50
45

38
34
30

26
24
22

19
17

15

13
12
11
10
9

Volume

92,000,000

54,000,000

32,000,000

18,000,000

Dec 98   Mar 99   Jun 99   Sep 99   Dec 99   Mar 00   Jun 00   Sep 00   Dec 00   Mar 01   Jun 01   Sep 01

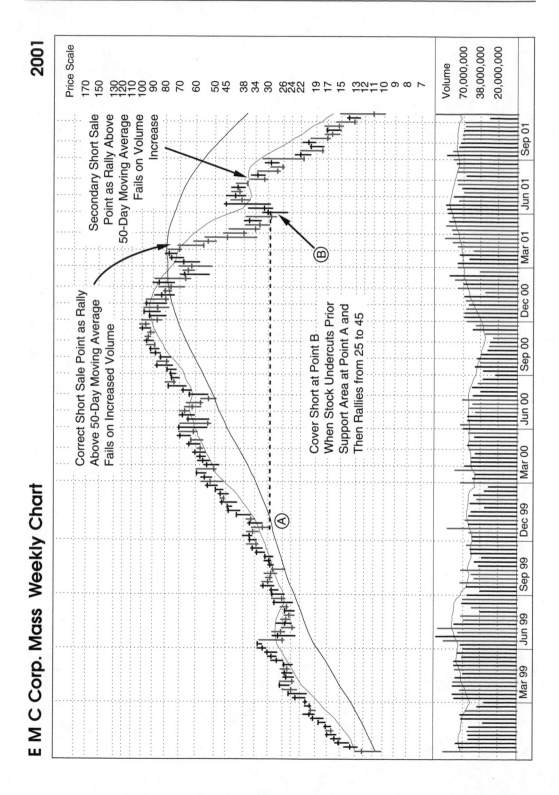

E M C Corp. Mass Weekly Chart

2001

Price Scale

170
150
130
120
110
100
90
80
70
60
50
45
38
34
30
26
24
22
19
17
15
13
12
11
10
9
8
7

Correct Short Sale Point as Rally
Above 50-Day Moving Average
Fails on Increased Volume

Secondary Short Sale
Point as Rally Above
50-Day Moving Average
Fails on Volume
Increase

Cover Short at Point B
When Stock Undercuts Prior
Support Area at Point A and
Then Rallies from 25 to 45

Volume

70,000,000
38,000,000
20,000,000

Mar 99   Jun 99   Sep 99   Dec 99   Mar 00   Jun 00   Sep 00   Dec 00   Mar 01   Jun 01   Sep 01

J D s Uniphase Corp. Weekly Chart

2001

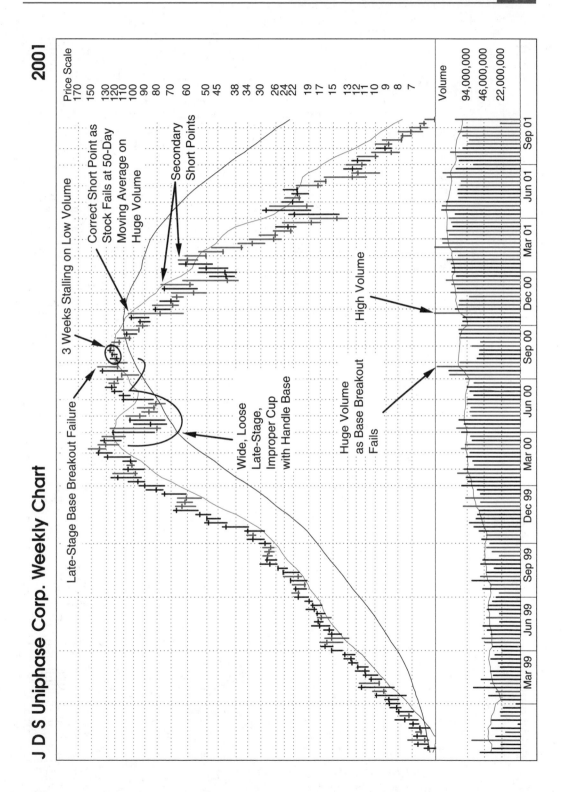

Price Scale
170
150
130
120
110
100
90
80
70
60
50
45
38
34
30
26
24
22
19
17
15
13
12
11
10
9
8
7

Late-Stage Base Breakout Failure

3 Weeks Stalling on Low Volume

Correct Short Point as
Stock Fails at 50-Day
Moving Average on
Huge Volume

Secondary
Short Points

Wide, Loose
Late-Stage,
Improper Cup
with Handle Base

High Volume

Huge Volume
as Base Breakout
Fails

Volume
94,000,000
46,000,000
22,000,000

Mar 99   Jun 99   Sep 99   Dec 99   Mar 00   Jun 00   Sep 00   Dec 00   Mar 01   Jun 01   Sep 01

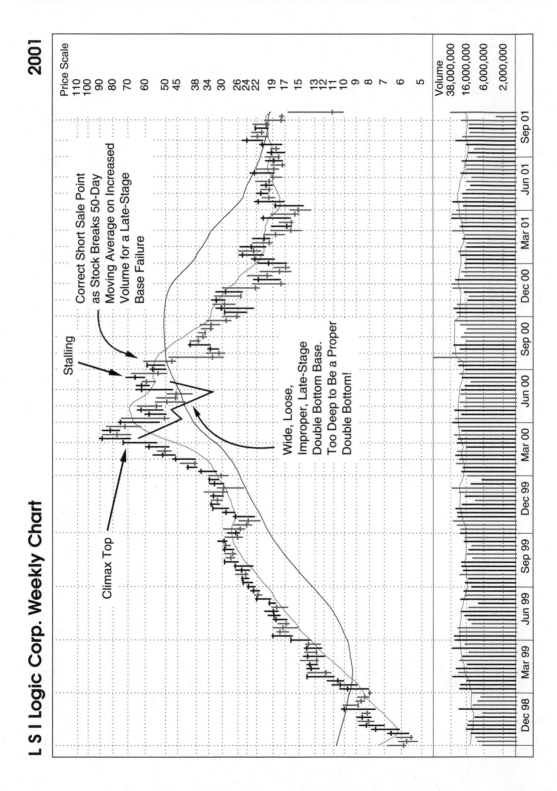

LSI Logic Corp. Weekly Chart

2001

Price Scale

Volume

Climax Top

Stalling

Correct Short Sale Point
as Stock Breaks 50-Day
Moving Average on Increased
Volume for a Late-Stage
Base Failure

Wide, Loose,
Improper, Late-Stage
Double Bottom Base.
Too Deep to Be a Proper
Double Bottom!

Oracle Corp. Weekly Chart

2001

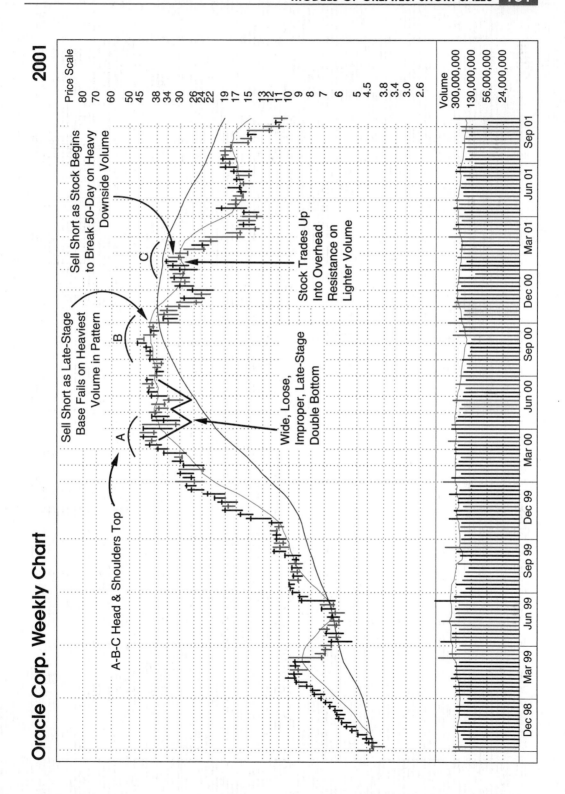

Price Scale
80
70
60
50
45
38
34
30
26
24
22
19
17
15
13
12
11
10
9
8
7
6
5
4.5
3.8
3.4
3.0
2.6

Volume
300,000,000
130,000,000
56,000,000
24,000,000

Sell Short as Stock Begins
to Break 50-Day on Heavy
Downside Volume

Sell Short as Late-Stage
Base Fails on Heaviest
Volume in Pattern

A-B-C Head & Shoulders Top

Stock Trades Up
Into Overhead
Resistance on
Lighter Volume

Wide, Loose,
Improper, Late-Stage
Double Bottom

A

B

C

Dec 98 Mar 99 Jun 99 Sep 99 Dec 99 Mar 00 Jun 00 Sep 00 Dec 00 Mar 01 Jun 01 Sep 01

Power One, Inc. Weekly Chart

2001

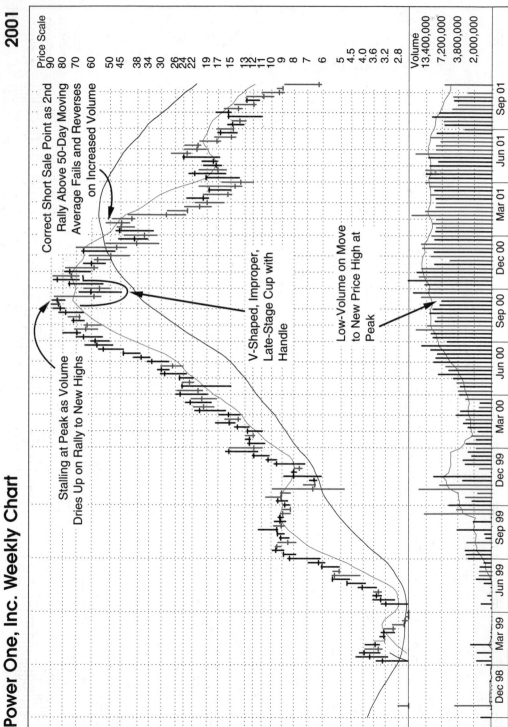

Correct Short Sale Point as 2nd
Rally Above 50-Day Moving
Average Fails and Reverses
on Increased Volume

Stalling at Peak as Volume
Dries Up on Rally to New Highs

V-Shaped, Improper,
Late-Stage Cup with
Handle

Low-Volume on Move
to New Price High at
Peak

Scientific-Atlanta, Inc. Weekly Chart

2001

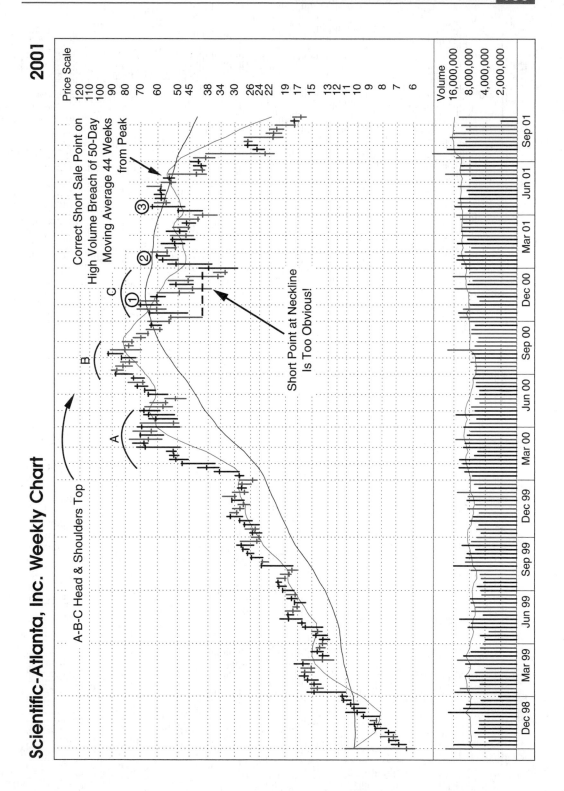

A-B-C Head & Shoulders Top

Correct Short Sale Point on
High Volume Breach of 50-Day
Moving Average 44 Weeks
from Peak

Short Point at Neckline
Is Too Obvious!

Siebel Systems, Inc. Weekly Chart

2001

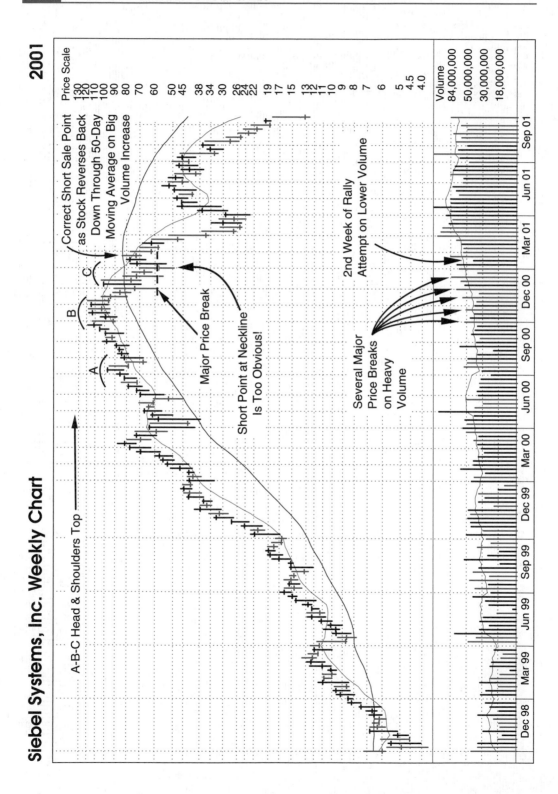

A-B-C Head & Shoulders Top

Correct Short Sale Point as Stock Reverses Back Down Through 50-Day Moving Average on Big Volume Increase

Major Price Break

Short Point at Neckline Is Too Obvious!

2nd Week of Rally Attempt on Lower Volume

Several Major Price Breaks on Heavy Volume

Price Scale
130
120
110
100
90
80
70
60
50
45
38
34
30
26
24
22
19
17
15
13
12
11
10
9
8
7
6
5
4.5
4.0

Volume
84,000,000
50,000,000
30,000,000
18,000,000

Dec 98 Mar 99 Jun 99 Sep 99 Dec 99 Mar 00 Jun 00 Sep 00 Dec 00 Mar 01 Jun 01 Sep 01

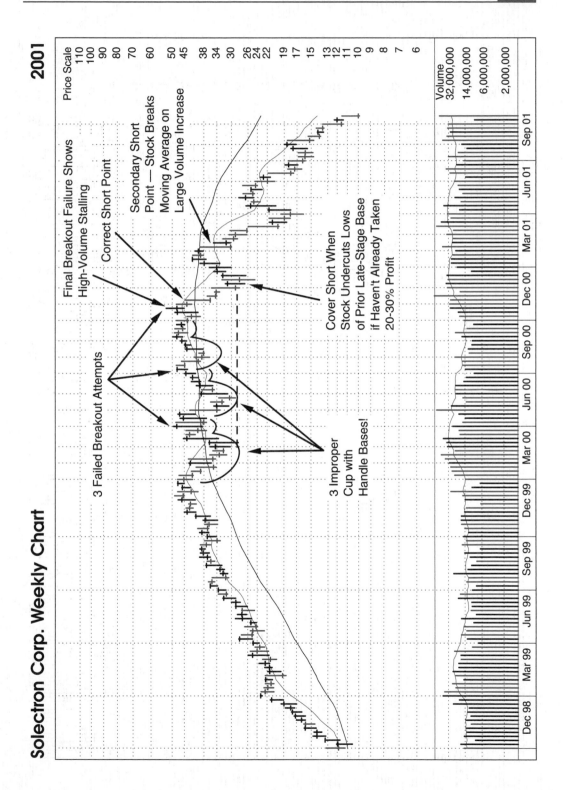

Solectron Corp. Weekly Chart

2001

Sun Microsystems, Inc. Weekly Chart

2001

A-B-C Head & Shoulders Top

A

B

C

Correct Short Point as
Late-Stage Base Fails

Correct Secondary
Short Point After
6 Weeks of Stalling
Action and 2 Rally
Attempts Above
50-Day Moving
Average

Volume Dies
on Move to New
Price Highs

High-Volume
Price Break

Stalling Action
and Inability to Rally
After Big Decline

Price Scale
100
90
80
70
60
50
45
38
34
30
26
24
22
19
17
15
13
12
11
10
9
8
7
6
5
4.5
3.8

Volume
120,000,000
54,000,000
24,000,000

Mar 99 Jun 99 Sep 99 Dec 99 Mar 00 Jun 00 Sep 00 Dec 00 Mar 01 Jun 01 Sep 01

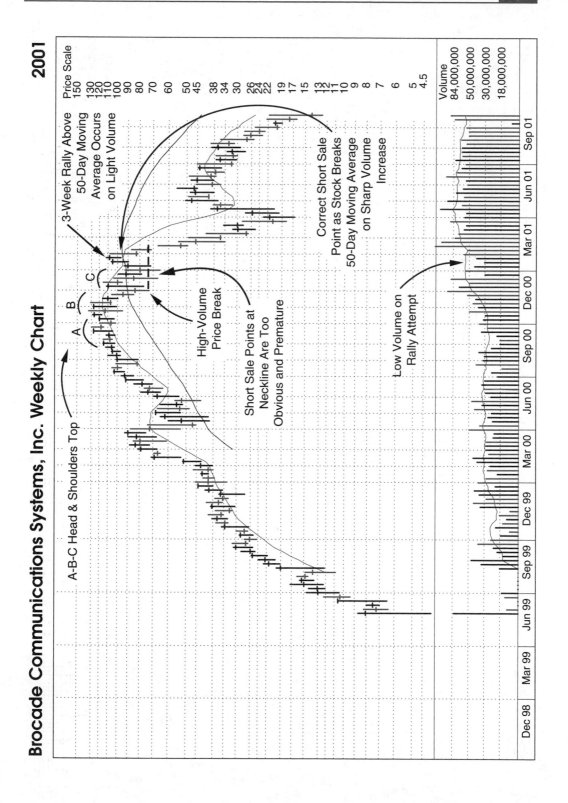

Brocade Communications Systems, Inc. Weekly Chart   2001

A-B-C Head & Shoulders Top

3-Week Rally Above
50-Day Moving
Average Occurs
on Light Volume

High-Volume
Price Break

Short Sale Points at
Neckline Are Too
Obvious and Premature

Correct Short Sale
Point as Stock Breaks
50-Day Moving Average
on Sharp Volume
Increase

Low Volume on
Rally Attempt

Price Scale
150
130
120
110
100
90
80
70
60
50
45
38
34
30
26
24
22
19
17
15
13
12
11
10
9
8
7
6
5
4.5

Volume
84,000,000
50,000,000
30,000,000
18,000,000

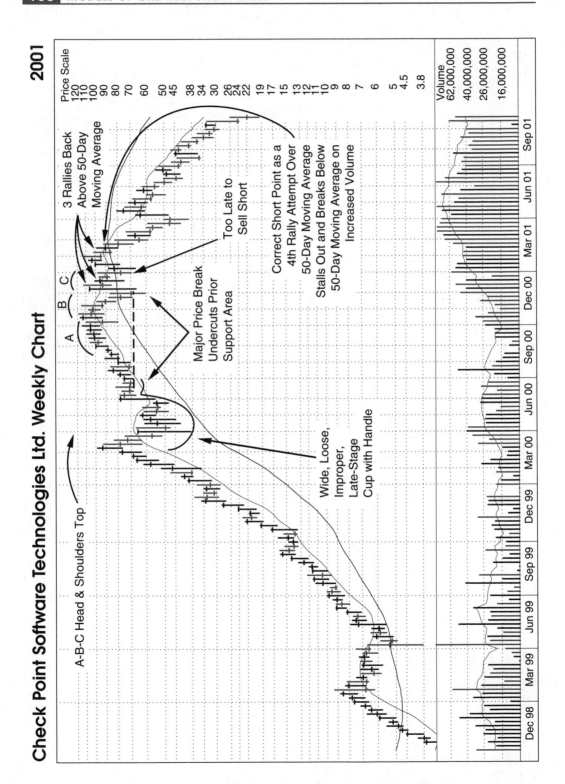

Check Point Software Technologies Ltd. Weekly Chart   **2001**

Price Scale

A-B-C Head & Shoulders Top

A B C

3 Rallies Back
Above 50-Day
Moving Average

Too Late to
Sell Short

Major Price Break
Undercuts Prior
Support Area

Correct Short Point as a
4th Rally Attempt Over
50-Day Moving Average

Stalls Out and Breaks Below
50-Day Moving Average on
Increased Volume

Wide, Loose,
Improper,
Late-Stage
Cup with Handle

Volume
62,000,000
40,000,000
26,000,000
16,000,000

Dec 98 Mar 99 Jun 99 Sep 99 Dec 99 Mar 00 Jun 00 Sep 00 Dec 00 Mar 01 Jun 01 Sep 01

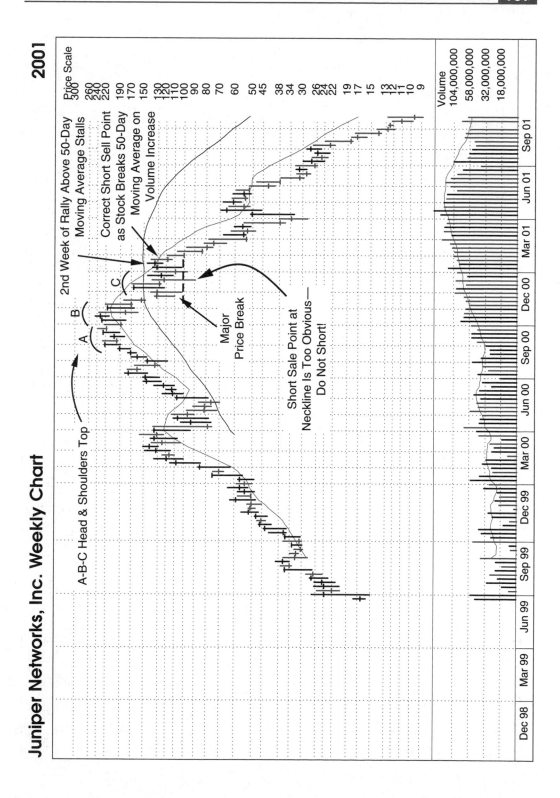

Juniper Networks, Inc. Weekly Chart   2001

A-B-C Head & Shoulders Top

2nd Week of Rally Above 50-Day
Moving Average Stalls

Correct Short Sell Point
as Stock Breaks 50-Day
Moving Average on
Volume Increase

A

B

C

Major
Price Break

Short Sale Point at
Neckline Is Too Obvious—
Do Not Short!

Price Scale
300
260
240
220
190
170
150
130
120
110
100
90
80
70
60
50
45
38
34
30
26
24
22
19
17
15
13
12
11
10
9

Volume
104,000,000
58,000,000
32,000,000
18,000,000

Dec 98   Mar 99   Jun 99   Sep 99   Dec 99   Mar 00   Jun 00   Sep 00   Dec 00   Mar 01   Jun 01   Sep 01

Mercury Interactive Corp. Weekly Chart

2001

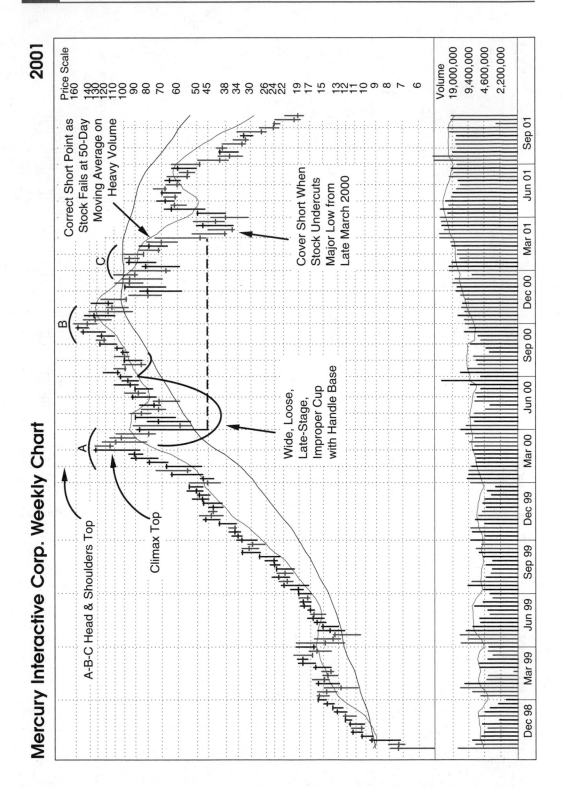

Price Scale

A-B-C Head & Shoulders Top

Climax Top

Correct Short Point as
Stock Fails at 50-Day
Moving Average on
Heavy Volume

Cover Short When
Stock Undercuts
Major Low from
Late March 2000

Wide, Loose,
Late-Stage,
Improper Cup
with Handle Base

Volume

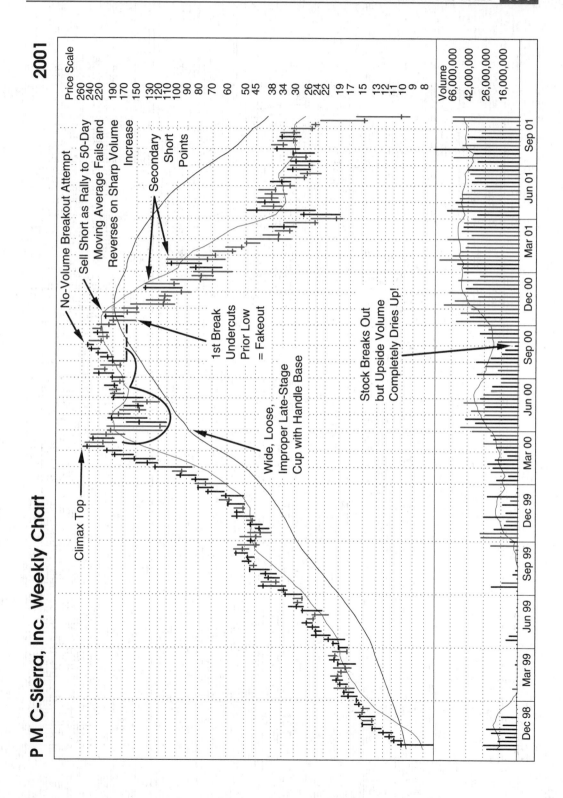

PMC-Sierra, Inc. Weekly Chart   2001

Qlogic Corp. Weekly Chart

2001

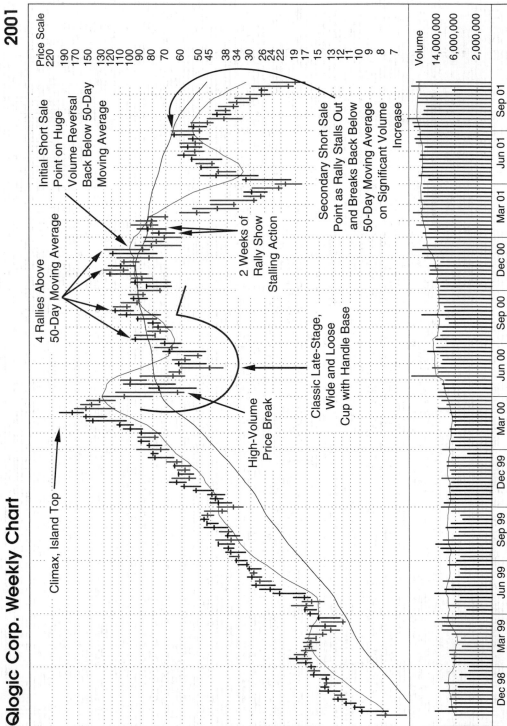

Price Scale
220
190
170
150
130
120
110
100
90
80
70
60
50
45
38
34
30
26
24
22
19
17
15
13
12
11
10
9
8
7

Climax, Island Top

4 Rallies Above
50-Day Moving Average

Initial Short Sale
Point on Huge
Volume Reversal
Back Below 50-Day
Moving Average

2 Weeks of
Rally Show
Stalling Action

High-Volume
Price Break

Classic Late-Stage,
Wide and Loose
Cup with Handle Base

Secondary Short Sale
Point as Rally Stalls Out
and Breaks Back Below
50-Day Moving Average
on Significant Volume
Increase

Volume
14,000,000
6,000,000
2,000,000

Dec 98 Mar 99 Jun 99 Sep 99 Dec 99 Mar 00 Jun 00 Sep 00 Dec 00 Mar 01 Jun 01 Sep 01

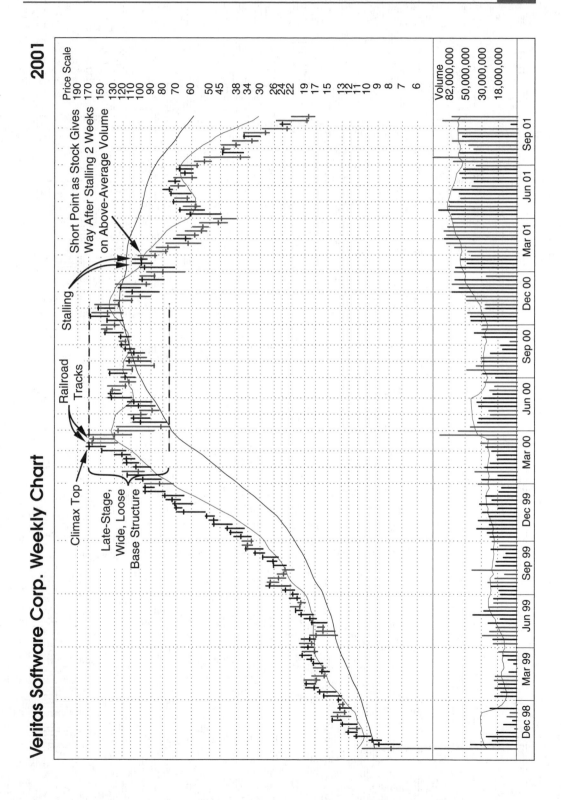

Veritas Software Corp. Weekly Chart

2001

Price Scale
190
170
150
130
120
110
100
90
80
70
60
50
45
38
34
30
26
24
22
19
17
15
13
12
11
10
9
8
7
6

Short Point as Stock Gives
Way After Stalling 2 Weeks
on Above-Average Volume

Stalling

Railroad
Tracks

Climax Top

Late-Stage,
Wide, Loose
Base Structure

Volume
82,000,000
50,000,000
30,000,000
18,000,000

Dec 98 Mar 99 Jun 99 Sep 99 Dec 99 Mar 00 Jun 00 Sep 00 Dec 00 Mar 01 Jun 01 Sep 01

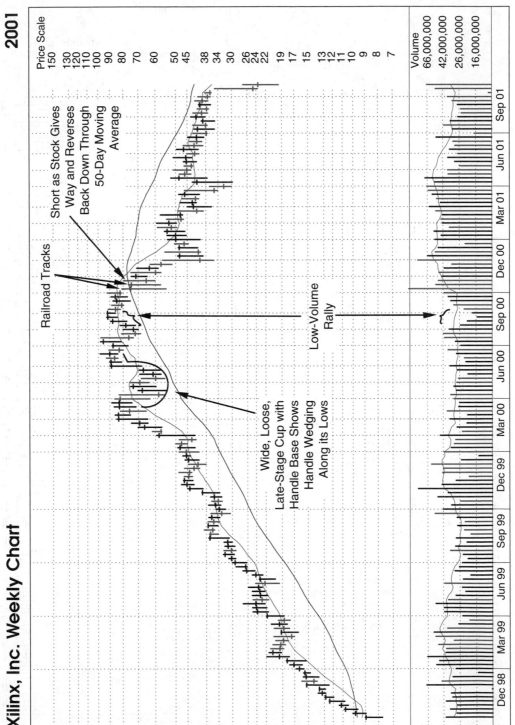

Xilinx, Inc. Weekly Chart

2001

Price Scale

Railroad Tracks

Short as Stock Gives
Way and Reverses
Back Down Through
50-Day Moving
Average

Low-Volume
Rally

Wide, Loose,
Late-Stage Cup with
Handle Base Shows
Handle Wedging
Along its Lows

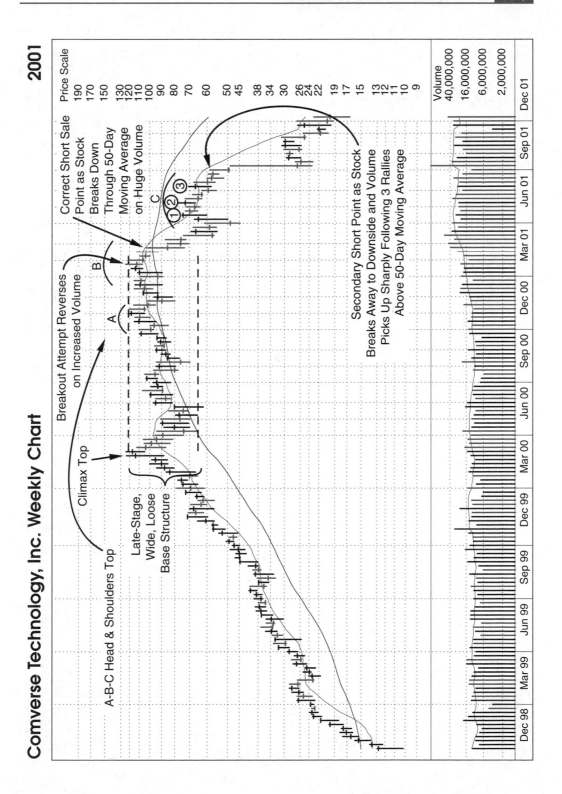

Comverse Technology, Inc. Weekly Chart

2001

Price Scale

Breakout Attempt Reverses
on Increased Volume

Climax Top

A-B-C Head & Shoulders Top

Late-Stage,
Wide, Loose
Base Structure

Correct Short Sale
Point as Stock
Breaks Down
Through 50-Day
Moving Average
on Huge Volume

Secondary Short Point as Stock
Breaks Away to Downside and Volume
Picks Up Sharply Following 3 Rallies
Above 50-Day Moving Average

Volume
40,000,000

16,000,000

6,000,000

2,000,000

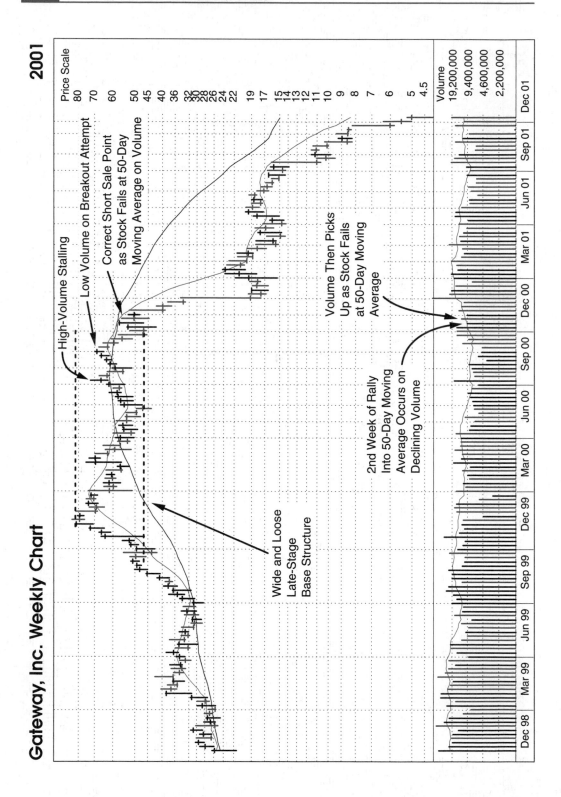

Gateway, Inc. Weekly Chart

2001

Price Scale

High-Volume Stalling

Low Volume on Breakout Attempt

Correct Short Sale Point as Stock Fails at 50-Day Moving Average on Volume

Wide and Loose Late-Stage Base Structure

Volume Then Picks Up as Stock Fails at 50-Day Moving Average

2nd Week of Rally Into 50-Day Moving Average Occurs on Declining Volume

Volume
19,200,000
9,400,000
4,600,000
2,200,000

Nextel Communications, Inc. Weekly Chart

2002

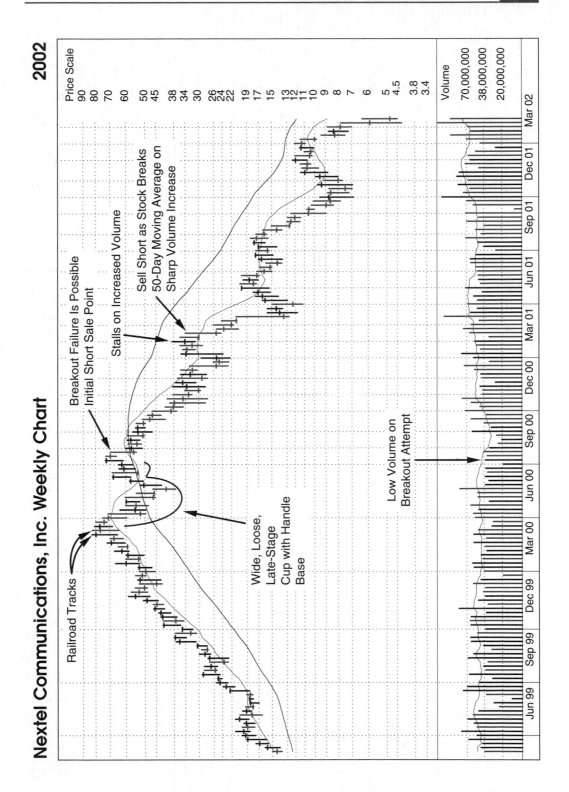

Price Scale
90
80
70
60
50
45
38
34
30
26
24
22
19
17
15
13
12
11
10
9
8
7
6
5
4.5
3.8
3.4

Volume
70,000,000
38,000,000
20,000,000

Railroad Tracks

Breakout Failure Is Possible
Initial Short Sale Point

Stalls on Increased Volume

Sell Short as Stock Breaks
50-Day Moving Average on
Sharp Volume Increase

Wide, Loose,
Late-Stage
Cup with Handle
Base

Low Volume on
Breakout Attempt

Jun 99 Sep 99 Dec 99 Mar 00 Jun 00 Sep 00 Dec 00 Mar 01 Jun 01 Sep 01 Dec 01 Mar 02

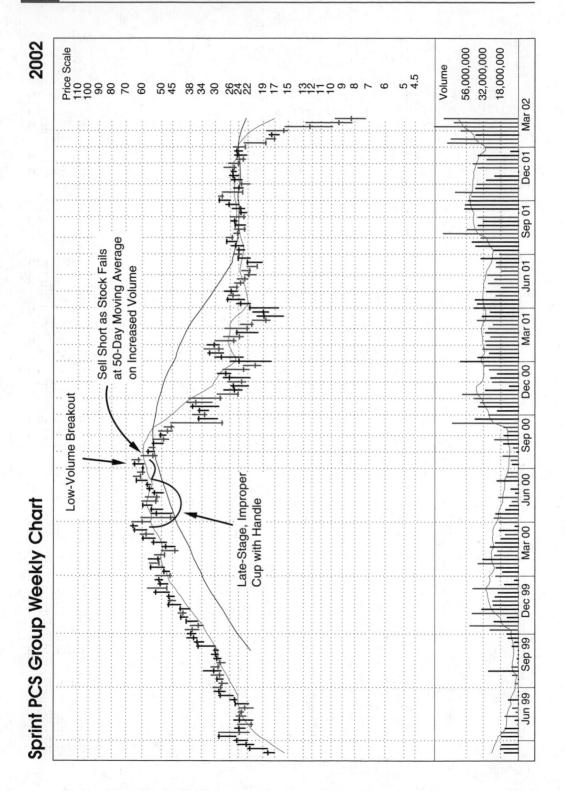

Sprint PCS Group Weekly Chart

2002

Price Scale

Low-Volume Breakout

Sell Short as Stock Falls
at 50-Day Moving Average
on Increased Volume

Late-Stage, Improper
Cup with Handle

Volume

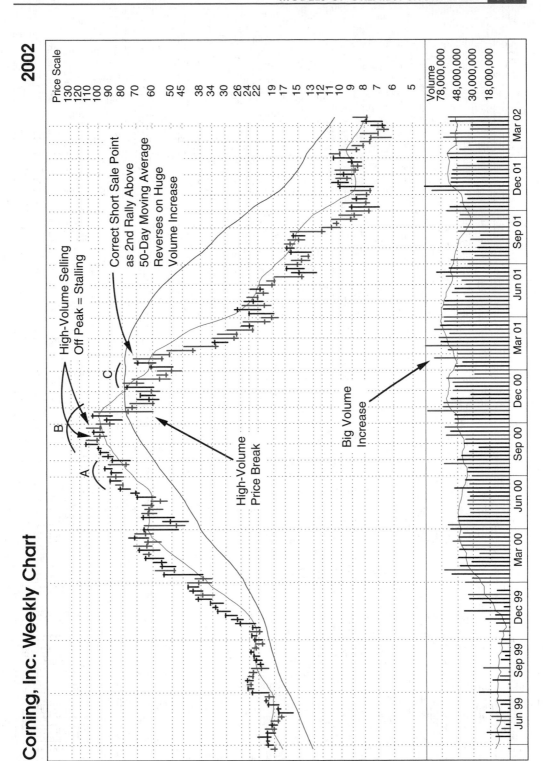

Corning, Inc. Weekly Chart

2002

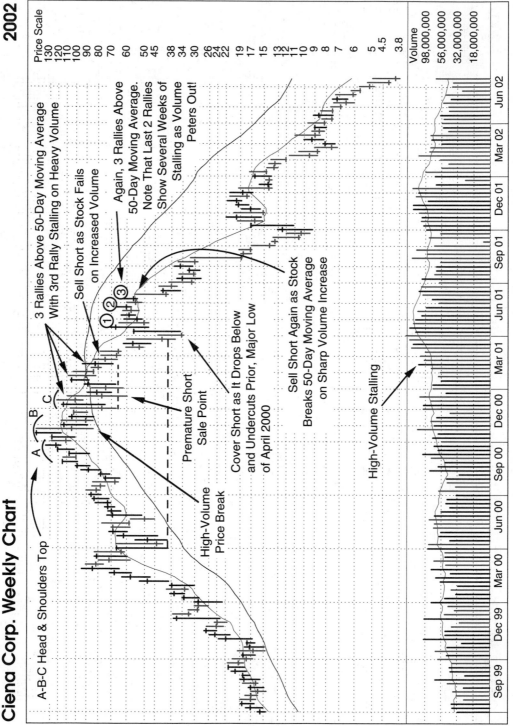

Ciena Corp. Weekly Chart

2002

Price Scale
130
120
110
100
90
80
70
60
50
45
38
34
30
26
24
22
19
17
15
13
12
11
10
9
8
7
6
5
4.5
3.8

A-B-C Head & Shoulders Top

3 Rallies Above 50-Day Moving Average
With 3rd Rally Stalling on Heavy Volume

Sell Short as Stock Fails
on Increased Volume

Again, 3 Rallies Above
50-Day Moving Average.
Note That Last 2 Rallies
Show Several Weeks of
Stalling as Volume
Peters Out!

A
B
C

① ② ③

Premature Short
Sale Point

High-Volume
Price Break

Cover Short as It Drops Below
and Undercuts Prior, Major Low
of April 2000

Sell Short Again as Stock
Breaks 50-Day Moving Average
on Sharp Volume Increase

High-Volume Stalling

Volume
98,000,000
56,000,000
32,000,000
18,000,000

Sep 99   Dec 99   Mar 00   Jun 00   Sep 00   Dec 00   Mar 01   Jun 01   Sep 01   Dec 01   Mar 02   Jun 02

Genzyme General Corp. Weekly Chart

2002

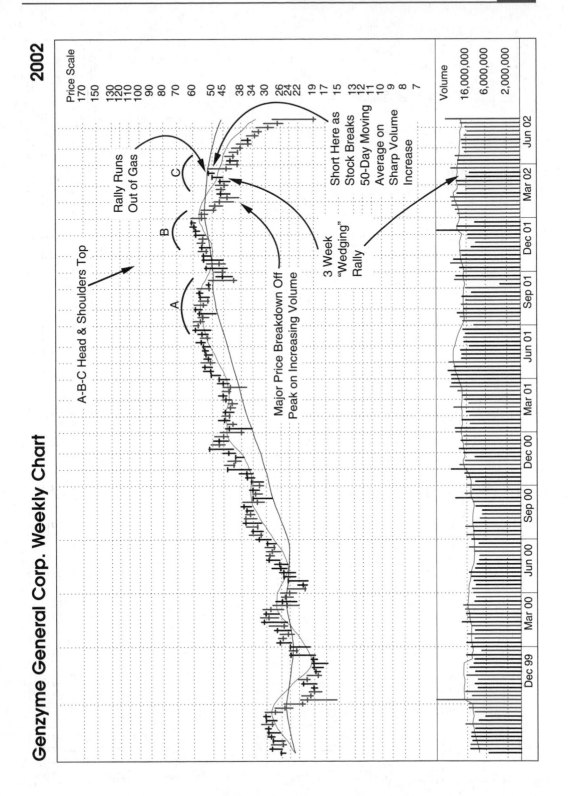

A-B-C Head & Shoulders Top

Rally Runs
Out of Gas

B

A

C

Major Price Breakdown Off
Peak on Increasing Volume

3 Week
"Wedging"
Rally

Short Here as
Stock Breaks
50-Day Moving
Average on
Sharp Volume
Increase

Price Scale
170
150
130
120
110
100
90
80
70
60
50
45
38
34
30
26
24
22
19
17
15
13
12
11
10
9
8
7

Volume
16,000,000
6,000,000
2,000,000

Dec 99
Mar 00
Jun 00
Sep 00
Dec 00
Mar 01
Jun 01
Sep 01
Dec 01
Mar 02
Jun 02

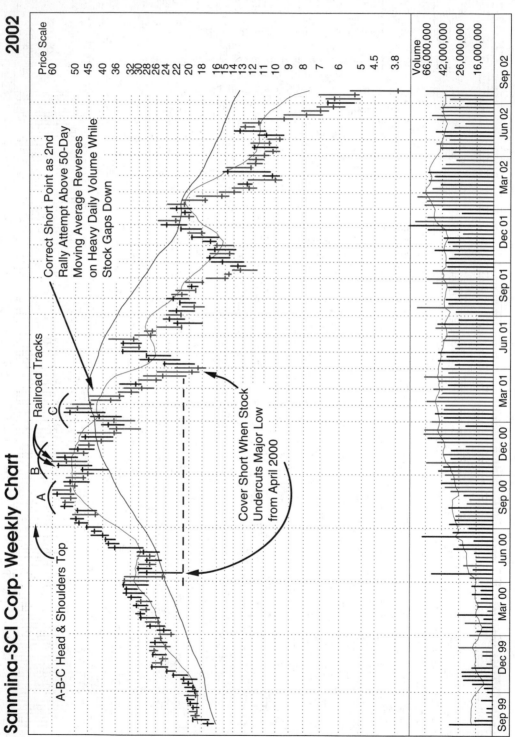

Sanmina-SCI Corp. Weekly Chart   2002

A-B-C Head & Shoulders Top

Railroad Tracks

Correct Short Point as 2nd
Rally Attempt Above 50-Day
Moving Average Reverses
on Heavy Daily Volume While
Stock Gaps Down

Cover Short When Stock
Undercuts Major Low
from April 2000

Price Scale
60
50
45
40
36
32
30
28
26
24
22
20
18
16
15
14
13
12
11
10
9
8
7
6
5
4.5
3.8

Volume
66,000,000
42,000,000
26,000,000
16,000,000

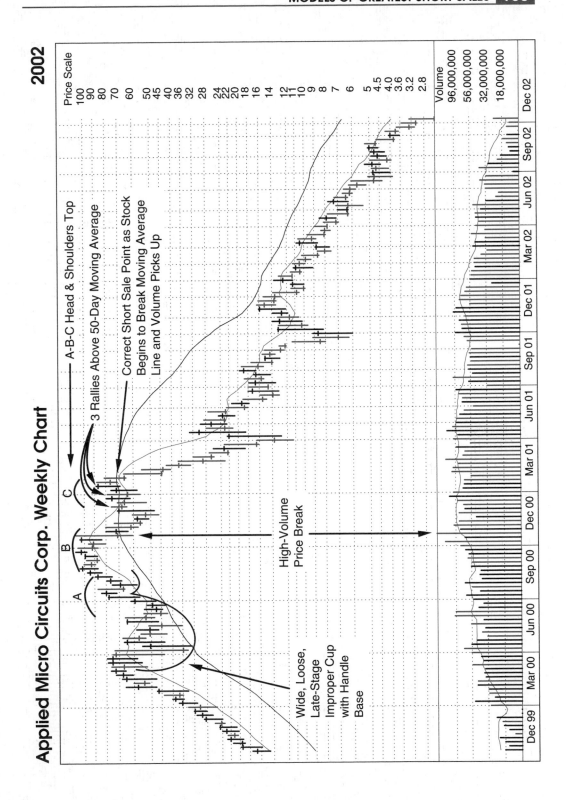

Applied Micro Circuits Corp. Weekly Chart

2002

A-B-C Head & Shoulders Top

3 Rallies Above 50-Day Moving Average

Correct Short Sale Point as Stock Begins to Break Moving Average Line and Volume Picks Up

High-Volume Price Break

Wide, Loose, Late-Stage Improper Cup with Handle Base

Price Scale
100
90
80
70
60
50
45
40
36
32
28
24
22
20
18
16
14
12
11
10
9
8
7
6
5
4.5
4.0
3.6
3.2
2.8

Volume
96,000,000
56,000,000
32,000,000
18,000,000

Dec 99 Mar 00 Jun 00 Sep 00 Dec 00 Mar 01 Jun 01 Sep 01 Dec 01 Mar 02 Jun 02 Sep 02 Dec 02

Career Education Corp. Weekly Chart

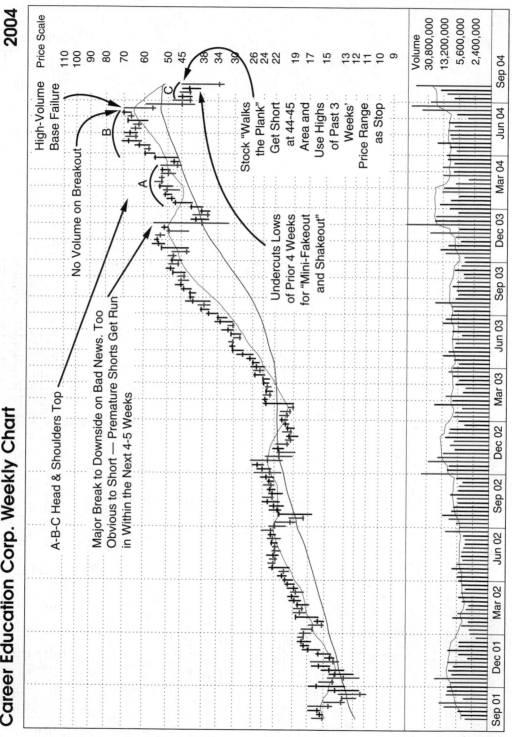

2004

Price Scale

High-Volume Base Failure

No Volume on Breakout

A-B-C Head & Shoulders Top

Major Break to Downside on Bad News. Too Obvious to Short — Premature Shorts Get Run in Within the Next 4-5 Weeks

Stock "Walks the Plank" Get Short at 44-45 Area and Use Highs of Past 3 Weeks' Price Range as Stop

Undercuts Lows of Prior 4 Weeks for "Mini-Fakeout and Shakeout"

A   B   C

110
100
90
80
70
60
50
45
38
34
30
26
24
22
19
17
15
13
12
11
10
9

Volume
30,800,000
13,200,000
5,600,000
2,400,000

Sep 01 Dec 01 Mar 02 Jun 02 Sep 02 Dec 02 Mar 03 Jun 03 Sep 03 Dec 03 Mar 04 Jun 04 Sep 04

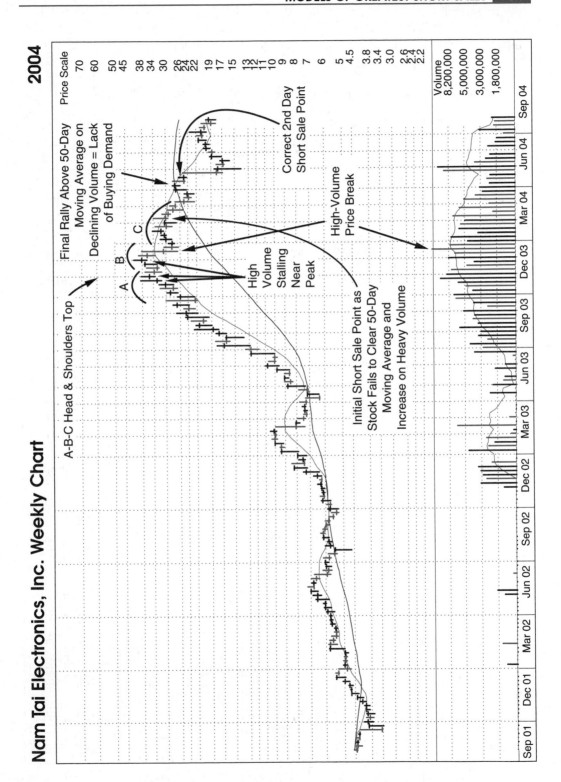

Nam Tai Electronics, Inc. Weekly Chart

2004

A-B-C Head & Shoulders Top

Final Rally Above 50-Day Moving Average on Declining Volume = Lack of Buying Demand

Correct 2nd Day Short Sale Point

High-Volume Price Break

High Volume Stalling Near Peak

Initial Short Sale Point as Stock Fails to Clear 50-Day Moving Average and Increase on Heavy Volume

Price Scale
70
60
50
45
38
34
30
26
24
22
19
17
15
13
12
11
10
9
8
7
6
5
4.5
3.8
3.4
3.0
2.6
2.4
2.2

Volume
8,200,000
5,000,000
3,000,000
1,800,000

Sep 01 Dec 01 Mar 02 Jun 02 Sep 02 Dec 02 Mar 03 Jun 03 Sep 03 Dec 03 Mar 04 Jun 04 Sep 04

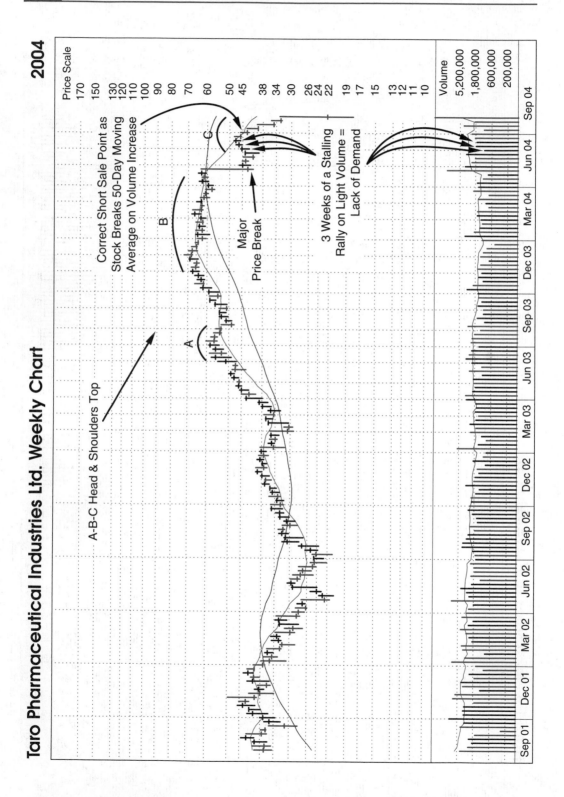

Taro Pharmaceutical Industries Ltd. Weekly Chart

2004

Price Scale

170
150
130
120
110
100
90
80
70
60
50
45
38
34
30
26
24
22
19
17
15
13
12
11
10

A-B-C Head & Shoulders Top

Correct Short Sale Point as Stock Breaks 50-Day Moving Average on Volume Increase

B

C

A

Major Price Break

3 Weeks of a Stalling Rally on Light Volume = Lack of Demand

Volume

5,200,000
1,800,000
600,000
200,000

Sep 01 Dec 01 Mar 02 Jun 02 Sep 02 Dec 02 Mar 03 Jun 03 Sep 03 Dec 03 Mar 04 Jun 04 Sep 04

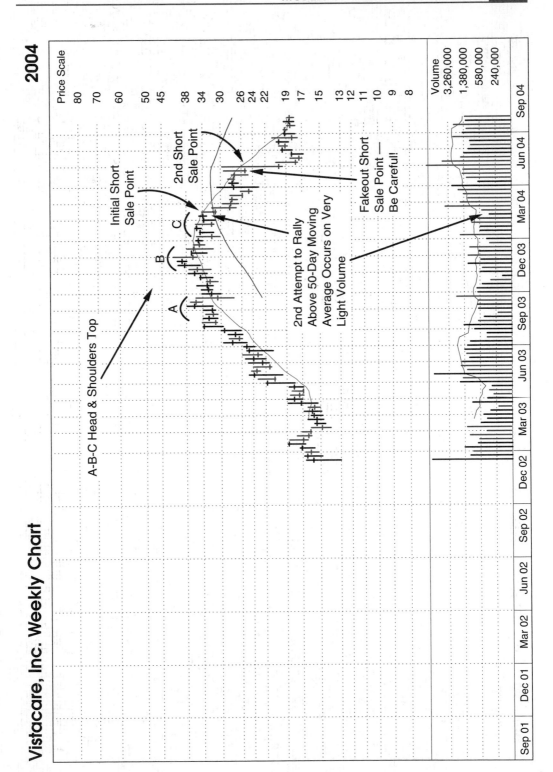

Vistacare, Inc. Weekly Chart

2004

A-B-C Head & Shoulders Top

Initial Short Sale Point

2nd Short Sale Point

C

B

A

2nd Attempt to Rally Above 50-Day Moving Average Occurs on Very Light Volume

Fakeout Short Sale Point — Be Careful!

Price Scale
80
70
60
50
45
38
34
30
26
24
22
19
17
15
13
12
11
10
9
8

Volume
3,260,000
1,380,000
580,000
240,000

Sep 01 Dec 01 Mar 02 Jun 02 Sep 02 Dec 02 Mar 03 Jun 03 Sep 03 Dec 03 Mar 04 Jun 04 Sep 04

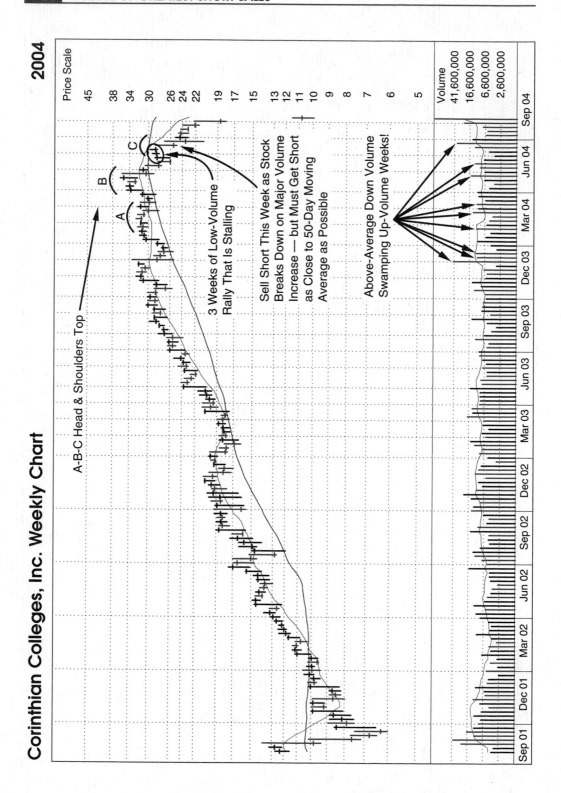

Corinthian Colleges, Inc. Weekly Chart   2004

A-B-C Head & Shoulders Top

3 Weeks of Low-Volume Rally That Is Stalling

Sell Short This Week as Stock Breaks Down on Major Volume Increase — but Must Get Short as Close to 50-Day Moving Average as Possible

Above-Average Down Volume Swamping Up-Volume Weeks!

Price Scale

45

38

34

30

26
24
22

19

17

15

13
12
11
10

9

8

7

6

5

Volume

41,600,000
16,600,000
6,600,000
2,600,000

Sep 01   Dec 01   Mar 02   Jun 02   Sep 02   Dec 02   Mar 03   Jun 03   Sep 03   Dec 03   Mar 04   Jun 04   Sep 04

Netease.com, Inc. ADR Weekly Chart

2004

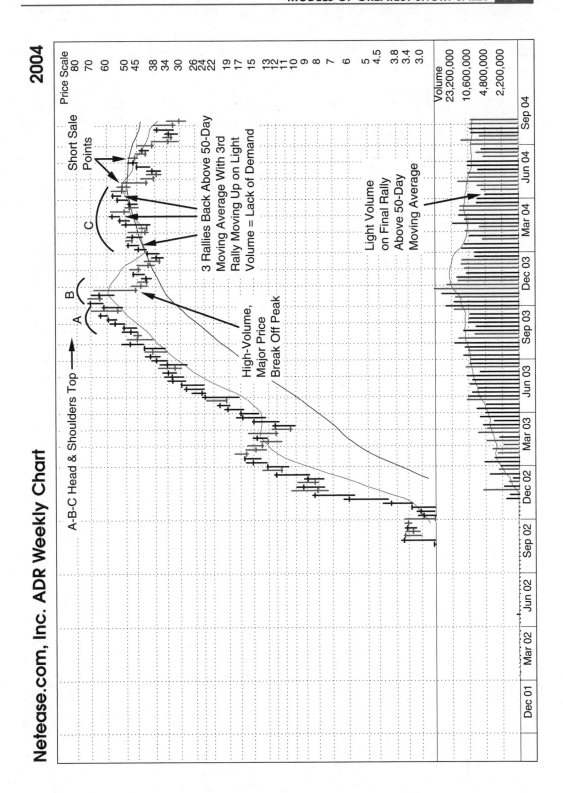

A-B-C Head & Shoulders Top ⟶

A
B
C

Short Sale Points

3 Rallies Back Above 50-Day
Moving Average With 3rd
Rally Moving Up on Light
Volume = Lack of Demand

High-Volume,
Major Price
Break Off Peak

Light Volume
on Final Rally
Above 50-Day
Moving Average

Price Scale
80
70
60
50
45
38
34
30
26
24
22
19
17
15
13
12
11
10
9
8
7
6
5
4.5
3.8
3.4
3.0

Volume
23,200,000
10,600,000
4,800,000
2,200,000

Dec 01   Mar 02   Jun 02   Sep 02   Dec 02   Mar 03   Jun 03   Sep 03   Dec 03   Mar 04   Jun 04   Sep 04

Sina Corp. Weekly Chart

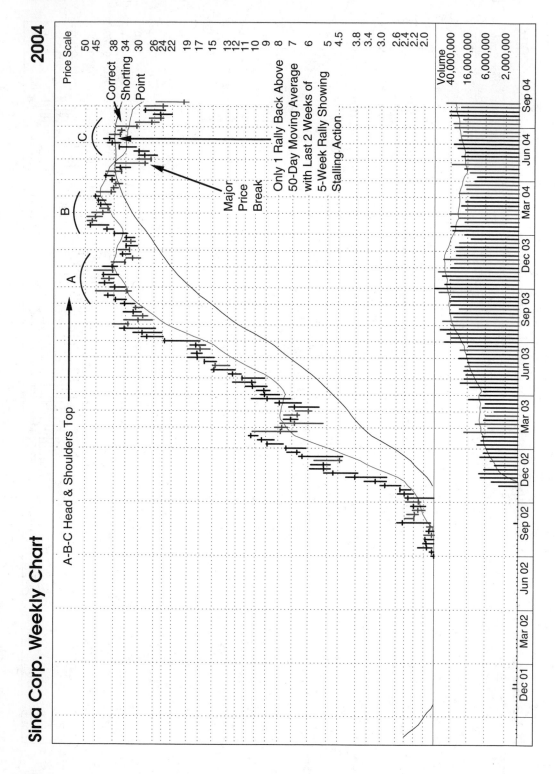

2004

Price Scale

A-B-C Head & Shoulders Top

Correct
Shorting
Point

C

B

A

Major
Price
Break

Only 1 Rally Back Above
50-Day Moving Average
with Last 2 Weeks of
5-Week Rally Showing
Stalling Action

Volume
40,000,000
16,000,000
6,000,000
2,000,000

Netflix, Inc. Weekly Chart

2004

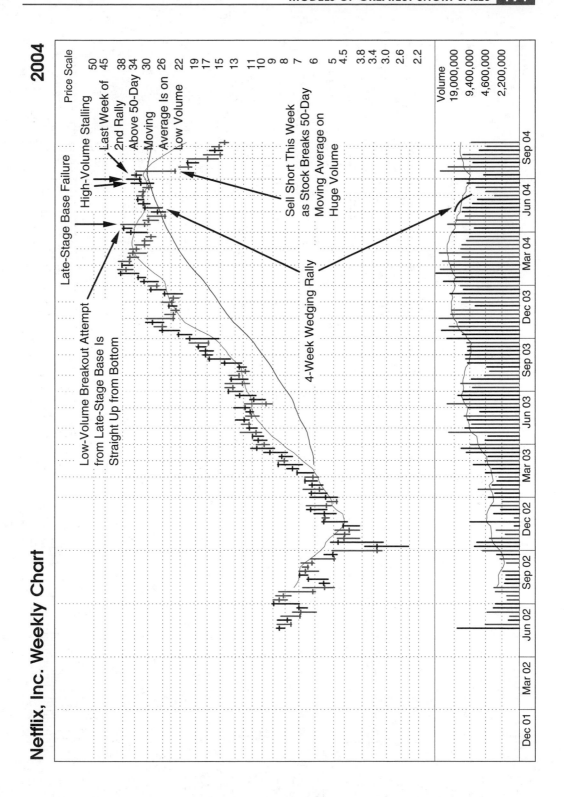

Price Scale

Late-Stage Base Failure

High-Volume Stalling

Last Week of
2nd Rally

Above 50-Day
Moving
Average Is on
Low Volume

Low-Volume Breakout Attempt
from Late-Stage Base Is
Straight Up from Bottom

Sell Short This Week
as Stock Breaks 50-Day
Moving Average on
Huge Volume

4-Week Wedging Rally

50
45
38
34
30
26
22
19
17
15
13
11
10
9
8
7
6
5
4.5
3.8
3.4
3.0
2.6
2.2

Volume
19,000,000
9,400,000
4,600,000
2,200,000

Dec 01   Mar 02   Jun 02   Sep 02   Dec 02   Mar 03   Jun 03   Sep 03   Dec 03   Mar 04   Jun 04   Sep 04

Krispy Kreme Doughnuts, Inc. Weekly Chart

2004

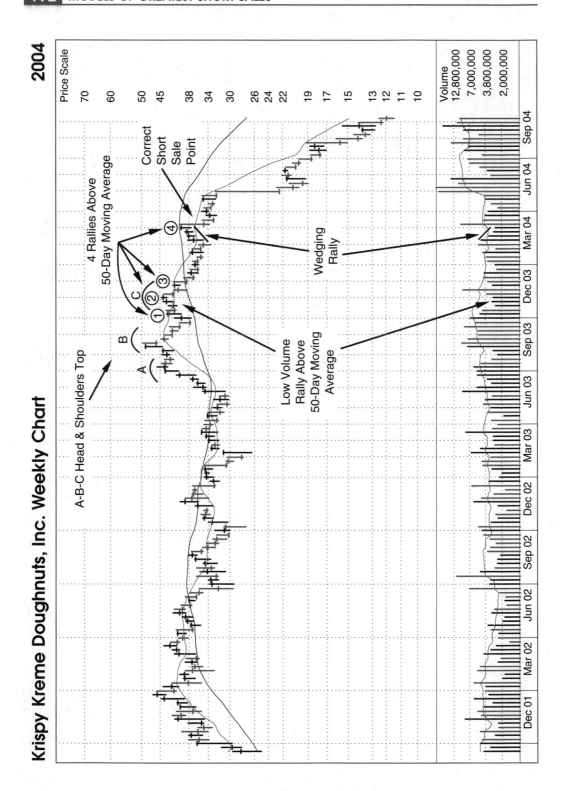

Price Scale

A-B-C Head & Shoulders Top

4 Rallies Above
50-Day Moving Average

Correct
Short
Sale
Point

Wedging
Rally

Low Volume
Rally Above
50-Day Moving
Average

70
60
50
45
38
34
30
26
24
22
19
17
15
13
12
11
10

Volume
12,800,000
7,000,000
3,800,000
2,000,000

Dec 01 Mar 02 Jun 02 Sep 02 Dec 02 Mar 03 Jun 03 Sep 03 Dec 03 Mar 04 Jun 04 Sep 04

Index